Reproducing the World
Essays in Feminist Theory

FEMINIST THEORY AND POLITICS
Virginia Held and Alison Jaggar, Series Editors

TITLES IN THIS SERIES

Reproducing the World: Essays in Feminist Theory, Mary O'Brien

Rocking the Ship of State: Toward a Feminist Peace Politics, edited by Adrienne Harris and Ynestra King

Sexual Democracy: Women, Oppression, and Revolution, Ann Ferguson

Reproducing the World

Essays in Feminist Theory

Mary O'Brien

Westview Press
BOULDER, SAN FRANCISCO, & LONDON

Feminist Theory and Politics

Published in 1989 in the United States of America by Westview Press, Inc., 5500 Central Avenue, Boulder, Colorado 80301, and in the United Kingdom by Westview Press, Inc., 13 Brunswick Centre, London WC1N 1AF, England

Library of Congress Cataloging-in-Publication Data
O'Brien, Mary, 1926–
  Reproducing the world / by Mary O'Brien.
    p. cm.—(Feminist theory and politics)
  ISBN 0-8133-0761-9.   ISBN 0-8133-0760-0 (if published
in paperback)
    1. Feminism. 2. Patriarchy. 3. Reproduction. I. Title.
II. Series.
HQ1154.027 1989
305.4′2—dc 19   88-10679
                                                                                          CIP

Printed and bound in the United States of America

∞ The paper used in this publication meets the requirements of the American National Standard for Permanence of Paper for Printed Library Materials Z39.48-1984.

10   9   8   7   6   5   4   3   2   1

To
Somer Brodribb,
who has gracefully turned this material
from chaos to order,

and for
Cath McNaughton,
without whose support I would never
be able to deliver

Contents

Preface

The publication of papers and lectures of the kind offered here is both an honor and a somewhat alarming invitation to self-criticism. Most feminists are united in the devotion to the theory of "collectivity," to the need for radical equity among feminists. At the same time, structural constraints nourish the male concept of "leadership" and "distinction" in a way that results in a sort of star system, nourished by mass-produced food at putative banquets and recycled feminist polemic entombed in the unrewarding format of the "conference paper." There is a lot of that stuff in my files, and the challenge to reproduce it textually tends to bring on a deep yearning to deconstruct the lot. However, the methodologies of deconstruction remain frozen in the dying languages of European patriarchy, despite the efforts of French women scholars to revitalize them. Further, the tendency of many feminists to worry about the ossification of the movement in the academy is largely a product of the class divisions in both liberal and socialist polities. In practice, the movement is active in many areas where both literacy and theorizing yield to the urgency of the lived experience of women's oppression in diverse cultural contexts.

Perhaps the greatest challenge to feminist politics is the need to reject those varied historical practices and imperialist yearnings which power patriarchal political and cultural machines. Yet I would argue that such a development has to be informed by theory, and the need to provide space and time for theorizing is urgent and most clearly available in the academy; though even there the price in personal fatigue is high. Whether or not the public lecture qualifies for inclusion in "practice," however, is a point on which there is no clear agreement: Socratic circles may extend their circumferences, but they remain circles. What we need is popular fiction, feminist comic books, day-care strategies which stress context rather than location, and a million other innovative political and social activities. Still, the significance of academic feminism may be over-stated. E. M. Forster, in *A Passage to India*, commented that squirrels might be in tune with the universe but are intelligible only to other squirrels, which might serve as a definition of the limits of elitism.

One aspect of the work that follows which does abate a preoccupation with heavy theorizing is the variety of audiences to whom these essays are addressed. Feminist academic careers do tend to a greater variety than conventional male ones, though there is a danger that as the movement expands it will also contract: the existence of "academic Marxism" is a fine cautionary tale. Many older feminists, like myself, came late to the academy, and this book reflects that more eclectic background. My twenty-odd years in midwifery and nursing are reflected here, as is my long and active association with British socialism. Furthermore, the fact that my academic career has developed in an institute for the study of education and that a large number of my students are teachers has also pushed me in certain directions: to questions of curriculum, for example, and to studies of the work of Gramsci which has informed the development of "hegemony theory." To be sure, there are many feminists who believe that patriarchal history and politics are infinitely barren, but I have found that the challenge of critique of patriarchal ideology is a spur to creative theorizing. I have therefore included in the collection some critical work in this area which was essential to the development of reproductive theory, which has been my major preoccupation.

Events, too, challenge theoretical creativity. When I wrote *The Politics of Reproduction* in the late 1970s, my analysis of what I was doing and why I was doing it *then* came from a personal observation that women's sexual and reproductive decisions were beginning to transcend the boxes which had encased them for centuries and that this had to be a "world historical event." This Hegelian/Marxist phrase I chose to interpret in a materialist way. World historical events must have a basis in some transformation of the "material conditions" of human life. The rather puny candidate I offered as fulfilling this condition was "the pill," noting that the ability of women to control their fertility was a very radical innovation. Frankly, I had no idea that the development of reproductive technology would be so radical or so swift, that the practice would outpace both the theorizing and the social changes which this revolution would initiate. Louise Brown was born in England while *The Politics of Reproduction* was accumulating rejection slips from patriarchal publishers, and without the pugnacious advocacy of Dale Spender, the book would never have seen the light of day. Now, of course, the problems of the development of this technology and the transformation of the social construction of human sexuality and reproductive power which accompanies it are central to feminist politics. The move, in a single decade, from the contraceptive pill and the "test-tube baby" to surrogate mothering and multiple birthing is one which creates an enormous challenge to women, not least in the fact that the liberation from compulsory childbearing has not broken masculine control of women's fertility. It may have enhanced it, and it has certainly sped up the process of industrializing it and confirming legal and medical--that is, conservative--male control, to say nothing of the bonus for capitalist accumulation in a giddy increment to the reproduction of production. Resistance to self-administered artificial insemination and "free-standing" abortion clinics are resistances to low-tech procedures which women can to some extent control.

These chapters, then, reflect only a small arc in the rainbow of feminist concerns. It is sobering to discover how repetitive one is. They also reflect the prejudices and narrowness of individual life experience: privilege--hard won but still privilege; ethnocentrism; preoccupation with theoretical issues; the cultural racism against which personal conviction is such an inadequate antidote; a celibate indifference to (or repression of) sexual issues. They are offered as a small contribution to ongoing feminist struggles to advance and support the reproduction and transformation of collective being-in-the-world.

Mary O'Brien

Acknowledgments

There is, of course, no such thing as a book produced by one person: the writing is but a part of a complex process of production. This involves many people: indeed, most of these chapters were conceived as lectures to feminist audiences in Canada, the United States and England. I have to thank all of the people who have invited me to write or speak to them over the last decade. Frieda Forman of the Women's Educational Resources Center attended to this writing and speaking with sisterly zeal.

I am also grateful to the feminist students, researchers and faculty of the Ontario Institute for Studies in Education who have created a feminist environment in which academic writing is stimulated and criticized in a very constructive way. Like all teachers, I learn continuously from my students.

The production of the book from scrappy manuscripts and dog-eared papers would have been impossible without the collecting, editing and general overseeing by Somer Brodribb, who has the ability to criticize constructively while re-habilitating at least some unmanageable sentences. Spencer Carr of Westview Press has given me much encouragement and the series editors, Alison Jaggar and Virginia Held, also brought their fine critical capacity to bear. Copy editing, surely an underrated art, I owe to Kathy Streckfus, who has the ability to force me occasionally to be clear without hurting my feelings, while Beverly LeSuer of Westview Press has made the mode of production a non-exploitive one.

For treating the anxiety which machines and discs and high-tech in general produce in me, I have depended on the skill and calm of Adele Sanderson. I have also been dependent on the skill and patience of those who have turned my messy manuscripts into the typed sheets which fill me with awe and envy: over the years in which these papers were written, I have been indebted to Peggy Bristow, Gail Buckland, Vivien Ching-Ako, Ruth Dawson and Jeanie Stewart.

PART ONE

Feminist Theory

1

Reproducing the World

The title of this essay, "Reproducing the World," reflects my wish to speak about what I--and many other feminists--see as a radical difference between feminist understanding, which has a relatively short public history, and the massive, dense intellectual current of male intellectual history--or, as I prefer to call it, male-stream thought. If there are certain topics which sum up these differences, then the nature of human reproductive relations and the perception of what the "world" is and might be are surely among them.

Thinking about the world; acting in the world; getting these two together: these are awesome tasks, or perhaps more accurately, constitute one task. An obvious way to go about it is to try to discover how our predecessors coped. However, our cultural heritage offers us history as the record of "man's" achievement. Studying male-stream thought is a bit like going on a diet. You have a sense that all is not as it should be--you're too fat, say. Now, common sense says that this is because you eat too much and if you ate less you would be thinner. But common sense is not highly valued in

The first version of this paper was read at the Simone de Beauvoir Institute of Concordia University, Montreal, in 1984. Developed versions have been presented subsequently at several feminist gatherings in Canada, the United States and England.

this man's world, so you see an expert or you read a book. This lets you understand how foolish common sense is: just eating less would be a counsel of ignorance, of not knowing how complex the chemistry is, the psychology, the sociology, the sex angle--vital, that--the normative, ethical, nutritional, aetiological, chemical, and recreational implications, theoretical possibilities, quantitative significance, vital statistics, and aesthetic deprivations. So you read your book, which tells you about all these complex relations and even gives you recipes. You go off to buy the stuff--the first shock usually comes with the discovery that restricted diets cost more than just eating. But it will be worth it, you tell yourself, if you can "master" it. The moment of truth comes on the day you look at your plate and say: I can't *live* on this.

Many of us feel that we cannot live intellectually on the dubiously nutritious diet of male-stream thought. Far more important, many of us feel that we may not be able to live for very much longer on man-kind's impoverished planet earth. If we are to survive as an earth species, to live in the world, we must constantly reproduce ourselves, our species, our planet, our living. Reproduction is multiple: it is reproducing the world.

Thinking about the world, acting in the world, getting the two together: that is the commonsense agenda for human survival, and it is far too important an agenda to entrust to experts or to books, and certainly to entrust to man-kind, universal man, the ruling sex, the combination of male narcissism, male violence, male dualism, and male dominance for which we use the short-cut word "patriarchy"--literally, the rule of fathers. I shall have something to say later about how uncertain a peg paternity is on which to hang the job of reproducing the world, but first let us talk about this world a little bit, and then about reproducing it.

It is, of course, quite difficult to think about the world-- planet earth--an insignificant speck in the universe, yet too large and too complex to be easily grasped or to be experienced whole. It is a great lump of volcanic rock and fecund earth peopled by folk who never seem to have been able to grasp two relatively simple truths:

1. We all as humans share the world, and share it with other species.
2. We need to constantly reproduce the world.

Perhaps, though, these truths are not so simple as they seem. First of all, *who* are "we?" The usual answer is "mankind." Second, *how* do we reproduce the world? Answer: by bullying "her" into submission to man's will. Who, then, is "man"? We are not all men, but we are all "Man." When I see this on my plate I cannot live on it either.

The usual answers to these questions are wrong, and precisely because male-stream thought has never been able to say who we are in all our communality and diversity, it has proceeded in the opposite direction, at least in terms of what man likes to think of as his crowning achievement, the development of "great civilizations." Historically, these "great civilizations" have several things in common (apart from the obvious one--that they do not last). Whether they be Greek, Inca, Roman, Confucian, Islamic, or Christian, capitalist civilizations, such sociohistorical conurbations share several important characteristics. They have all been imperialist, racist and sexist; they have all relied on class divisions of an oppressive kind. Structurally, they have all made some kind of division between public and private life, between urban and rural life. They have all rested on the exploitation of human labor, human sexuality, human greed, and human endurance. They survived by force and succumbed to greater force, driving chariots of fire over all resistance to universal man's will, defined at specific moments in history by the strongest military and most economical men. These forays have left behind a geography, cultural artifacts, diverse languages, and heaps of ashes: after all, the logical consequence of a chariot of fire is a heap of ashes. They have also bequeathed us their myths, their lies, and their strange silences--the silences of the women, of the slaves, helots, eunuchs, and dead soldiers. We do not know who they were, these silent people, for we know them only as spirits: universal man, of course, is big on spirit and confident that his will to power is exemplary, his heroes representative, and his empires secure.

The "great civilization" to which we belong shares these general characteristics, except perhaps that we know a little more about the links between ideology and learning. At least we had better know if we want to know anything at all: the "university" is, after all, the school for universal man, and the price of admission is knowledge of his achievements. There are problems with this system, to which I shall return, but I first want to stress what I see as the major differences between Western civilization and its predecessors and contemporaries. The most obvious of these are related to economic production and to that particular deportment toward knowledge of the world which we call the scientific approach.

Economic theory--"in principle," as men like to say-- potentially includes the idea that we all share knowledge of the world, at least the knowledge that we must produce in order to meet certain biological needs. Economic production is a dialectical process in which material conditions and labor, both mental and manual, interact to "reproduce" individuals on a daily basis. Yet modern economic--namely, capitalist--production does not in fact produce to meet needs but to maximize profits, while Communist economies struggle with the fair distribution of a plenitude which they have not yet quite managed to produce. Conjoined with scientific economics, which has no trouble at all in understanding "objectively" that riches work for the good of all, even when the majority learn more about work than riches, scientific capitalism has produced extremely sophisticated forms of imperialism, racism, sexism, and exploitation. It has also produced an extreme form of separation of public and private: the nuclear family appeared at one time to be the final solution to the problem of species reproduction, but statisticians have more recently had to categorize the antithesis of kinship, the so-called "one-person household." Nonetheless, the nuclear family as a mode of organization of the social relations of reproduction joins up with extreme individualism, in which capitalism identifies each of us as an abstract purchasing choice in an imaginary free market in which our communality is expressed in a war for the best bargain. Who are *we*? We are consumers of goods, and the harder we choose to work, the more goods we acquire to decorate our isolated "homes." We do not "make" a home, we buy one--the construction and the real estate industry have done it all for us, provided that we ransom our earning power to the kindly neighborhood banker or landlord.

As far as knowledge is concerned, we are taught that there are two important things about it. It is cumulative (like profit), and it is objective (like market choices). Perhaps the *second* thing which most forcibly strikes women who enter the knowledge market is the *abstract* nature of knowledge. This has come to be known in feminist discourse as the problem of dualism, the knowing of the truth of any one thing by its separation from and its epistemological reliance on its opposite. The *first* striking thing, of course, is that knowledge is a male prerogative. The question is whether these two--the dualism and the masculinity--are related. It does not take long to discover that the "big things" are dualistic in a particular way: mind (abstract), body (material); culture (abstract), nature (material); science (abstract), common sense (material); public life (abstract), private life (material); intellectual work (abstract), manual or domestic labor (material); money (abstract), poverty (material); art (abstract), experience (material). If we also add man (abstract), woman (material), does that make sense? Not if we speak of particular men--our friends, lovers, oppressors, dependents--but certainly if we speak of universal man--the generic component in the identification of the species as "mankind," the man who makes history, who fouls up our grammar, who takes arms against nature, who has produced knowledge, who is made in the image of God. I am not speaking here of sex roles, nor the division of labor, nor of neurosis, nor of phallic imagery. I am speaking of abstract universal man, that metaphysical jello which is supposed to bind us all together in our communality, to represent our totality. I do not like to see that jello on my plate either: I cannot live on it.

The first "simple" truth, then, that we all share in the world, is hidden from us by the misidentification of the "we" as mankind. The second truth--that we have to reproduce the world, is hidden because the reproduction of the world has two relations embedded in it: the daily reproduction of individuals and the ongoing reproduction of the species. In a stunning reversal of the actuality of birthing, we find that this process is perhaps the only instance in which man is material and woman abstract, where man provides what John Milton liked to call "the holy seed" and woman suspends her personality so that abstract "nature" can do "her" stuff.   Perhaps all this is not so stunning: we remember that Adam fell upward while Eve fell downward in the effort of inaugurating history.   We are told, in my culture, that Adam was the first man, and it is considered simply bitchy to note that he was also the last man to be certain that the children were his: he was the only game in town, but even then was nervous of serpents and bad spirits. But let us not be distracted by metaphysical spareribs and applesauce.

"Reproduction" is a pregnant word. Recently I met an old friend of the Marxist persuasion who had read my book *The Politics of Reproduction*, and she rebuked me for apostasy: I have evidently misunderstood the meaning of reproduction, for she told me that I would know that reproduction is the production of production.   What, then, I asked, is birth? Birth, she said, is of nature and not of history--a classic pronouncement of not only the patriarchal ideology of dualism but of its ultimate inadequacy. But I must say a few words about Marx, whose intellectual achievements are still for me exciting.   Marx is important for many reasons, theoretically because he achieved, by virtue of a critique of Hegel's lively idealism, an important leap over some of the fixations of dualistic thinking.   Western man, having identified to his satisfaction (and occasional despair) the bifurcations of human experience, then froze them, as it were, in thought.   Man's mind had triumphed over the disorderly waywardness of mute matter by categorizing and naming its dualisms and then contemplating their inevitability with his mind's eye.

But the basic dualist perception of material and abstract remained a battalion of abstract truths which could only describe the actual world. The point, Marx said, trenchantly and correctly, was not to describe the world but to change it.

There are no eternal truths--there are human ideas, and human ideas are not plucked from eternity into time but emerge from the sensuous experience and necessary labors of men, who make history. Marx, in his attempt to add material conditions to Hegel's dialectic of God's mind and Man's mind, provided in principle a strategy beyond abstract thought to make the useful notion of dialectical study apply to actual rather than metaphysical history. He did not quite succeed, for he did not move beyond patriarchy. Marx did not recognize "man" as an ideological abstraction, and he did not recognize that "history" is not composed of only individuals and classes, but of individuals and species. Traditional dualisms were phony, Marx argued; they served the interests of ruling classes who were happy enough with a certain measure of popular fatalism. No dualism was absolute: what we actually experience is *contradiction*, and contradiction can be *mediated*, that is to say, acted upon by unifying thought with action. Furthermore, dualisms are not eternal verities but products of the particular problems which the species encounters in its efforts to meet the necessities of material existence--fundamentally, Marx argued, the necessity to produce our subsistence. Our understanding of our world is concrete and historical; it is a form of consciousness grounded in material realities. Consciousness itself must struggle with the contradiction of sensuous experience and rational thought which are integral to its formation. The material conditions of existence are never experienced directly, individually, nor totally, for these conditions and the effort to understand and transform them are together the reality of *history*. Individuals cannot grasp the totality of understanding history unless they approach it in an aware way. But such awareness comes only in transcending the individual in the collectivity in class struggle to negate class. Moreover, the conditions of life and the formal modes of production necessary to sustain a species change historically, and classes stand in different relations to the productive process. Historically these classes are engaged in struggle, because for most of its history the species has been beset by the specter of scarcity. Marx believed that communism would abolish scarcity and therefore abolish class, but the condition of the negation of class division was struggle-- the long historical struggle for scarce resources but the struggle for the abolition of class structure that has been generated historically in the course of that struggle.

The great merit of Marx's work is that it takes the material world as the condition of existence and human activity as creative. Marx resisted the liberal isolation of "free" individuals, asserting instead the reality and consciousness of class solidarity; he also resisted the definition of the world as a problem for intellectuals. What is real is movement, process, history, and subsistence, and this activity is in the world, not in heaven, not in mind. One of the great defects of Marx's work is the partial nature of his notion of history--mode of production follows mode of production in providing subsistence for the reproducing of man on a daily basis. The daily reproduction of the *species* in the birth of *individuals* is not perceived as an essential dialectical moment of historical process, which of course it is: dialectical relations are by definition relations of universal and particular. Marx understands the need to mediate contradictions, especially those of nature and history on the universal level and worker and capitalist labor on the particular level. "Mediation" being understood as "struggle," Marxist man is permanently doomed to an agonistic relation to the natural world, and class struggle therefore becomes the *only* strategy of historical liberation. Marx, despite his brilliance, occupied the standpoint of abstract universal man, a fatal flaw in a "materialist" perception of history. Marx misses the "we-ness" of the sharing of the world and misunderstands the nature of the reproduction of the world. Nature is to submit to man, species reproduction is to remain forever stuck nondialectically in the mindless world of nature, and women will presumably never recover from the "world-historical defeat" inflicted upon them in the abstract anthropology of Engels.

Feminist scholarship is now honing in on the problem of reproduction, of birth, of the historical significance as well as the emotional trauma of motherhood. Earlier feminist theorists--and Simone de Beauvoir in particular--accepted the conventional masculine evaluation of motherhood as theoretically uninteresting. Marx and Engels understood the sexual division of labor as "natural": that is to say, not of history, not in the Marxist sense "material," and immune, presumably, from historical injustice. For Marx, materialism is a science of history and birth can tell us nothing of history. The fact that reproduction, like production, is a historical structure raised on the material pangs of appetite is lost in the realm of what patriarchs know and experience. Men do not experience birth labor, and without control of women's sexuality, then cannot know who their children are. They do not labor reproductively, so only productive labor counts for Marx in the reproduction of man's world. Through productive labor, Marx argued, men know the natural world, work on it, and change it. In doing so, men change themselves, but they also unify themselves in shared necessity and social response. For Marx, labor is a response to individual necessity which *becomes* social historically: labor moves from the natural to the socio-historical. History is not an accumulation of ideas in practice, but the history of practice which teaches us to think. *Ungrounded* theories are, in both senses of the word, immaterial. They tell us nothing of the world except that we have a social arrangement that has separated intellectual and manual labor, and we need to understand why this happened. This need is addressed by the theory of class struggle.

The problems of reproducing the world are practical problems, but we cannot begin to redress them until we understand them. To understand them, we need knowledge, but the knowledge and the theories of knowledge bequeathed to us by male-stream thought are inadequate. Universal man does not live in the world: he is a product of mind. His appearance in the world comes in the guise of *ideology*--patriarchal ideology--which is willfully and energetically transposed from the realm of fantasy to the realm of truth to justify the very real power which men have in the world. This is the power to regard their relation with the natural world as an antagonistic one; the power to define women as part of nature; the power to divide public from private life; the power to insist that men must rule each of these domains; the power to define the continuity of the species as a "motherhood issue," unscientific, boringly self-evident, an unconscious product of biology-in-action--a plateful of gall and wormwood, suitable intellectual diet for women.

There are two things, in my view, which feminist theory must do before we can plan strategies to resist this negative, powerful, and ultimately destructive force based on the power of men to define themselves. This does not mean we have to sit back and think before we can do anything at all. Marx was surely right in describing history as a unity of thought and action, and the particular unity of thought and action which insists on reproducing the world in its wholeness is the historical force which we call feminism. This is not a force which is waiting in the wings. Feminism has already redefined revolution itself. Although revolution has long been understood as violence in the public realm, feminist revolution is a nonviolent revolution of the private realm. Evidence of it is seen in what its most implacable enemies-- the New Right--perceive as an assault on the traditional family. Feminist revolution overturns the ideology of patriarchy at a fundamental level by insisting on unifying biological necessity with politics. This notion has nothing at all to do with that tired patriarchal whipping horse, biological determinism. It is okay in patriarchal terms to base whole philosophies on natural realities, as Marx and Freud and death-haunted existentialism do. Somehow, birth process, women's sexuality, race, sexual preference: all of these are without history and, according to patriarchy, are apolitical. Feminism is therefore not only transforming the lived conditions of the private realm, but insisting on and organizing around the principle that the personal is political and that the separation of public and private is a death-dealing power play which must be stopped. But it is not, of course, doing so without resistance, and it has managed to upset conservative forces--economic, militaristic, religious, political--a great deal!

Resistance mounts as feminists proceed to examine the relation of public and private life as a dialectical and historical relation grounded in the realities of gender relations. Men and women do not see that childbirth and the social relations and forms of consciousness to which it give rise are a dialectical and historical process. Thus Hannah Arendt, with her argument that childbirth is animal or, much as we admire her, de Beauvoir's perception of childbirth as "a useless or even troublesome accident."[1] We women have only just begun to assert the need to pose historical questions from our own experience, to ask the forbidden questions and proclaim that if the theory does not fit, that is because of the limitations of the theory and not the inadequacy of female intellect. For example, we do not yet ask what, if all labor creates value, is the value produced by reproductive labor. Is this value not in some sense--a sense to be analyzed--the value of the individual life poised in dialectical contradiction to the life of the species? Why are we so diffident in insisting that women's experience and women's labor create and, in the teeth of patriarchy's contempt for life, sustain certain human values which do not sit well with those whose political imaginations choke in the mouths of cannons? Why do we not give the lie to the claim that birth is merely a biological happening, when our sex has universally created reproductive cultures which structure this event in variable but persistent sets of social relations between mothers, sisters, children, midwives, friends, neighbors and, intermittently, men? Why do we acknowledge the validity of class consciousness and neglect the structure of gender consciousness? Why should we accept the notion that ideological hegemony is sustained at work and school and in political action when we know quite well that the hand that rocks the cradle does so to the alien rhythm of male self-interest and masculine oppression?

Analyses of those ensembles of social relations in which the biological necessity to produce is transformed to the cultural needs which make history have a tendency to fade into abstract economic structuralisms: these relations cannot be adequately explained in terms of class hegemony, nor of intellectual imperialism, nor of any other one-sided ideology.   Production itself has no "antithesis" in Marx's otherwise scrupulous dialectics.   If we are to argue that neither productive relations nor reproductive relations can be reduced to biological determinism of a reflexive kind or to abstract idealism of an ahistorical kind, then what we must show is that the *process* of reproduction is dialectically structured and that this process stands in contradiction to the productive process in specific ways. I have attempted this demonstration, still at a very abstract level, in *The Politics of Reproduction*. What I have argued there at some length is that reproduction is historical, material, and dialectical. Let me summarize very briefly this analysis.

Maternity is a product, in the first instance, of human sexuality.   The human activity of reproduction, however, unlike universal sexuality, is differentiated genderically. This differentiation is no mere truism, for it is the material ground of reproductive consciousness. For women, the birth process is *mediated* by labor.   Childbirth is a mode of alienation mediated in women's labor. Historically, on this mediation is built varying sets of social relations which meet the needs of mother laborer and the new needs of the helpless product of reproductive labor, the infant. Like all *necessary* labor, reproduction creates two things: value and new needs. The historical development of structures to define this value and meet these needs is varied, but their ground is the reproduction process itself. For women, giving birth is a unity of knowing and doing, of consciousness and creative activity, of temporality and continuity.

Paternity is a quite different phenomenon. The essential moment of paternity is also alienation, the alienation of the sperm. As this alienation is *not* mediated, is fundamentally abstract and involuntary, it must be given meaning by abstract knowledge rather than by experience. It must then be concretized in social process, the most primordial form of which is the male appropriation of the child. The fact that this appropriation is oppressive precisely because it is at the same time the appropriation of women's *labor* embedded in the child is obscured by the fetishisms of patriarchy. Paternity is fundamentally ideal, and as a matter of knowing rather than doing, it must be understood as historical discovery: at some unknown historical moment the unmediated relation of man and child is discovered to be both integration with and alienation from reproductive process. Paternity is thus a historical discovery and an ideal phenomenon, rooted in "knowing" but also in not knowing.

This contradiction--knowing in general but not knowing in particular-- leads to considerable flexibility in the cultural definition of the alienated father, quite a different experience from that of the integrated mother. Paternity may be said to be ungrounded idealism, while maternity can be said to be grounded materialism. Paternity is tyrannized by the abstract, it responds by tyrannizing the concrete. The historical contradiction which mediates the dialectics of reproduction is thus universal alienation of individual men from the species, and it is the cultural mediation of this contradiction which historically becomes the structure of "the family" and the ideology of patriarchy. Paternity is not simply a psychic yearning any more than alienation is a neurosis, it is an epistemology, a system of knowledge of a concrete experience of practical alienation, which is the ground of male reproductive dialectic. Universal man is an abstraction drawn out from the universal experience of men as uncertain fathers, as outcasts from species continuity, as individuals who do not "have" but "acknowledge" children.

The alienation of woman from child occurs at the involuntary moment of birth process. This mode of alienation, however, is categorically different from that of men in that the separation of woman and child is *mediated*: maternity, unlike paternity, which is abstract and dualistic, is concrete and integrated. It is mediated in the first instance by individual reproductive labor and in the second instance by the historical creation of reproductive relations grounded in integrative labor. Childbirth constitutes a mediated dialectic which unifies thought and action, and creates an integrated rather than an alienated relation of women, species, and value produced by reproductive labor, the value of life as such. This value has been obscured in cultural relations in which abstract man has been denaturalized by a real live brotherhood working together to ground man's abstract universality of reproductive experience in a culturally structured *right* to appropriate women's reproductive labor and to redefine their own exclusion from species continuity as freedom. This process is a matter of historical record. The abstracted father is reintegrated through the concreteness of patriarchal culture, a culture which devalues life in an endless preoccupation with death and destruction, which appropriates and exploits women's labor and women's children, and which symbolizes itself in the triumphant and idealized contours of the penis rampant, the icon of man's first historical subversion and transcendence of natural necessity.

The first historical change in the process of reproduction, then, is in the discovery of paternity and its dialectic of alienation and freedom. The second and quite recent change is the removal of the involuntary component of female reproductive labor, a historical development which grows out of the dialectics of production and reproduction. A developed knowledge of cause and effect in general and of the relation of sexuality and reproduction in particular is the condition of paternity, the development of maternal control of conception is the condition of female control over reproductive process. I believe that a first priority of feminist politics must be to wrest control of reproductive technology from men, just as, long ages ago, men partially but effectively wrested the control of sexuality, children, and the social construction of gender from women.

Materially, we are as a species compelled to take notice of the dialectically related necessities of production and reproduction. Patriarchs, responding to the genius of Karl Marx, will acknowledge the need to produce and to create social relations and historical modes of production. They will not, however, accord any cultural or historical meaning to the need to create social relations of reproduction, muttering darkly about biological determinism and reductionism and other epistemological sins. To be sure, in ages of totally involuntary pregnancy such a view is understandable, though it still ignores women's centuries of struggle to control their own fecundity. The task was never rendered easy: apart from the technical difficulties, ideologies of male sexual rights or conquest and myths about gender differentiation of sex drives have contributed to millions of unplanned pregnancies. In the new age of contraception and reproductive technology, the male "potency principle" is as outmoded and bizarre as old Malthus's population theories. Those on the Left who castigate Malthus without noticing their own patriarchal premises and class fixations cannot make sense of reproductive technology, which they understand as just another development of the market system. Not recognizing the family as a historical phenomenon grounded in reproductive gender relations, for example, they think of family forms as changing in response to modes of production. Liberals think of these new technologies as extensions of free personal choice.

Yet the dialectics within and between production and reproduction are now doing much more than maintaining class antagonisms or gender antagonisms. They are making the fundamental human task of reproducing the material world and its population highly problematic. With ecosystems and genetic patterns subject to ignorant neglect and blind technological twiddling, human history and human individual survival become pawns in the maw of technocrats. The political infrastructure to control these processes is struggling to find strategies to analyze these realities and politicize them. This is a task which only feminist politics is equipped to take seriously. To be sure, feminist politics can be and is distracted by liberal individualism and class struggle. A better deal for women individually and in class terms constitutes a vital strategy, but only if it is seen in the context of the larger historical imperative. That imperative, of course, is to reproduce the material world and our historically conscious species. It is an urgent task, involving knowing, doing, acting, thinking--above all, working together to maintain international cooperation and universal momentum in feminist politics.

NOTES

[1]Simone de Beauvoir, *The Second Sex*, translated by H. M. Parshley. (New York: Bantam Books, 1953). p. 26.

2

State Power and Reproductive Freedom

In 1975, a slightly irregular graduate student--white-haired, post-menopausal--I was faced with that most complex modern version of a male puberty rite. I had to write a thesis. After several years in school, I realized that I had not the slightest idea of how to do this. As in all ritualistic procedures, uncertainty and cabalism are used to heighten the nervous tension: one is told one must do it, one can do it, but one is never told how to do it. Some kind of alchemy will be fused with institutional approval to produce what is referred to as an original work of scholarship. Now, if my studies had taught me anything, they had taught me that there were precious few original works of scholarship around: I even had a deep suspicion that Plato and the authors of the Book of Genesis had been cribbing from a lost oral tradition, exploiting the absence of copyright law. In fact, the only really original stuff that I had read was the new feminist writing by Millett and Firestone, but this had not found its way into any of the reading lists that I had ploughed through. Further, there were no faculty who had actually

Reprinted with permission from *Canadian Woman Studies/les cahiers de la femme* 6, no. 3 (Summer/Fall 1985), pp. 62-66. An early version of this paper was presented to the National Association of Women and the Law conference, "Who's in Control?" in Ottawa, 1985.

read this work, and in any case they thought this stuff (which they had not read) was "derivative," they told me.

Derivative from what? I asked. Cold Look. From the tradition, I was told. It took about three minutes for me to understand that what this meant was that the tradition was essentially and exclusively masculine. Mainstream thought was not main stream but male-stream thought. I had, of course, recognized much earlier, before I went to school at all in fact, that I wanted to do a feminist thesis, but I had not thought much beyond providing a critical proof of the generic one-sidedness of the vaunted tradition. In this spirit, I had done quite a bit of research for a thesis on John Milton. Milton comes into the curriculum of political theory not as a poet but as a pamphleteer. During the bourgeois revolution in England, Milton wrote pamphlets for Puritan Liberalism; he was even assigned the task of writing the justification for the execution of the King, which is as fine an omelette of law and ideology as one could ever hope to swallow. But he also composed polemical pamphlets on divorce, advocating divorce by consent, which sounds progressive until one finds that only the consent of the husband was at stake. Not surprising, by the man who used all that poetic power to libel Eve and Delilah. Milton wanted to escape from his own nasty marriage to a much younger but not especially submissive wife. But I was bored with this self-righteous puritan before I even thought about what I may say in a thesis, except that I was impressed by the note of hysteria which crept into his voice when he spoke of paternal rights and the power of the "sacred seed", the true source of life. Fathers would decide, fathers had the *right* to decide the fate of "their" children and "their" wives. The great liberal imagination had its limitations. I noted that Milton was able to argue that women could be sexually "unfaithful" without in any way threatening the legal rights of the husbands to the issue of their wombs, whatever happened to the *amour propre* of the uxorious husband of the Miltonic muse. But of course, children were of law for men and merely of nature for mothers. It would be many years before Somer Brodribb and Sheila McIntyre introduced me to the legal precept of "The mother is always certain. The father is he to whom the marriage points" (*Mater semper certa est: pater is est quem nuptiae demonstrant*) and to the perception that paternity is a legal fiction rather than, like maternity, a human truth grounded in the materiality of reproductive experience.

But Milton's ideological ramblings, the prose issue of Adam's rib and Lucifer's rebellion, did set me thinking about birth and the implications of the uncertainty of paternity. I had just spend five years reading political philosophy, pondering on notions of power and community, of law and of consent, of states and constitutions, of tyrannies and parliaments, but I had read very little about birth. There were, of course, Locke and Hegel and such characters, eloquent of the subject of hereditary power and its evils and hereditary property and its goods, but silent on the historical nature of birth. There was not a total neglect of the natural and biological worlds among political theorists--Machiavelli dreaded nature for "her" inconstancy and uncertainty, and Marx in fact rooted his whole philosophy on the material basis of our need to reproduce ourselves and our species; but species production for Marx was a by-product of productive forces. Aha! that was true . . . wasn't it? We have to eat to live at both the individual and species level, and to eat we must work--or some of us must work. Labor. The core of Marx's epistemology. But when I said that word labor my understanding went right back to my days as a midwife, and I knew that there was more than one kind of labor. In fact, my first immediate understanding of labor was that labor which brings forth the child. Maybe I could write a thesis about that? In fact, I did, but not without a great deal of preliminary struggle.

The struggle came about because I had been taught, in the male tradition, to think dualistically. We understand things by their opposites, or we must separate one thing from the other thing before we understand why it is that particular thing, or we must simply face the fact that we as individuals are doomed to be dualistically constituted because we stand opposed to "The Other": Sartre at his most hysterical extreme, clawing his way out of all these slimy holes of otherness. Even my heroine, de Beauvoir, posited otherness as absolute. So when I tried to think systematically about birth, I was distracted by this otherness, this separation of nature and history, of mind and body, of family and state, of self and others. I had further been taught that to ascribe causality to the biological world was to endanger man's free will. I didn't care too much about man's free will, which I thought to be both exaggerated and abominably abused, and in any case, the midwife in me said again and again: birth is cultural, it is a unity of natural and cultural processes. Labor is real. Women may not be able to stop what they are doing, but they *know* what they are doing. They are conscious of themselves as reproducers. There is such a thing as reproductive consciousness, and it differs between men and women. Male consciousness is alienated from the process of reproduction. Man is related to his child only by thought, by knowledge in general, rather than by experience in particular--whereas motherhood is a unity of consciousness and knowing on the one hand, and action (reproductive labor) on the other.

It is in this way that I came to develop the notion that not only were the *cultural* forms of the social and legal relations of reproduction historical, but that actual process of reproduction, the integration of doing and knowing which women experience and the separation which men experience, are historically developed forms of consciousness. I was nervous of this judgment--would I ever dare to show it to my already nervous thesis committee--did I actually believe it myself? If so, why?

I was outraged that none of the works I had read paid any attention to the historical and philosophical aspects of human reproduction, the meaning of the event, the necessity for women's labor to reproduce the species in history. (In political theory, the state is defended as man's supreme achievement, that which transcends such dubiously human events as birth, livelihood, bodily well-being in the glory of law, order and power. In making the state, men believe themselves to be making history.) Yet, surely birth is a substructure, a condition of history, surely it is an act, a conscious act of labor? Surely it is not mere biological event but human action? But of course, it is a *woman's* act, and few women had written any of the books I had been reading for years, and few formulated the power and the glory of the state.

Why is it important that birth be understood as historical? Because it is the ground of certain sets of social relations which, I was convinced, needed to be changed, and change is what history is about. Birth itself may be a natural phenomenon, but in fact a great deal of history--in culture, certainly in law, in ideology--has been piled on it. Yet birth process itself was regarded as changeless, and therefore by definition historical, natural, contingent, occasionally miraculous but usually uninteresting. In and of itself, birth process has no meaning--until men give it one.

In my analysis of the history of birth process, as opposed to the social construction of child rearing or marriage or legal forms which arise from it, I discovered that birth process, when understood as a unity of knowledge and practice, rather than an animal accident, had changed only twice. The first change, a long time ago, was the discovery of paternity, with all its contradictions of alienation and freedom. Paternity is not present to consciousness in an immediate way, and therefore must have been discovered in historical time and discovered in the mode of causality. The second, indeed the historical condition which I believe has led many feminists to turn to the process of birth with new understanding, was the change wrought by contraceptive technology on a potentially universal scale in our time. In 1975, I and many others could see that this development was enormously significant, that it was what Hegel called a "world-historical event," a happening which would transform not only ancient institutions but which would bring about transformations in our consciousness of ourselves, our bodies, our historical and social being. The questions were: what kind of changes, and who would control and direct these changes? How could a state designed to transcend mere birth, crude biology, deal with this historicization of the ahistorical with the politicization of the pre-political? In fact, the state has no difficulty in doing this, for its willing surrogates, the medicine men, the legal establishment and the scientists, are all ready to face down the possibility that

reproductive technology might serve to establish reproductive
control for women.

I should note that then, just ten years ago, what I meant
by contraceptive technology was the pill, but I had read
Brave New World, and knew it would not stop there. Frankly
I had no perception of the speed of development, that in 1985
we would be dealing with artificial insemination by donor,
contract mothering, freeze-dried sperm and a scientific
dramaturgy played out on the stage of petri dishes. I had
rather naive visions that reproductive technology would
liberate women, usher in reproductive choice and transform
the social relations of reproduction fairly directly. I don't
believe this was fundamentally wrong, but my timetable was
a little sanguine. What was inseparable from the technology
question was the question of power and of control. Men have
always defined the social parameter of the forms of
reproductive relations. They have also controlled
technological development. It is this old male control of
production combined with newer control of reproduction
which makes the development of reproductive technology a
political question, a historical event of a momentous kind
and a renewed struggle for reproductive power. The
implications are awesome. There is no single issue which
unifies the human need to produce for survival on an
individual basis and to reproduce for survival on a species
basis in the way that reproductive technology does.
Reproductive technology makes the marriage of capitalism
and patriarchy fecund. There is no issue which throws down
the challenge to women to seize control of their usurped
reproductive power in the way that this issue does. There is
no issue in which the holding in balance of the laws of the
natural world and the law of the historical world offers us
radical choices and possible transformations of such a
fundamental kind. I believe that the powerful development
of the women's movement in recent years is grounded in the
transformation of our reproductive experience and is not a
wave or a spasm but a new unity of species and self-
consciousness: feminists understand that these changes
require a newer, braver, more just world if they are to be
humane and liberating. They also know that we do not have

a just world, we do not have the rule of justice. We have the rule of men, patriarchy, a historical megalosaur which does not yet recognize that it has earned extinction. This man's world has consigned the condition of history--birth--to the world of nature, which man understands as enemy. It has constructed the institution of the private realm in which the tasks of birthing and rearing can be controlled by man's grandiose projection of his universality into the state, the public realm. This man's world, in which birth is animal and death is splendid, in which destruction is noble and conservation soft-headed, this man's world in which control of production and reproduction are the political and economic tools of patriarchal survival, this man's world in which the unifying concept of species itself is fractured into divisions of gender, race, wealth, sexuality in a mammoth exercise of divide and conquer: this is the world which created the processes in which women could be oppressed but not obliterated, in which children could be claimed and named but not necessarily cared for, the process in which the alienated fathers consolidated a legal claim to real power over their reproductive lives. This power over women is clearly not enough: mankind now aspires to buttress that control with the mastery of the natural world, the scientific and technical control of species reproduction, the ultimate triumph over the treacherous inconstancy of nature and her accomplice, woman. Reproductive technology and the technology of species destruction are conjoined in a lethal alliance which would negotiate the gap between individual and species by destroying both.

We must never for one moment believe that we are dealing here with pure technology, any more than we believe that Star Wars is pure science. These are the strategies of a ruling gender dizzy with the power of denying the grounds of human being in the labor of birthing women. This is not, of course, to say that reproduction is in any sense sacred, that it cannot be tampered with, that it is beyond human transformation. Women in particular have clear interests in controlling their reproductive powers, of making choices, of ameliorating the physical agonies of reproductive labor. This is to say that the way to go is in the sane and humane

utilization of technology in the interests of the species--not in
the interests of a scientific-industrial state designed by the
patriarchy to maximize men's power, to glorify violence, to
reap profits, to mutilate the good earth's abundance. Can
one think of a more sterile ambition for any civilization than
that of "conquering space," the colonization of emptiness?
Can one think of robotic heroism? The old ideology of the
creative power of the divine seed, the sacred seed, pales
beside the notion of automated procreation.

It is against this frenzy that the feminist movement lives
and grows and struggles. The changes in reproductive
process are both grounds of and challenge to the feminist
movement. This is not another sectarian revolt. Feminism
has redefined revolution. Always understood as a violent
upheaval in the public realm, revolution in feminist terms
becomes a non-violent but radical revolution of the private
realm, a struggle which breaks down the barriers men have
built to control women. Now there are political advantages
in redefining revolution, not least of which is the fact that
antagonists don't really see what is happening. Politicians
think of us as a new voice--shrill, of course, women are
always shrill--a new vocal "minority" to be wooed for votes.
Employers think of us as a reserve labor force, but now on
the uppity side, needing to be disciplined by low wages and
part-time participation in the job of earning our, after all,
less demanding livelihoods. Some men think of our liberated
sexuality as their escape from the bondage of the private
realm and the responsibility inseparable from the continuity
of species in the love and care of children. The New Right
thinks we have accidentally freed ourselves from comfortably
mindless constraints, and should be desperately agitating to
have them put back in place. Despite all of this, the
transformation of the social relations of reproduction, of
gender identity, of women's political sophistication, the
development of sisterhood, the challenge to knowledge itself:
all of these slowly and painfully proceed. And there is joy in
it notwithstanding.

There are also problems galore. Some of these come from
the historical hegemony of men which has left us with a
legacy of one-sided concepts and speechless languages, which

make it difficult to conceptualize our history: to assert the validity of our consciousness and experience, to recover the history of the species' continuity, given reality by women's reproductive labor; to assert a different time consciousness, a new ethics, a sense of unity with nature and life which denies conventional patriarchal preoccupations with crude causalities and violent confrontations, with objectivity eroded by death wishes and subjectivity identified with power. Who is to do all this? Who is to attack all this? Who is to destroy it? Who is to replace it? Women, we answer, and such men who can transcend their own history. But who are women? Here, we stand face to face with the misogynist interpretation of patriarchal history, the pro-masculine essence of the state and of knowledge. Edward O. Wilson, the great white father of sociobiology, asserts that "the female of the species is quintessentially a producer of eggs." Quintessence, you will recall, was the fifth essence posited by the ancients as the substance forming entities not obviously composed of the four elements of earth, fire, air and water which their science had identified. Quintessence was also thought to be the substance of which the heavenly bodies were formed. This does not seem to be the sort of ascription Wilson had in mind (although my friend Milton would have been quite happy with a quintessence for the sacred sperms). Wilson means essential but more so, and commits this etymological gaffe in his desire to suggest that egg producing is not only an essentially feminine task, but the only significant thing we do. This view of women as essentially breeders, preferably of healthy children with clearly accredited fathers, is the quintessence of patriarchal ideology--a substanceless substantiation. The assertions of the historical significance of reproduction, of the reality of reproductive consciousness, of the moral nature of the mother-child bond: all of these are in danger of slipping into the crude causality and abstract determinisms of sociobiology (and its new step-son, bioethics) if we de-historicize them, if we try to cram them into patriarchal categories of language and thought. The separation of the child, the unknowability of biological parenthood which men experience, produce birth as a causal concept of men's minds rather than as an issue of women's unity of consciousness, experience and reproductive labor. In their birthing potential, as mothers, as midwives, as carers, women unify nature and history in a way not accessible to masculine experience. We cannot use their abstract notions to construct the society which validates our real collective consciousness as women.

Yet, that alien experience has formed our culture, an alienation which now sees no contradiction between biological and technical determinations, which are as crude in conception as they are sophisticated in execution. The crisis in reproductivity has projected its patriarchal momentum and muddled morality upon the ancient practice of abortion rather than on the crucial contemporary problematics of reproductive technology.

Women's struggles to control their own bodies are historic struggles, and are central to the abortion war, but it is not women who have defined abortion as the single locus of reproductive politics. This strategy serves to deflect attention and energy away from the deeper and more important issue of reproductive technology, which is a more powerful weapon of control in terms of patriarchy, which doesn't eat up law officers of the state, and which has a potential for the generation of profit, thereby making it attractive to the ruling class. The abortion struggle is ideological in that it produces a clash between two opposing abstractions, the emptied perceptions of Right and an equally empty ideology of pure life. This is a difficult and often divisive issue for women because the whole business is trapped in ideological formulations: pure life on the one hand and the concept of right on the other, which, without the legal verification which gives content to right, becomes merely an assertion of "natural" right, pure empty right pitted against pure dehistoricized life. The liberal solution to this impasse, a retreat to situation ethics, is not very satisfactory; the conservative position of sticking mindlessly to patriarchal ideology is even less so.

We cannot bring change by changing the meanings of words, but we cannot identify political strategies or ethical positions by starting with ideological definitions. I would argue that the definition of "life" which patriarchy has produced is grounded in men's existential separation from species continuity rather than women's integrative experience of birth. If "life-as-such" is an absolute value then we must never swat a fly, fumigate a fungus, catch a fish, nor boil a quintessential egg. This is why the concept of Right must be added to the crude affirmation of life but right itself is a political legal concept of a quite murky kind.

Human life, of course, is presumed to be "different" from other forms of life, a difference which men have usually attributed to the possession of rationality--a quality more satisfactory in theory than visible in practice--and the exercise of choice, which is dangerous in women who have no rationality. All of this has led to extraordinary fights over when in fact a foetus becomes human.

This obscure and abstract debate can only take place in a world in which men have usurped the right to give meaning to experience, including the experience from which they are biologically excluded, that of giving birth. The transformation from life in general to human life in particular comes, I would argue, in the concrete labor of women. (Marx defined labor as the creation of value, but he did not heed the value produced by women's reproductive labor.) This work is a unification of bodily labor with human consciousness, a unity of knowledge and experience which defines the human as the species which knows what it is doing in the act of giving birth: it is creating value, the value of human life, a cultural and individual value which is consciously experience by the laboring reproducer. Life-as-such can have no moral value, for value is a good which rests on a conscious interpretation of the experience of being in the world and of working in the world. The infant, produced by a combination of labor and consciousness, of culture and biology, of women and nature, is the human reality of life as opposed to that abstract "quintessence" of life--undifferentiated, brute and without consciousness. The foetus *in utero* is all of these things, and the notion that it is already human from "conception" is one which rests solely upon the limp fallacy of the procreative power of the alienated sperm, the "holy seed" of patriarchal ideology that bestows life. Abortion is neither a right nor a crime, but a

very difficult existential choice related to our human
participation in species continuity, our women's perception of
the unity of life and living, complicated by the fact that
heterosexual relations are conducted in such a grotesquely
adversarial way. It is an odd world in which we casually
destroy millions of people, the valuable products of women's
reproductive labor, and find these killings ethically
defensible, while we become violent in the defence of a
collection of cells unvalorized by labor and uninterpreted by
conscious human experience. It is an odd world, too, in
which men are taught to value mere gratification as
essential to man-kind's greater density.

   All of this deflects our attention from a much more vital
issue, that of reproductive technology. Women are
understandably ambivalent about this; childbirth is no fun,
whatever the subsequent joys. Technology, a male preserve,
is a device which may award to men that control of the
species reproduction which has been available to them so far
only by strategies for controlling and privatizing women.
This is not a reason for blind resistance to technology, but it
does mean that we must address the implications of
reproductive technology seriously and thoughtfully. Perhaps
women will eventually gain by the escape from the hazards of
labor, but the species may lose from its blindness to the
ethical dimensions of childbearing, usually dismissed
contemptuously in the phrase "motherhood issue."
Motherhood, more broadly understood, may well be the
ethical issue of the coming decades, with the implications of
caring and conserving life which men have taught women to
understand as mere sentiment, but which in fact have a
capacity for mediation of dualism, for integration, for
reproducing the world--a capacity which is absent from the
sterile deductive categories of axiomatic and syllogistic
ethics.

   It is good to see women breaking down the barriers of the
legal profession, not only in terms of careers, but in terms of
bringing to legal knowledge and to legal practice the insight
and determination of women's practice and feminist vision.
It is by law, after all, that the patriarchal states built their
cultural hegemony, consolidating the power of the father in

the legitimation of children, placing the existential bonds of legal marriage on women, legislating male power and tacitly or even overtly legitimizing violence in the family. From the judge on the bench to the cop on the beat, from the statesman in public to the patriarch in private, men's laws have ruled women's lives and appropriated women's children as soon as they were old enough not to need a mother's toil and patience, though they never grow old enough not to need her sacrificial love. And it is to the law that the reproductive technocrats turn for the legitimation of their procedures, for the patent of approbation and the license to exercise the ultimate control, that of the reproduction of the species. The women's movement at this moment in history needs a voice in law, and it is good to be here and know the voice is speaking, neither ex cathedra nor pontifically, but in sweet tune with the aspirations of women in all walks of life. We need that voice. As a movement, we need your knowledge and your political commitment, your sense and your concern, to mount the necessary critique of and resistance to robotic technological hysteria of the new baby-farmers. We need your help to understand the processes and strategisms in which male control of reproduction is being consolidated and how to challenge that. But most of all, we need you as all women need each other, to fight the good fight which will transform patriarchal legalism to feminist justice, justice for us, for our children and for our species.

3

Abstract Thought and Feminist Theory

What I want to address here is how to do theory. The limitations imposed by the deep-rooted sexism of language and thought have been much discussed by feminists, but what I want to look at is abstraction as both a proceduring--"abstracting from"--and a noun--"the abstract." I am sensitive to this issue because my own work has been criticized as abstract; at the same time, I cannot envisage a mode of theorizing which is not in some sense an act of abstracting something from something. It is not, in my view, a question of whether to theorize. We do have minds and generally assume that our experience has some meaning. The question is *whose* meaning.

Theory is the use of mind to explain, encode, or distort the real. At its worst it can be an act of domination and terror-- it can be theorized that Jews are unfit to live, that women are mindless, that where there is no penis there is no sexuality, that nature is an enemy: all of these are familiar theories and have been put into practice with all too real results. Is it not then a danger that the process of

---

An early version of this paper was presented to the National Women's Studies Association conference at Douglass College, Rutgers, The State University of New Jersey, 1984.

abstraction of meaning is in practice quite arbitrary and hopelessly drenched in ideology and prejudice? In practice, abstraction is the central methodology of theorizing. In all phenomena or interactions between phenomena there is a little something not immediately present to the senses which, theorists have argued, gives meaning to objects, people, acts, interactions, events, to reality in general. This uncovering of meaning is done by means of the active inquiry of mind into meaning, essence, particularity, universality, sense-- whatever.

Of course, it has always been claimed that true truths--"objective" truths--are demonstrable. The scientific approach is to theorize a relation and then test it, either experimentally or empirically. However, theory as hypothesis has rather limited scope (which is a pity, as such procedures are currently being used to "test" species destruction). There are old and new questions with which such a strategy cannot deal; for example, What is truth? Or, What is patriarchy? We can, of course, *describe* patriarchy, and it is important that we do so. The meaning of patriarchy is in one sense the definition by others of what women are. Patriarchy, however, is also a historical phenomenon; it is not "natural," however much it presents itself as such. So what is the history of patriarchy and what, then, does "history" mean? These questions raise a wide range of issues, and we have tended to turn to male theorizing--that of Marx, for instance--to tell us what history is, and then we adjust this theory to "include" women. Yet all theories of history are surely abstract in the idealist sense if they neglect the empirical condition of continuity over time, of species reproduction, of the birth of individuals, and the maintenance of the species. Here we see the complexities of abstraction very clearly: having abstracted the process of reproduction from history, patriarchy has rendered history abstract. History, in having its meaning only in "the mind of man" has no meaning in the lives of ordinary people. The current threat to history, the end of history, is no longer a prose poem to titillate the romantic male imagination. It is a very real possibility, neither hypothesis nor abstraction but concrete history: the bang is in fact far more likely than the whimper. Feminists theorize that this historical situation is related to patriarchy, but it is crucial that we be able to say how. This explanation must involve, at the very least, abstracting from patriarchy the meaning of its destructiveness, the underbelly of the historical "progress of man."

How in fact can we know anything, given that we have only patriarchal tools to work with? Patriarchal theories of knowledge are hopelessly contaminated by prejudice, self-interest, and sheer error--the mixture of falsity which we call ideology, or "ungrounded" theory. Perhaps the greatest fraud of patriarchal abstraction is the myth of objectivity and the reliance on "rigorous" method to overcome the real problems of knowing. How fond of "rigor" men are! I think what rigor means is not permitting anyone to disagree with you. It embodies a theoretical claim that methodological rigor is the systematic application of mind to reality. But rigorous objectivity is just as often prejudiced abstraction--taking out of phenomena those qualities in accord with the theory or simply the interests of the observer: reality is colored less by the objective mind than the ideological and abstract nature of patriarchy's most successful abstraction, the notion of universal man.

Feminism aspires to put thought and experience together in a coherent way. The materialism which we associate with Marx tried to do this, and Marx's definition of history is at least promising in that it recognizes that history is a unification of theory and practice and tries to ground that praxis in real conditions of human life. Unfortunately, it was men's theories and men's actions which engaged Marx, and although the need to produce subsistence is recognized as a continuing undercurrent of necessity in the process of making history, Marx had no doubt that it is men who make history. He limited historically significant praxis to economic production and the social relations arising therefrom, but he identified men, or perhaps Man, as productive workers. The social action to which Marx accorded greatest significance-- class struggle--is also man's fate. In all this, Marx created an abstract history in two ways. First, he simply abstracted women's work and struggle from history; second, he understood correctly that human history is materially grounded in the necessity to produce subsistence but did not recognize the related necessity of species reproduction. Marxist man labors to make history without ever getting born or raised to adult manhood: he is abstracted from history and life process. There is no recognition of species continuity and the development of social relations of reproduction as material conditions of history. Here, Marx shares the general theoretical proposition which is central to patriarchal thought: men *transcend* life process to make history. This is the theoretical leap which validated the notion of universal man as superior to the mere male of the species.

The question is not one of demonstrating that all theory is sexist and partial: all thought abstracted from life and the reproduction of individual and species life is doomed to abstraction in the idealist sense. The idea is real in the heads of men but is separated from the reality--from the truth--of history as material continuity over time. It is at this point that abstract "universality" replaces concrete community.

The question is how to uncover ways in which women's reality can be thought about (with a view to transforming it) that avoid the separation of realities of women's lives from the truth of their lived content. "Pure thought" is the stuff of ideology and thought control, abstractions willfully reconstituted in a world by theories purporting to be based on truths. For example, Nietzsche's gnomic utterance: "Suppose truth is a woman, what then?" The answer for universal man is: nothing.

Yet we cannot regard abstract thought as fraudulent, comical, elitist, or totally unreal. We think, but language and modes of thought in which we are soaked ensure that we think in terms of otherness. Thought has no power in and of itself; it must be unified with action to insist that one interpretation of truth--the hegemony of abstract man as the maker of history--prevails. The material consequences are, of course, enormous. In Western society, the powerlessness of the many is masked by abstract generalizations which have been raised to political "truths" of a most problematic kind:

all men are free, all people are equal, nature is abstract but man is real--all of that stuff. The power mechanism by which such palpable lies can be presented as a truth is itself an abstraction, that curious non-entity which we call the state. The state is the ultimate abstraction of power from the many transformed into the "truth" of the government by the best--a proposition descending from antiquity which serves the concrete few in the consolidation of power abstracted from the many. The state is the triumph of male will to power writ large in invisible ink.

We must not confuse the all-too-real trappings of political power and social oppression with their abstract justifications. The state masks its abstract nature by huge edifices of an administrative and manipulative and, where necessary, coercive kind. The state itself is a concept, an abstract principle of continuity rendered as vital entity. This abstract state provides a continuity that is abstracted from the actuality of biological reproduction in which men are marginal and uncertain actors and reconstituted as man's great achievement in rational social organization, in making history. The state can appear as real only if it can represent itself as a rational objectification of power. But power itself becomes an abstraction if separated from the living creatures who do have the capacity to act on the world. Power belongs to the community, and at certain points in history has been actualized in community activity. The state precludes this organization of power in which production and reproduction are perceived as essential. The state abstracts these powers from people in general and awards them to particular men in the name of universality. Community is dehumanized so that it can be abstractly masculinized and transformed into an abstract power called "the state."

The social and historical expression of this power is settled upon those who are able to appropriate the "right" to govern. Predictably, such rights are abstractions and downright lies: that superiority rests in morality, wealth, gender, color, heredity, brute force, greater intelligence, and all kinds of "objective" factors. In fact, the consolidation of the real power of the community rests entirely on coercion, and the myth of state power is an enabling device to convert natural and sociable community power to artificial and social elite domination.

The state, both as concept and ideology, legitimates and procures consent to the abstraction of power from community, and in doing so develops procedures, practices, and precedents for the consent of the governed to this state of affairs. To be sure, states seem to work more successfully where this consent is procured by more subtle means than mere force, but the guns in the attic are not at all abstract and are always there should the need arise. The obscuring of the abstract nature of the state in the notion of legitimacy is accomplished by the development of social and political symbols, institutions and ideologies which enable the powerful to hang on to power and organize consent to these arrangements. In democracies, an important part of this process is the involvement of citizens in the process. The state, for example, controls and funds education, but the system is set up so that teachers and, to a lesser extent, parents and students are given the opportunity to acquire some influence in decision making processes; but these participants bring to this exercise a carefully bred conception of ultimate powerlessness. The construction of curriculum appears as a diffuse and even haphazard affair until members of the community attempt real strategies of control. The struggle to introduce feminism into the curriculum, for example, has to lurk under the pallid--and abstract--guise of "women's studies," and critical class studies are labeled "political economy." Only when established can these forms for knowledge acquire legitimacy, and then at the price of cleaving to established theories, methodology, and acceptable pedagogy. Nonetheless, such studies are subversive and call for a state response, which generally takes the form of giving public encouragement to the less radical forms of such inquiry. Threats to the concrete symbols of the abstract state--wealth, decision making, war waging, value systems-- are met with a number of strategies, the most effective of which is to define and realize the usefulness of such studies in terms of economic success within the state structure. The result is that getting funded and having the study published in elite circles defines research success and all is further diluted in the realities of "policy making."

The abstract state acquires its veneer of reality, then, by strategies which impoverish both community and individual powers by appropriating human activity for "national survival," by which is meant the political hegemony of gender, class, and race. For the state to appear as rule, community must appear as abstract, a point which Nancy Hartsock's work has rendered more clear to me than anyone else's.[1] Indeed, when one speaks of the relation of real community and abstract state, it is much more common to be asked: "What do you mean by community?" than it is to be asked what one means by the state. The lived social relations of individuals appear as abstract and problematic, while the theory and practice of the custodians of the abstract concept of the state appear real. Personality cults are endemic to modern states, and the British Queen, the American president, Stalin, and Hitler are different versions of the political strategy of concretizing the concept of state and justifying the means of coercion, at whatever level of brutality they are exercized. But these "heads of state" (pure mind?) also replace birth (women's concrete labor) as representations of continuity over time. Collective symbols (e.g., "the party," the aristocracy) tend to political instability and usually lead to the Strong Man appearing.

All of these issues are addressed by political theorists in a variety of ways, from the spiritual arrogance of the ultramontane to the earnest voting analyses of behavioral scientists. Some of these findings are useful in a limited way, but the role of patriarchy is central to none of them. Yet patriarchy might well be the truth of the abstract state, not only in terms of the reality of male political power, nor the exclusion of the private realm from public life. The abstract state not only renders community abstract, but also does the same to individuals. This abstraction is achieved by the concept of universal man making history; in other words, the identification of the species as male. Here we see the two senses of abstraction very clearly, both as active verb and abstract noun; men have abstracted women from their *concept* of history (they clearly cannot be obliterated from actual historical events), thus rendering history itself as a concept, a product of mind, an abstraction. The difference

between actual history and the concept of history is similar
to the contrast of living community and abstract state.
Concepts liberate mind from the discipline of the real. Male-
stream thought offers no explanation of why this is
necessary, why mind and reality must be seen as separate, as
dualist, as alienated from each other.   Marx offers an
analysis of alienation based on the particular construction of
work by capitalism in the form of wage labor which is
persuasive but partial. He is right in saying he only turns
Hegel upside down, for he does not actually challenge the
notion of the dialectic of ideal and material or, in older
vocabulary, mind and matter. The models are the same; only
the *hierarchy* of thought and reality is inverted. Both are
incomplete, for community is rendered abstract. For Hegel,
the state has its reality in the symbolism of the hereditary
monarch; for Marx, the state is the executive committee of
the ruling class.

The question is a simple one but very difficult to pose in a
culturally acceptable way. Is the lust of men to persist in
double-dealing abstractions a product of the fact that they
are male? There is no cultural difficulty in the suggestion
that women live oppressed lives in the private realm because
they are women.   Nothing prevents such tautological
abstraction in the rules of the patriarchal political game.
Women remain abstracted from community as developed by
patriarchy because women are of nature, and nature is
abstract. By this is usually meant that while nature is
objectively there, she (sic) has no meaning unless man gives
it to her. The awarding of meaning is rewarded by control;
power is the product of the act of awarding meaning, which
is understood as the abstraction of a meaning which is there
waiting for man and his mind to explicate it. *Why* does man
then first of all create an abstraction of himself, a notion
which transcends actual collectivity in favor of the concept of
universality?   Why is community itself first cleansed of
women, who inhabit a different private realm? To ask this
in a less abstract way, what is it about men's experience that
gives them the sense of the reality of abstraction in the first
place?

I have argued elsewhere that men are in a concrete sense abstracted from the vital process of species continuity by virtue of the process of biological reproduction. The uncertainty of paternity is a significant material form of alienation, and fatherhood is a nonabstract form of extraction from significant action. There is a sense in which male species integration stops dead at the moment of ejaculation. Historically, at some time birth had no meaning for men. In constructing a social meaning for paternity, men did two things. They experienced themselves as abstract, and they abstracted a self-interested meaning from this abstraction. They then proceeded to enact the social conditions which support this process. Separation from the species came to be expressed in two abstract categories: superiority and power--superiority to all other species and to women, power to abstract and define what is "essential" to the giving of meaning.

Universal man organized in abstract states has to give reality to his nonreality by denial of the everyday, the commonplace, the exceptional, the different. There is only man. At moments in history he is weighed down and depressed by this responsibility, but as it is essentially an abstract one, he soon gets his confidence back, at least for a while. Abstract universal man is an achievement of mind, but must be translated by social and political action into that constellation of oppressions of the biological world which we see in patriarchy's dread and fear of biological realities. The very suggestion that anything is biologically determined or even grounded in natural necessity is unworkable for man, which is one reason why Marxism has never been concretized as politics. Men are, as fathers, alienated from life process, and they have regarded this as a concrete strength: the price is the abstraction of historical process from its bond with species reproduction, the odd notion that birth is insignificant while death is some kind of fetishistic triumph. The life of man, ungrounded in time or substances, has to develop an ambience of abstraction in which to solemnly proclaim its meanings and its truths. The state is the historical state of alienated paternity dedicated to the historical task of explaining the "riddle" of existence while denying meaning to the praxis of birth.

Thus, universal man and abstract state are said to make sense and to make history, and the copulation of these two abstractions permits patriarchy to give birth to itself. All this is said to make sense--theoretically. It is a massive achievement, the giving of certainty to paternity and the cultural creation of the patriarchal state. It can be transformed only by a concrete turning toward community and life, integration of people and the natural world, to a practice which integrates the web of species and persistence with the realities of personal and social being. Such a strategy requires a theory, the theory that species and history have value, that a living ethic of care can be transformed from abstract pathos to historical practice. Feminism is the historical force which makes this kind of claim and is thus the only current progressive force in history, perhaps even the first progressive force. What we must now do is theorize how that theory can be transformed into practice, but we cannot postpone action while we theorize. This is precisely the dualism which has been central to patriarchal practice. It is this practice which has made history but which is now stale, tired, zonked with violent technology and technologies of violence. The theoretical relation of personal and political is fun in speculation, useless if the division of the two creeps back. It is very vulnerable in cultures where the transformation of private life and ultimate life is swifter and more satisfying than the transformation of public life. But feminism has to do both: we cannot abstract the movement from politics just because we don't much like the patriarchal model. We must not only do both, but must also understand the relation; after all, in theory and practice, the political is personal, too.

NOTES

[1]Nancy Hartsock, *Money, Sex and Power* (New York, London: Longman, 1983). See my review in *Women's Review of Books*, vol. 1, no. 7 (1984), pp. 9-11.

4

The Tyranny of the Abstract:
Structure, State, and Patriarchy

Over the centuries, patriarchal ideology has changed its mind quite often as to what is both the nature and object of knowledge. This process is a great deal more complex than the simple opposition of idealism and materialism. The object of knowledge has been understood variously as wisdom, meaning, essence, or simply information. While all of these forms persist into our own times, the modern feminist search for knowledge about women--philosophical and in a nonsexist sense carnal--takes place in the context of a developed modern consensus that knowledge is in some sense knowledge of structure. The perception of structure as the condition of being able to know in the first place is common to diverse modes of inquiry: matter itself, mind, society, psyche, history, myth, spirit, and language are all understood as accessible to knowledge by virtue of having structure, so much so that the rage to uncover structure has itself become a belief, an ideology called structuralism. The perception of a structured relation of mind and world is common to habits of thought which are otherwise locked in mortal combat.

Earlier versions of this paper have been presented at Atkinson College, York University, at Brown University, and to the Canadian Society of Women in Philosophy.

Idealism, whether or not it knows itself as such, continues to attribute structure to the inquiring mind with its ability to abstract structure from any given phenomenon. Materialism regards the structure of history grounded in necessity as the object of knowledge of the world.

E. P. Thompson, in his lively and acerbic polemic against Left and Right structuralism, has argued persuasively that both of these share certain destructive characteristics.[1] His basic argument, if I may express it rather cryptically, is that structuralism destroys structure. Thompson is especially incensed by what he sees--correctly, in my view--as the betrayal of Marxist materialism by Althusserian structuralism, a formulation of process-as-such in which people as thinking, acting makers of history are obliterated by an abstract construct of process, the last instance which, like Godot, never comes. Structure, posited as logically prior to and intellectually superior to both empirical experience and humanist aspiration, tyrannizes over both. Thompson's indictment of Althusser, Popper, and their followers shows, in an admirable fusion of reason and passion, the way in which the structuralism which is supposed to give an account of the truth of social structures actually dematerializes history. The work of the historian and the social scientist becomes irrelevant as elaborate philosophical structures supersede the events on which they are imposed. Thompson obligingly provides a diagram of Althusser's motor of history, felicitously cast in the medieval mode of an orrery in which a creaky mechanical determinism makes theoretical claims to have uncovered the meaning of events.[2] I want to extend Thompson's critique and argue that in the tyranny of abstract meaning over concrete experience lurks the ancient but persistent tyranny of a specifically male dualism, of the failure of patriarchal culture to reconcile meaning and action, mind and body, theory and practice, idealism and materialism and all the familiar instances of dualism over which epistemologists brood.

Thompson underlines the important distinction between structure, which is a real product of human action in response to the needs and conditions of human life, and structuralism, which is the ideological practice by which the

Platonic quest to define ideas as real and appearance as error has been carried into the age of high tech. He does not, however, analyze the roots of this dream in which the abstract tyrannizes the real.   His own empirical historiography claims to understand what happened from a Marxist perspective carefully laundered of Hegelian stains by the detergent of British empiricism.   The fundamental question of *why* the understanding of process, structure, mind, or history is so intransigently dualist is not addressed. Abstract dualism is the lynchpin of theoretical practice, while concrete contradictions are the reality of historical struggle. Despite Marx's attempt to mediate this separation, dualism remains a given structure and structuralism, and the history of male-stream thought can be understood at one level as an effort to *think* Humpty Dumpty back, whole, on his well-grounded wall.   Thompson, himself a scrupulous avoider of sexist language, has elsewhere written an extremely useful history of class development,[3] yet in all these 900 odd pages, the participation of women in the making of the English working class gets rather short shrift and even then mainly in terms of their economic function in cottage industries, or as unskilled rivals threatening the livelihood of honest male tradesmen. Thompson presumably shares the general view that men make history without ever getting born, for in the idealist structure of male-stream thought which Thompson does not ultimately transcend, birth has no meaning until it is thought about, and it is too banal and naturalistic to induce thought. As for Althusser, no messy issue of flesh and blood is permitted to spill on the orrery of this poor man, who was constrained to murder his wife, it is reported, because she got on his philosophical nerves.[4]

The persistence of abstract dualism in male-stream thought is something more than the merely ontological exile of women, as Jill Vickers has shown.[5] Women have been defined dualistically as "other," and the material division of public and private spheres is intransigent because it expresses a dualism which men see as eternal rather than as a historically structured contradiction which must be mediated in praxis.   However, while the arguments of antiquity as to whether structure is born of necessity, of nature, of mind, or of the gods are unresolved, the character of discourse on structure was indubitably transformed by the advent of science. The confirmations that the universe itself and its tiniest building blocks are structured does not, of course, immediately cancel all notions of metaphysical causation: such considerations caused much anguish to men like Newton and Keppler, who solved the problem in a way which has ironic resonances for women, for they simply separated their private religious selves from their public scientific selves. Nonetheless, the notion of the structure of matter as an object of empirical science poses the question of structure in various ways without resolving at all the question of whether structure is primordially the product of mind or matter, of contemplation or action. The presence of structured phenomena as the objects of scientific inquiry is generally accepted as a precondition of science, but science sweeps the unresolved dualisms under a number of closely woven metaphysical rugs, an option which is not open to serious social scientists.

It is not proposed to mount here a plea for a return to chaos, or to that Paradise which men lost with considerable angst quite some time ago. As far as social science is concerned, structure is the precondition of knowledge just as much as it is for physics. Structure, as Thompson argues, is the product of the historical creativity of the race in response to certain basic necessities inherent in human history. The relation of need and/or necessity to structure is a dialectical one: structures such as kinship relations, economy, the state, education, armies, and so forth are real, composed of real live people going about the business of species survival and of meeting the problems which history presents to them; but a tendency to coalesce need and necessity is endemic to materialist analysis. Structures, ideal and empirical, are subject to change, controversy, conservation, and manipulation. The ways in which this has happened are the subjects of empirical inquiry by historians. The question of the conservation or destruction of existing social and ideological structures is the very stuff of politics. Questions of the limits and possibilities of structural*ism*, however, constitute a debate among intellectuals, and it is at this point that the whole complex business of the status of social structures shows its perennial tendency to slip into abstraction. What we call ideology is in fact a deportment toward social structure which gives priority to the control of definition, meaning, and model rather than to the needs and actions of real people.

The notion of structure is not one which feminists have embraced with a great deal of enthusiasm. If social structures indeed arise from human needs, who needs patriarchal structures? The answer is historically clear: men appear to need patriarchy, and are still passionately engaged in the defense of patriarchal structures as "natural" phenomena. However, by that curious sleight of mind which bedevils perceptions of structure, it is argued that patriarchy is natural and necessary not on the grounds of men's nature but on the grounds of male ideas of women's naturalness. Like all structures, patriarchy is supported by webs of social meaning and a well-developed ideology, though the concept of ideology and the practices which support it partake of the same kinds of fact/value, principle/prejudice indeterminacies which structuralism itself epitomizes. Nonetheless, real structures of patriarchal ideology and practice exist in almost all societies, and certainly in those societies which claim to have achieved "high" levels of civilization. If, however, it is true that the need for structure rests on universal and identifiable human necessity, any claim which patriarchy might make on grounds of necessity, or even created need, must be challenged to identify itself, whether it arises in a historical, anthropological, or socioeconomic context. Unrooted in necessity, patriarchy is structural*ism*, and its structures are therefore grounded in ideology rather than necessity, in male interests rather than universal masculine historicity. Structures, further, create much more than the language in which they are expressed or the institutions they nourish. They produce ontologies and epistemologies of non-being and non-thinking in which abstract universal man claims a valedictory historicity.

With what one might call a structuralist irony, the analytical and conceptual tools which are available to

feminist scholarship to address these opacities have all been
forged in the man-serving workshops of male-stream thought.
While this issue raises a number of methodological problems,
it also raises questions about the universality of patriarchy
as both ideology and as concrete social relations and specific
cultural practices. Further, at a time when the structure of
patriarchy is being clearly eroded by the political and
intellectual vitality of feminist praxis, what specific, concrete
modes of historical necessity are involved in such erosion?
Such considerations challenge far more than the institutions
and ideologies of patriarchy. They challenge, for example,
the assumption that structure closes the gap between the
ideal and the real; for, with the exception of Engels' generally
rather feeble attempt to posit private property as the
determinant substructure of patriarchy, claims that male
supremacy is necessary have never been persuasively
explicated. Structure involves the relation of diverse
phenomena and the coherence of a structure clearly lies in
the relation in question. Structure is never simply
immediate nor crudely empirical; it is fraught with
contradictions which must be analyzed, given meaning, and
mediated in praxis. Dialectical logic has the merit of making
it possible to distinguish between contradiction, which is
integral to everyday life and may be mediated in praxis, and
dualism, which is eternal, given, and abstract. This is not,
however, a distinction which patriarchy makes, for as I
argued in *The Politics of Reproduction*, the material ground
of patriarchal dualism has never been explicated.

The fact that patriarchy apparently rests on no
demonstrable material necessity is perhaps the reason why
dialectical materialism has been so reticent in examining
gender relations. The truth is that in a conceptual sense
patriarchy is as abstract and fundamentally irrational and
useless as the orrery of Althusser. Biological sex
differentiation is not the material base of patriarchy, for
patriarchy, the grand abstraction, has insisted that biology
has no historical meaning. Atoms may be busted, deserts
grow, wingless creatures fly, black holes appear in the
universe, infinity turn finite, and structure rearrange itself
in the binary mode which is the new fount of truth to which

we must adjust our social life: changeless in all this flux is immutable biology, impervious to mind, indifferent to historical praxis, yet somehow the domain of real, live, but essentially ahistorical women. This mute and mindless presence differentiates species members by sex in such a way that the social relations of reproduction are perceived as differently structured from all other social processes: gender relations are willfully designated as ahistorical, as abstracted from history, as prestructural. Such relations therefore must be separated from the creative flow of history, ensconced in a "private realm" where utilitarian events without interest or meaning occur. To be sure, some modes and disciplines hold that gender relations do change, but such change must be wrought from outside of reproductive experience, and the social determinants which impinge upon them are presumed to do so incidentally--for example, in the needs of a transformed mode of production, some kind of natural disaster, specific property relations, or a riotous romp[6] into "poststructural" mythologies in which discourse has to bear all the burdens of constructing meanings. Any attempt to examine reproduction of the species as a necessary substructure of history, or to assert that there is such a thing as reproductive consciousness, is likely to be treated with the special contempt reserved for those vulgarians who have not yet transcended biological determinism. Biology, of course, represents matter which does not matter, for it is immune to transformation by the serious attention of the thinking man.

This practice of defining the real as abstract and the abstract as real has produced a number of arbitrary rules for intellectual work that are so thoroughly entrenched that it is very difficult to transcend them. When I first started to develop a dialectical analysis of biological reproduction, the question that I was most often asked was, "But isn't that biological determinism?" As the answer was in some sense clearly "Yes," it proved necessary at that time to rethink the whole notion of biological determinism. Such an endeavor turned out to be not only an intellectual one but a political one. My friends of the Left assured me that in even asking questions about biological determinism I was opening the

door to the justification of sexism and racism.   My
acquaintances of the Right accused me of denigrating man's
spiritual essence. Both were agreed that human history is
the transcendence of biology, that biology represents the
abstract tyranny of a natural world which must be
overthrown with Machiavellian energy if man is to
restructure himself, to make history. This perspective raised
a number of questions: are not large and impressive bodies
of contemporary thought predicated on specific biological
realities?   Is not the basic premise of Marxism the
proposition that people must eat?   Is not psychoanalysis
grounded in human sexuality? Does not existentialism build
its abstract nothingness on the concrete inevitability of
individual death?

Patriarchy answers these questions with looks of pity,
words of scorn: these are precisely those factors which have
been transcended by man and his history, his strength of
body, mind, and spirit.   What then of the necessity to
reproduce the species? Has that been transcended? This, it
appears, is a different order of necessity. Men do indeed
transcend it but women, alas, do not, yet it is precisely this
actual "transcendence," this cultural mediation of men's
separation from species reproduction, which is the material
base of what we now call patriarchy.   The most familiar
version of this transcendence in my culture is perhaps that
represented in the events in Eden, in which Eve fell
downwards and Adam fell upwards. Women are not capable
of this sort of levitation.   We are supposed to live in a
nonmediated relation with biological process which defines us
as less than human, as inferior creatures who do not make
history as active agents but have babies as passive patients.
The reproduction of the human species evidently is not,
strictly speaking, a human activity, and certainly not a
historical praxis. This is by no means simply an ideological
absurdity; this regrettably nontranscendent endeavor (as it
has no place in human history) must be *abstracted* from
history and the world.   It must be hidden, it must be
structured in such a way that its necessary social relations
are of a different order from all those other social structures
which may be created, vitalized, and transformed by thought

and/or action.   Species reproduction must, in a word, be privatized.

The mediation of patriarchal structure and patriarchal structuralism is a very complex affair.   Apart from the question which I have already raised of the grounding of this structure in necessity, there are many promising fields of inquiry concerning the relation of patriarchal structure to other structures, the logical validity of patriarchal propositions, and the relation of patriarchy to language. Feminology must raise these issues in new ways.   For example, one might propose the hypothesis that the separation of biological continuity from historical process over time is the root of the dualistic fixations and delusions of transcendence which are the staples of male-stream thought.   One might meditate on the proposition that the universal privatization of the creation of life is the source of the public carelessness with individual lives, which is the ugliest aspect of patriarchal hegemony.   The truth is that we are timid about raising such questions because they are ruled out of order by the canons of male intellectualism, and women are faced with the compelling need to know in circumstances in which knowledge has become a commodity peddled by patriarchs in a highly controlled market dedicated to the principle of unfair competition.   Yet we must know and we shall.   Doris Lessing says: "We were learning, we old ones, that in times when a species, a race, is under threat, drives and necessities built into the very substance of our flesh speak out in ways that we need never have known about if extremities had not come to squeeze these truths out of us."[7]

The threat of which Lessing speaks, of course, is the threat to the survival of the species, which is another of those topics arbitrarily assigned to the irrational realm of those mad people who are too stupid to understand that the ruling class and the ruling sex will save us with technology. It seems that technological determinism, unlike the old black magic of biological determinism, is acceptable.   Indeed, reproductive technology is to be the final solution to the "problem" of the control of reproduction.   Patriarchy is evidently still not able to resist the charms of final solutions. One wonders what it takes.

What, then, is to be done? Specifically, what is to be done by feminist intellectuals? Clearly, the critique of patriarchy, of its historical structures and its ideological structuralisms, is a legitimate and urgent task. Such a critique must, as my friend and colleague Dorothy Smith properly insists, be undertaken from the standpoint of women. The ground of that standpoint, however, is pot-holed with patriarchal bullets, and the questions of theory and method are urgent ones. Received intellectual traditions are suspect, yet they form the ambience in which we live. The problem is especially acute for Marxist feminists. Marxism offers at least the possibility of the mediation of dualistic structures in the unity of dialectial logic and political action. The standpoint of women is, for individual women, a class standpoint, and Marx's articulation of the historical creativity of class struggle is enormously useful. Yet demasculating Marx is no easy task. Marx never deviated from the perception of biological continuity as mute, brute, and characterized by infinite regress, the position which he articulated in the Third Manuscript.[8] For example, one might argue, rather technically, that history, must have at least two identifiable substructures if it is to be understood as dialectical contradiction rather than abstract dualism. This is not a proposition which Marxists receive with anything but a bored perplexity. Nonetheless, I would argue that this is precisely the case: there are many realms of created need but only two realms of historically dynamic necessity. Expressed dialectically, that is to say that in terms of the opposition of particular and universal, these realms are the survival of individuals, from which arises the structures of economic production, and the survival of the race, from which arises the structures of the social relations of reproduction. Production and reproduction stand in dialectical opposition to each other, and to attempt to wrest a materialist law of dialectical development from only one of these realms of necessity is to doom the resultant formulations to abstraction, to convert historical structures to an abstract structuralism of a most tyrannical kind.

Of course, the whole question of whether Marx actually proposed a structuralist model of substructures and superstructures is a complex one. It is also, I think, an irrelevant one. Marx is not here, and if he were he would be different. What is here is a collection of Marxisms, vulgar or rigorous, and a few samples of Communist states. None of these arouse particular feminist enthusiasm. In particular, the proposition that Engels has somehow done for the social relations of production the same kind of exhaustive and satisfactory analysis which he and Marx did for the social relations of production is as absurd as a claim that the Soviet Union has liberated women.[9] Engels stops women's history before it starts. Historical evidence shows, for example, that the nuclear family is the specific form of the social relations of reproduction in capitalist societies. This does not justify a claim that the *only* content of family relations which is interesting to Marxists is the production of use value, the exploitation of working women, and the sexual division of labor. The reproduction of the race is reduced in such a formulation to a given necessity, understood as the abstract reproduction of labor power and having as its main interest, for Marxism, its effect, on wage calculations. For most Marxists, the relation of family to mode of production is at best reflexive and at worst reductionist. The crucial role of the family in ideological reproduction seems to be better understood by Parsonian structuralists than by Marxist sociologists, and the fact that the ideology of male supremacy is rooted in the family was better understood by Freud. All of this permits the dogged evasion by the Left of the reality that women of all classes are oppressed by men of all classes.

Ultimately, the legitimacy and the usefulness of structuralist conceptions rests upon the grounding of social and cultural structures in material necessity. Much of the confusion of masculinist theorizing rests upon the ludicrous premise that biology is abstract or at least uninteresting, the grounds for such a claim resting on variations on the theme of the eternal dualism of the human and natural worlds. Only a worldly mediation of this contradiction can make history. By mediation is meant some combination or other of thinking and doing. I apologize for making such an obvious observation, but it is precisely the "ordinariness" attributed to abstract dualist structurings of reality which are the key

to understanding the "obvious" proposition that men make
history and women don't. The arbitrary substitution of
historically generated *needs* for biologically generated
necessity is the process by which such propositions as, for
example, a claim that the continuity of species is the
precondition of human liberation over time can be dismissed
as uninteresting truisms of a trivial sort, despite the fact
that species survival is increasingly problematic.

Marxism does not ultimately transcend the contradictions
which do indeed exist in modes of production: a materialist
view of history cannot simply ignore reproduction and gender
struggle as ongoing by-products of class struggle. Economic
activity reproduces the individual on a daily basis, and thus
economic activity is indeed a substructure of history, but
productive activity is primordially individual and only
becomes social historically. Reproductive activity is
essentially social but has been "naturalized" historically. At
the level of necessity as such, Marxism, like Hegelianism, is
partial: history is the mediation of the contradiction between
the (particular) individual and the (universal) species, the
dialectic of reproduction and production. Neither class
consciousness nor gender consciousness can be subsumed into
one another; both are materially grounded consciousnesses.

The question of the individual is one which produces
dreary knee-jerk responses from many Marxists: anguished
cries of bourgeois subjectivism and psychologism rend the air.
The cacophony mounts as feminists proceed to examine the
relation of public and private life as a dialectical relation
grounded in feminine perceptions of necessity. To be sure, the
polemic against liberal individualism, with its constant
substitution of free trade for free people, is one which
feminists have properly shared. Yet we must not become so
absorbed in these important tasks that we neglect to ask
other questions. We have only just begun to pose our
materialist problematic from our own experience, to ask the
forbidden questions. For example, we do not yet ask what, if
it is the case that all labor creates values, is the value
produced by reproductive labor. Is this not in some sense to
be analyzed--the value of the individual life poised in
dialectical contradiction to the life of the species?

The question of reproduction has become a vital one for women in light of the full control which patriarchs see in the galloping development of reproductive technology. The single-mindedness with which the conservative high priests of patriarchy concentrate on the issue of reproduction demonstrates a clear understanding by the Not-so-New Right of the major threat which feminism poses to male hegemony, but we must be alert to the fact that while the abortion struggle has been going on in the public realm, patriarchal states have turned with enthusiasm and funds to stealthy genetic engineering and experiments with extra-uterine pregnancy. The search for safe contraceptives appears to have been abandoned in a series of decisions as obscure as the original decision to develop oral contraceptives. The implications of this are clear, for nothing demonstrates the inhuman coupling of capitalism and patriarchy more clearly than the development of a population corporation to provide a final solution to the abstraction of man from the process of species continuity.

Let me quote once more from Doris Lessing. She is speaking of the gradual demoralization and apathy of the people of Planet 8 as they recognize that their planet is dying. Perhaps, they think,

> It would be better if children were not born at all, not in this terrible time. And . . . when a species begins to think like this about its most precious, its original, capacity, that of giving birth, of passing on an inheritance, then it is afflicted indeed. If we are not channels for the future, and if this future is not to be better than we are, better than the present, then what are we?[10]

What we are, of course, we women, is that future. We always have been, but we have been tyrannized by the concrete structures of abstract man and his abstract state. There is some urgency about the task of structuring the world anew on the material basis of life as value, of reintegration of the natural and historical worlds. If this is biological determinism, so be it. Women have more important work to do than *defining* patriarch--the work of structuring the social and political realities in which the heretofore abstract dialectics of species continuity are rendered concrete as a necessary substructure of history.

NOTES

[1]E. P. Thompson, *The Poverty of Theory and Other Essays* (New York: Monthly Review Press, 1978).

[2]Ibid. pp. 99-102.

[3]E. P. Thompson, *The Making of the English Working Class* (Harmondsworth: Penguin Books Ltd., 1974).

[4]For a discussion of the integration of Althusser's homicidal activity with his tyrannical abstractions, see Geraldine Finn "Why Althusser Killed His Wife," *Canadian Forum* (September/October, 1981) pp. 28-29.

[5]Jill Vickers, "Memoirs of an Ontological Exile: The Methodological Rebellions of Feminist Research," in Angela Miles and Geraldine Finn, eds., *Feminism in Canada: From Pressure to Politics* (Montreal: Black Rose, 1982), pp. 27-46.

[6]For a feminist critique of poststructuralism as masculine ideology, in particular the works of Foucault, Derrida and Lacan, see: Somer Brodribb, "Nothing Matters: A Critique of Post-structuralism's Epistemology," Unpublished Ph.D. Dissertation, 1988, Ontario Institute for Studies in Education, University of Toronto.

[7]Doris Lessing, *The Making of the Representative for Planet 8* (London: J. Cape, 1982), p. 24.

[8]Karl Marx, *Third Manuscript*: "Private Property and Communism," Dirk J. Strulk, ed., *The Economic and Philosophical Manuscripts of 1844.* See also Mary O'Brien, "Reproducing Marxist Man," in Lorenne M. G. Clarke and Linda Lange, eds., *The Sexism of Social and Political Thought* (Toronto: University of Toronto Press, 1979).

[9]Frederick Engels, *The Origin of the Family, Private Property and the State* has been the object of much excellent feminist critique. For summary and citations, see Nancy C. M. Hartsock, "The Feminist Standpoint: Developing the Ground for a Specifically Feminist Materialism," in Sandra Harding and Merrill B. Hintikka, eds., *Discovering Reality* (Boston: D. Reidel, 1983), pp. 283-310.

[10]Doris Lessing, *The Making of the Representative for Planet 8* (London: J. Cape, 1982) p. 39.

5

Redefining Revolution:
Women and Socialism

I always think of myself as a bona fide proletarian, though I recognize that there are enough contradictions in that claim to satisfy the most ravenous of dialecticians. I mention it, though because the claim is based firmly on familial reality: in Scotland, where I grew up, the consciousness of one's class was very commonly based upon family rather than on personal participation in a mode of production. Indeed, the big problem for my family was participation in a mode of production at all, for this was the 1930s when subsistence was perceived as a much deeper problem than class exploitation. Low-level economic survival, a fatalistic belief in hierarchical order, and overt state encouragement of the notion of personal inadequacy as the direct cause of social insecurity all contributed to the defusing of socialist and revolutionary passions. Since then, a more sophisticated development of ideologies of upward mobility has further depressed the poor and weakened socialist activism. In the 1930s, we all saw trade unionism as the preferred road to socialism, but very few women workers were unionized. My own early socialism was induced, I think, mainly by the

---

Paper presented to the Socialist Scholars Conference, The City University, New York City, April 1987.

61

discovery of the Left Book Club and the Fabian Society, and
perhaps from a rather mysterious precociousness which upset
my family a lot. However, the notion of the family as the
material base of one's status in the class system was, and is,
a powerful mode of consciousness which theoretical Marxists,
from Engels on, have seriously trivialized. It was the
intersection of family status and economic fatalism which
eventually led me, thirty years later, to undertake an
analysis of cultural modes of reproduction as materially
based phenomena, despite the long-standing myth that
economic activity--which is based on the need for individual
survival--is somehow material, while reproduction--based on
primordial sexuality--is not.

  In partriarchal ideology, the notion that the social
relations of production leap from nature into history
is respectable. The social relations of reproduction are
not seen to have this dialectical vivaciousness but
relegated to sitting lumpen in the private realm, which is
of course grounded in nature rather than developed
in history. However, notions that economic and cultural
structures mediate between material necessity and
forms of consciousness in the process of making history
is a specifically patriarchal ideology. What is often
thought of as the transcendence of biology in history is thus
celebrated as a male achievement. The species' need--to say
nothing of the historical need--for the creation and
maintenance of new people is perceived by men as something
outside of them, which indeed, after ejaculation, it is. The
facts that reproductive process creates modes of
consciousness which are mediated in the dialectics of
historically constructed gender; that this process is a
dialectical process in theory and a mode of struggle in
practice; or that the enduring presence of family forms are
simply not reducible to a mode of production appears to be
invisible to men. All of this goes unanalyzed, perhaps
because in reproductive process they are nonlaborers and
patriarchal consciousness is fundamentally an alienated
consciousness, an ideology. Men cling to an ontological and
immaterial view of birth process, from which of course they
are literally alienated at the moment of orgasm. Yet they

have constructed historically the ideology of male potency on the material ground of the alienated sperm, and they have built an elaborate and pervasive definition of our species as *man*-kind.

This abstract and speculative nonsense precludes a materialist analysis of the contradictions between productive and reproductive social forms. I believe that these abstract causalities are the reason why socialism has never been able to fulfill its political promises: it is radically one-sided because it is politically radical and conservatively patriarchal, refusing to invest Marx's great effort to provide us with the tools of a living logic of contradiction in anything but a now increasingly ahistorical theory of historical process. A revolutionary consciousness must clearly be a collective consciousness capable of a dialectical analysis of production *and* reproduction. If we want to be philosophically fussy, then we can note that this pair represent a classical contradiction of the general and the particular. Reproduction sustains the species, production sustains individuals, and I do not believe we can hope for radical change, for revolution, unless we restructure both. I began this essay with a discussion of socialism as a familial inheritance precisely because I want to make this point.

The basic historical contradiction within historical modes of species reproduction is that between family and polity, the so-called public and private realms. Kids like me did not have our sense of injustice and outrage, of hatred of power and exploitation conveyed to us in the family *because* the family somehow stood in a sort of mediator role between individual and community, or somehow was a mere reflector of a mode of production. Throughout history the private realm has itself stood as an oppressive mode of production and gender oppression, and it still does in most societies. But what can the family teach in terms of creative politics when it is the breeding ground of the politics of patriarchal power, of maternal selflessness, of violence? The family is patriarchal praxis, with all its ancient litanies of transcendent masculine ego trailing its Oedipus complex from the joy of sex to the crudities of masculine hegemony.

It seems to me that Left consciousness, with its vision narrowed to the reality of class warfare and bourgeois guilt, will never mount a revolution that makes of its politics a passionate agenda. It cannot transform public greed which poses as private enterprise while private masculine uxoriousness still exists as the natural haven of universal man.

Men and women have fought together in the past, resisted together, died together in the cause of the more equitable distribution of the world's goods, in the cause of ridding themselves of oppression, in the cause of saving their children. These activities have brought about radical changes in both public and private social structures, but none of them have yet addressed the central problem of the family. This is old-fashioned male supremacy, patriarchy, the power of men over women's wealth, women's children, women's bodies. The family is quite literally the life and death of patriarchy: it is the place where men are taught that violence is ethical. There they must embrace the idiocies of the noble death of the soldier as their fate and their glory. It is small wonder that the family itself is so often the practice field of violence. The second thing the family must do is replace dead soldiers, and it was extraordinarily astigmatic of Engels to think that the main purpose of the family was that of providing a conduit for property. The largest portion of the human beings who have lived historically have not had and still do not have any property except the sons who will replace the fathers who are stupid enough not to see through the ideology of militarism. Are there real alternatives to the socialist notion of moral good achieved by class warfare and violent revolution?

The absence of alternatives is, I believe, the source of the failure of socialism to fulfill its humane promise. "Democratic socialism" of the European and Canadian kind has reached accommodation with capitalism. The only political movement which believes in nonviolent revolution is feminism. To be sure, there are partial movements which advocate nonviolent solutions to particular problems: liberalism with its vague ideologies of legislated equity; the peace and environmental movements; the gutsy remnants of cooperative retail movements; lesbian and gay liberation, and all those folks who cannot find rationality or morality in nation-state politics or available political ideologies. It is my view that feminism is strong and growing stronger because it has a material base, but this view contradicts a socialism that believes the word "material" relates only to productive activity. The historical/material base of contemporary feminism, in my view, is the transformation wrought in the hitherto biologically defined process of birth. Reproductive technology (RT) is not just a stage in the development of technology in general, which has previously been concerned with material production within an expanding notion of subsistence and warfare. The impact of RT is on individual reproduction and thus far exceeds the experimentations and intellectual analyses of gender relations and contraceptive techniques for which millions of my sex were burned at the stake not that long ago. The search for control of reproduction for women by women is witchcraft; the establishment of capitalist-patriarchal control over women's fecundity is science. It is better described in old Hegel's phrase, "a world-historical event," for RT transforms the material base of the patriarchal family, providing only the *potential* for rational population policies but the current *actuality* of big science and big business on a lucrative binge, blessed by a strengthening of "pro-family" politics, which are in fact crude patriarchal expressions of self-interest.

RT is revolutionary in a way about which we have not yet thought enough. For men, it solves an ancient problem: *not* the accident of sterility but the question of the certainty of paternity, the great unspoken animator of patriarchal social forms, and particularly of the felt male need to control women's bodies. For women, it is much more radical. On the one hand, it has been pointed out that women may finally be expendable, though why the highly complex technology of creating artificial wombs rather than the reproduction of comparatively simple sperm should be perceived as the only way to go is simply another instance of masculine ideological assumption/presumption. But this revolution is new, and the strategies and politics of it are only in their very early stages and frighteningly complex. However, they must be dealt with.   Clearly, this situation in itself transforms the very notion and act of revolution.   Patriarchs, including socialist patriarchs from Marx on, have defined revolution as violent action in the public realm.   The current feminist revolution is therefore not seen as revolutionary for a number of reasons: it is not violent; it is very narrow so far in its class focus, and its major gains have been for middle-class women; it is a bourgeois phenomenon, although it is catching up in socialist   countries.   As   the   Nairobi[1]   conference   so hearteningly showed, feminism is growing in Third World countries in impressive and culturally appropriate ways. The disturbing aspect of reproductive technology is that it is being applied quickly and unevenly and under the control of male lawyers, doctors, and scientists, male politicos, and good old dad, even with his confidence a bit shaken by low sperm counts.   But make no mistake about the significance and political passion around these issues.   This is a revolution whose major impact is on the private realm.   The threat to the patriarchal family has now been confirmed by the daddy of all daddies, the pope himself.   The transformation--known as the breakdown--of the family is manifest and by no means universally beneficial to women.   But   there   are   spots   in which the potential of this peaceful revolution of the private realm can be seen.   For some women there is a marked increase in control of fecundity and the transformation of the family, especially with the new technology which allows self-insemination for any woman with a turkey baster and a good man friend.   I would suggest that the possibility of women controlling their own fecundity is radical in the deepest sense, and that the shock to the patriarchy is the shock of a revolution   in   the   private   realm--a   new,   different,   and immensely complex historical transformation.

What I think socialists have to do is to expand the notion that a specific mode of oppression and a very limited strategy--class struggle and class war--can transform history. We have to transcend the partiality of the ideological corsets in which these concepts are hooked and address ourselves to all modes of oppression: by race, by ethnicity, by sexual orientation, and above all by the oldest and most recalcitrant oppression, that of gender, which crosses the lines of all other oppressions. No one in this world is untouched by nor can evade gender oppression in the way that, for example, whites, the rich, the straight, the apolitical, and the uncaring can transcend other struggles by refusing to notice them. The development of RT, in my view, forms a historical and material base for the development of reproductive consciousness and reproductive revolution. The sneer that feminism is a "bourgeois phenomenon" is pathetically irrelevant, demonstrating only a theoretical paralysis held, alas, by those who have forgotten that dialectical materialism is a theory of *history* and that socialism is a politics of universal collectivity. Karl Marx, for all his brilliance, inherited from Hegel the notion that history could be completed, a much more ominous notion in the age of technology than it was in the age of industrial fabrication. RT has the effect of doing for the materiality of reproductive processes what industrialization did for productive process-- laying bare the historical dialectic in a triumphant extension of men's hegemony over the natural world.

Many men continue to deride feminist analyses as mere apocalyptic scenarios produced by that well-known women's epistemology of hysteria. It really is up to us women to do the hard theoretical and political work which can transcend outdated dialectics for the crucial dialectical materialism of production and reproduction. The question of strategy becomes vital, and a new theory of revolution is called for. It must not only be original, in that it rejects violence and militarism, but also militant, which in women is known as hysteria. This is okay--the politics of birth and womb have a promise no longer visible in the necromantic, poststructural politics of the heroic death, which spits in the teeth of socialist humanism. And in fact, this strange and redefined mode of revolution is under way. Men have always defined revolution as violent action in the public realm waged by graduates of patriarchal families, schools for the right and duty of men to be violent. The new and novel revolution is not yet noticed, for it is a revolution in the first instance of the private realm. As in all revolutions, the revolutionaries themselves provide the major casualty lists, and the evolution of the family which is currently in process certainly has destabilized the social realities of thousands of women: some "liberated" men may toss off their traditional responsibilities, while others become sperm donors and surrogate husbands and fathers. But let us not make the mistake of underestimating the ideological vitality and political clout of this new mode of revolution. It has two major aims: to wrest control of reproductive process from the corporate scientific elite, and to reconstruct a caring and shared notion of parenthood in an assault on patriarchal power. This revolution is still in its primitive stages, and the new social realities which must be developed to deal with changes in the material base of reproductive relations is at about the level of the peasant revolt in terms of class struggle under developing capitalism. But as the technology moves much faster, so must the political response; hence the precipitousness and extraordinary vitality of feminist growth which too many socialists in my environment are still shrugging off as a bourgeois fad. I suggest we turn our praxis to the very serious analysis and response to the reproductive revolution, or we shall be cruising into a fictionalized class struggle as impotent raiders in a lost ark.

NOTES

[1]The United Nations End of Decade For Women Conference and Forum, 1985.

6

Collective Pilgrimage:
The Political Personal

I have been asked how the women's movement has influenced my work. When I thought about that, I found how difficult it is to think in that way because I just don't see two things, two processes. The feminist movement and my work as a teacher and a theorist are not related--they are in fact fused. This has been so for many feminists since the bold declaration 25 years ago that the personal is political. But I think it is even more than that. Feminism creates a new view of the world, of our lives, of our ambitions, of knowledge itself. The masculine tradition of knowing, of trying to understand anything, is one of "making distinctions," of separating things out from their context so that they can be looked at one at a time, so that they can be defined and understood as objects. Our male-manufactured culture is full of these divisions, including not only the well-known separation of nature and culture, of mind and body and-- perhaps most important to our topic--the division between our private lives and our public lives. This distinction has served men well: it enables them to conduct large parts of

---

A public address given at the Centre for Women's Studies in Education, Ontario Institute for Studies in Education, in 1985. Reprinted with permission from *Canadian Forum* (May 1986), pp. 5-9.

their own lives in a secretive way and call that public life. When I grew up, it was customary for most men, for example, not to tell their wives how much they earned, where they had been--though one could often deduce that by the way they smelled--or even how they voted or who their friends were. Despite all this, they called women "the secretive sex," but as they also regarded women as incorrigible gossips, it was very confusing. Men have not ever been much bothered by the contradictions in their view of women, which they have used mostly as a justification for their own superiority: male "definitions" of femininity always say more about men's illusions than women's realities.

Perhaps it is the very fragility of the notion of superiority, the sense that it might not be true, which has accounted over the centuries for a great deal of male bombast and reliance on simple violence to resolve any sneaking feeling that their superiority was not as obvious as they have been taught it is. But in any case, this separation of who we are at home and who we are outside of the home is one which feminism has challenged. In challenging it, we also challenge this whole notion that separation of things makes it easier to understand what they mean, the whole self-serving logic of cause and effect. I would find it really weird to say that being a feminist has *caused* me to do certain things in particular ways. I don't, for example, teach women's studies *because* I am a feminist; I don't try hard to overcome the prejudices which male society has taught me with regard to such things as racism, as fear of otherness in sexual orientation or language or culture because I am a feminist. I don't struggle against the "common sense" which says that power relations are the only way to create an orderly social life or that there are some problems which can only be solved by violence because I am a feminist. I struggle with all these things because I experience feminism as a way of life: if it is a "cause," it is not the kind of cause which we associate with separate effects; it is a moral and political cause, a set of social relationships which changes one's view of the world, which "takes over" one's life, not in a dictatorial sense, but in the sense of learning together how things are related rather than teaching how they are separated. Teaching and learning are not separate "roles" for women, but two sides of one petal. Feminism is a way of beginning to know and experience the possibility of coherence in our lives. Such an integration of life and history can only be winkled out by collective action from the fragmented, broken up view of reality which men have made. This has a lot of significance for the way we live. For example, we cannot accept as "truth" propositions that might is right, that violence is natural, or that the good earth is there as "our" [i.e., "man's"] imprisoned plaything, and we can ravage it, despoil it, take what we want and leave "someone else" to clean up our mess. The "someone elses" who clean up messes have so often been women, and women's very intelligent claim that it would be easier not to make the mess in the first place has not been recognized as the good sense it is, but has been called nagging. An honorable occupation, in my view, but it has to be done in public as well as private, and preferably by a strong and united community of nags rather than by single voices.

I have in fact been fortunate in my own life in that I have always lived with women. In fact, much of my personal share of life's misery has come from the fact that I didn't know for a long time how fortunate I was, and kept trying to fit into uncomfortable behavioral corsets of conformity. My mother left my brother and myself when I was four, an event which caused me some anguish until I was old enough to analyze what kind of man my poor, weak father actually was. But he was fortunately serving the British Empire, which made him arrogant but kept him far away. I lived with his three sisters. Then, in my teens, I entered the nursing profession and lived for half a dozen years in nurses residences. After I had slogged through nursing training-- which in those days took longer than a Ph.D.--I shared houses with other nurses, and in fact I still live with another nurse. For about the first twenty years of this kind of life of sisterhood and fun, the women's movement was not especially visible, though there has always been among nurses a sort of contradictory seam of experience composed of great pride in the history of nursing and the tradition of service and a

seething resentment against poor rewards, long hours and
the arrogance of the medical profession. In my own case, I
eventually became a nursing administrator, and the fun was
replaced by that wrenching futility of responsibility without
authority which eventually drove me out of the profession.
Nonetheless, the years of experience of living with, working
with and deeply respecting women seasoned me well to greet
the upsurge of feminism like something I had always known
was struggling for a clearer place in history.

The other aspect of my own experience which I think
prepared me for the feminist renaissance was my long
association with socialist politics. I'm not sure now what
turned me to socialism, except perhaps that my father was
that peculiar British anomaly, the working-class Tory. But I
think, too, that my passion for the written word was a major
factor. I had an important great aunt who introduced me to
Shakespeare as a child, and a lifelong love of language
which, as a feminist, I now feel I sometimes practice as a sort
of secret vice, telling myself that I'm really doing feminist
critique when I am often just indulging in pure aesthetic
pleasure. Patriarchy thrives on its own contradictions!
However, Shakespeare's work is hardly a road to socialism,
and that road appeared, I think, because of the political
struggles of the depression in the 1930s and my proletarian
sense of deprivation and outrage. Like all of the children I
knew, I was expected to go to work at fourteen, but I suppose
we were a little bit upwardly mobile, for I did not go to a
factory or a shop, as my aunty did, but to lick stamps in an
office. In fact, had it not been for the war-time "emergency"
I would never have become a nurse at all; admission
requirements were slack because of all the mayhem going on.
As it was, I met in nursing a couple of committed socialist
quakers and turned my reading appetite on socialist
literature. I thus discovered shadows of the long
underground history of women in the socialist movement. I
also acquired a hero, Bertrand Russell, which made me a
pacifist and an ardently ignorant devotee of "Free Love." As
you can imagine, I was relatively bruised in the process of
discovering that it was never free, this love, and not always
loving. It was, however, decades before I knew about Dora

Russell. After the war, I joined the Scottish Labour Party, and began to work in earnest in parliamentary politicking. I also discovered the women's section of the Labour Party, which talked of its heroines and its loving memories of the suffrage battles while the men tried to pin on the section the job of fund-raising through sales and other "events." The "Events" committee was seen by the men as the suitable sphere for women socialists, but I learned good lessons in how to keep the boys right. I had actually been nominated to the parliamentary candidates roster in 1957 when the crises broke in both the capitalist and Communist camps. The Suez affair and the invasion of Hungary took me out of patriarchal politics forever, with their greedy self-interest and the political bankruptcy which offered no route but violence, violence and more violence. I decided to come to Canada, simply because I felt that Europe was hopelessly decadent and corrupt, soiling its cultural inheritance in a desperate attempt to resist American takeover of the capital markets. So I retired from politics for some years and went back to reading Marx and other socialist literature, worrying about why I couldn't bring myself to marry, becoming a nursing administrator, and cultivating women's friendship.

But the lust for knowledge persisted, and I started to take classes at Sir George Williams in Montreal and, when I moved to Toronto, at Atkinson. I started with Shakespeare, of course, but soon discovered that, in my immodest opinion, none of these academics knew and lived his work like I did. One was counting commas in *Hamlet* on a primitive computer; mistakenly, I was more shocked by the rape of the text than impressed by the technology. Then came the 1960s, and I watched with some bewilderment the apostles of the new free love, and ached a bit for their ultimate disillusionment. But then came feminism, growing steadily from the eternal underground to start its new and, I think, final pilgrimage to a better world. I don't know when I resolved to go back to school and to write a feminist thesis. I know I had a lot of trouble finding a committee and I realize now that I frightened quite a lot of people. Had I been an ordinary graduate student--a young male, that is--my proposal to rework the whole of philosophy could have been dismissed out of hand, and would have been. Had I been a young woman, with very scanty support in the men's world of political science, I doubt if I would have attempted it. But here I was, grey-haired, forty-five, and battle scarred, telling young academics that I had to revise Hegel and Marx--from a feminist perspective. And as I battled for my intellectual integrity, suddenly they were there, the women. Students, underpaid part-timers, secretaries, black women, lesbian women, Latin women, women who had been standing alone, reviled and laughed at every time they stood up to protest sexist language, course biases, unfair labor practices.

It was in the unlikely act of writing a doctoral thesis that my life, lived as a constant and often devastating battle with incoherence, suddenly jelled. Just like the lift you get when you're stirring the jam which seems to be getting thinner and thinner, when suddenly the wooden spoon feels that resistance, the color deepens, the texture richens, the frothy bubbles become a deeply satisfying, ever-thickening roll--my thesis topic began to jell in just this way. As I discussed it with the women who were not qualified to supervise it and tried to explain it to the men who were, I began to see that it was not "my" thesis. Life has to be lived in a certain way if all the pieces can come together, and for me it was the historical context of feminism that made this possible. Here was the self-educated working-class kid, refusing to accept conventional interpretations of experience for the good reason that they made no sense and I hadn't been indoctrinated early enough. Here was the erstwhile free-lover, finally understanding the ruinous perversity of separating sexuality from social life and from species life and, often enough, from the joy of unifying one's body with one's feelings and one's mind. Here was that starry-eyed young nurse, learning the error of believing that the social construction of caring for others meant the belittling of the self, who did not know the difference between an exploited skivvy and a proud servant; here was the good-time friend who thought that the essence of a good time was just getting the right guys there and who had taken women's friendships for granted; here was the socialist who believed that social and political change was a public affair in which men of good will could overcome their baptism and confirmation in the paths of violence to create the utopian community in which women would magically gain equality; here was the cynical administrator, believing that competence could be some kind of substitute for morality. Here, above all, was the midwife, who had watched the magic of a new birth without realizing that she was watching the most profound and necessary level of the making of history. Above all, here was the critic who delved into the history of male versions of wisdom and said, "I don't believe it"--and finally discovered that she was not alone.

This is not the accepted "objective" framework for what academia calls "the development of a thesis project." But then, the whole history of thinking in the male tradition consists of a radical and self-defeating individualism: sit in a hole in a wall somewhere and meditate and then write down what you have thought. So serious and lonely is the act of thinking for men that they have frequently felt it necessary to lock themselves up in man-centered and putatively celibate communities to do it. Lonely pilgrims, these great men, weighed down with the weight of their brains, their learning from other men, and the immense burden of their self-regard. To be sure, solitude is an important part of the intellectual life, but it is not one whit more important, and is probably much less important, than solitude for the mother of small children--and not, for her, only when she is too tired to think. But thinking in the abstract--a great masculine value, this capacity for abstract thought--is being in nothingness in the most radical way. What does one think about? Oneself and one's being, if we are to believe the philosopher who said "I think therefore I am." Even if we extend the notion to that of unifying thinking with action, there is not much to do by oneself. Bringing my own quite ordinary woman's life experiences into my intellectual labors was ultimately to understand that intellectual labor is essentially collective labor. My regard for Marx is because he understood this; my critique of Marx has been that for him the socialist collectivity was still that shadow army known to patriarchal history as "mankind." I could not make sense of my life under that rubric: my significant others had all been women, and it was the collectivity of women, the feminist movement, which was giving me the insight and the courage to say, not, "I have something to say" but "we have something to do."

And we have always done things--agonizingly and to the point of exhaustion and even death, we have worked and borne children, and thought and acted and wept and laughed and loved and hated and sung and danced and worked and worked, we women. But the things we have done have been considered inconsequential, particular and paltry, necessary but boring, not making history but making men comfortable. Patriarchy, at least in the West and the North, but also in other parts of the world, have divided up men's work and women's work along evaluative lines, work done in separate places. Men make history in public; women are the handmaidens of nature in private. Men achieve, women serve. In Euro-American culture, this ancient separation of the private from the public takes the form of the patriarchal family against the capitalist or Communist state. What I have tried to do in my academic work is to show that this separation of public and private is a historical creation rooted in the reality of sexual difference but developed in the cultural reality of an artificial construction of gender. We call patriarchy patriarchy because we recognize that it is in *paternity* that men have justified their self-defined superiority and their advantageously self-serving rights and privileges. Yet it is also in paternity that they face the reality of their own negation, the uncertainty of knowing who their children are. This is clearly of importance to them, for they have gone to all the historical effort of creating a private realm in which their paternity is protected and their women guarded from other men. The truth is that paternity is power and property acquired without labor and quite the opposite of motherhood, which is hard physical work as far as birthing and nurturing children is concerned. Paternity separates men from the actual world into which women are integrated through the act of birth. Men's and women's work is valued differently, and women's work takes place under the supervision--which may be benign, tyrannical or violent--of men, has traditionally taken place in the private realm, and is ultimately maintained, as all power is, by the threat or practice of a right to be violent.

We are often asked: where is the women's movement? What is it doing? Isn't it being reduced to the economic and power ambitions of individual women who care nothing for less fortunate women? These are the siren songs of an enemy skilled by centuries of practice in the usurpation of women's capacity to define themselves. Battles must be fought where we are in practical everyday terms, and where women are historically and with relatively limited variation is in the private realm, even when they are working hard in the public realm, too. I believe that what is not yet clear enough to be sure of, but what seems to be happening, is that feminism has created a completely new version of revolution. Revolution, as patriarchy has defined it, is violent action in the public realm--death and chaos on the barricades and glory steeped in blood. This activity has never challenged the separation of public and private, even where it has transformed both. The feminist revolution is so novel that it has not yet been named, for it consists of non-violent action in the private realm, now understood as essentially part of public life. It is becoming clearer, surely, that the "separation" of public and private, of family and polity, is artificial. The state, the economy and the family are spermogenetic triplets and the transformation of any one is the transformation of all. Feminism is transforming the family in a radical way, and we have difficulty in seeing the profound significance of this, for we are rightfully wary of family-based ideology. Indeed, the significance of the non-violent revolution of the private realm often seems much clearer to the desperate opposition on the far right than to us, who engage in this struggle day by day and sometimes do not take seriously enough our most profound revolutionary insight: that the personal is political.

And of course, the private is not private. It is institutionalized and has an elaborate set of myths and ideologies and "normal" practices to prop it up, a set which we call by the name of patriarchy. It's even difficult to talk about it sometimes, and the notion that there is no private life makes us properly nervous. But the real distinction I think we have to develop is not between private and public but between public life and intimate life. I talked a few moments ago about the felt need for solitude, and one might add sensual and emotional needs of an intimate nature. But the intimate life feminism presupposes is struggling to develop as something other than a power relation, and the family as we know it is just that. It is the locus of power for every man, and patriarchy is a crude form of biological determinism, for all its philosophical pretensions. Private life as we have it in our historical experience links privacy to property, so that owning a modest house or plot becomes some sort of justification of the principle that others should privately own great chunks of the earth's resources. I think this must change and in this way I remain a committed socialist, and cannot see any other economic arrangement that makes sense. Private life and private property are essentially exploitive. But I would argue that traditional socialism has not seen the relation of polity, family and economy clearly enough, and that feminism is the only political movement which has any chance of making the radical historical transformations necessary if we are to stop the ultimate rape, the rape of the planet.

I called this chapter "Collective Pilgrimage." What sort of pilgrimage is it? Pilgrimages, traditionally, are collections of individuals united by faith going somewhere or other to have that faith affirmed. The word has religious echoes. I would not want to deny that the feminist movement is rich in spirit, but it is refreshingly free of icons and idols of saints and prophets, and surely women have had a historical bellyful of the frauds of martyrdom. The goal of our collective pilgrimage, I believe, is the pilgrimage itself, the discovery of ourselves and of our sisterhood, the knowledge of collectivity and diversity which is the condition of the new and complex form of revolution which we are creating in so many different ways. It is the rejection of competition for complementarity, of egoism for respect, of struggle to shake off the invidious distinctions between us which we have inherited without creating new ones of our own. It is the complex project to integrate the natural and cultural worlds before they are blasted asunder, and at the same time to recognize that, just as we have redefined revolution, we have redefined politics as project rather than power, as creativity rather than ruthlessness. We do not underestimate the pressure, and we are not sure we have the time left, but we are sure that we shall never give up until we have developed the way.

To make our history, our story, we must create a living legend of women doing the thing which we are always told by men we cannot do: working together. It is, of course, easier said than done, but we who have had so much doing and so little saying in the past are developing strategies and constructing ways of expressing our projects and our desires. Feminism is not a subculture; it is a revolution. I expect the boys to remain bewildered for a long time yet before they grasp the historical significance of what we do. I hope we don't all drop with fatigue--making history is a tiring business. I hope, too, that the material world lasts long enough for us to establish the coherence of our social lives with our natural one. I hope we can find the energy to resist the powerful "thrust" to bury birth in technology controlled by powerful men. There is plenty to do. We all do different bits. Just like domestic labor: we've had lots of practice for the new kind of revolution.

PART TWO

The Critique of Patriarchy

7

Resolute Anticipation:
Heidegger and Beckett

Suppose Godot's a woman, what then?

Clearly, a speculative question, and to ask speculative
questions in our time is to antagonize a substantial part of
the scholarly establishment. Feminist scholarship, however,
has learned that the canons of enquiry which have developed
from the history which men have made do not necessarily
provide the answers to questions arising from female
experience: quite often, indeed, such questions cannot even
be formulated. Phenomenology and existentialism proclaim
an openness to Being and Knowing, so in the context of these
kinds of philosophical investigations perhaps such a question
might be asked. It is asked here in such a spirit, and it is my
further intention to ground this speculation in another. This
is the notion that Samuel Beckett's tragi-comedy, *Waiting for
Godot*,[1] can be understood in an important way as a
dramatization of Martin Heidegger's *Being and Time*. If that
is too much for tidy minds, then at least I would want to
argue that these two works address the same problems and
share a conceptual vocabulary in a way which enriches and
clarifies both. I shall also argue that the "tragic" aspect of
Godot emerges less from the famous existentialist void and
more from Beckett's critical and poetic perception of the
significant absence of the facticity of femininity and
reproductive being from Heidegger's account of time and,

indeed, from the history of philosophy in general. After all, what is more comical, or more tragical, than men's ancient longing to "make themselves?" Philosophy, both ideal and material, has not found women's praxis in giving birth interesting; rather, it has sustained a nagging death fetish, a preoccupation with finitude. Death without birth is not only abstract and unrealistic, but signals an odd unwillingness to give meaning to species persistence as the material substructure of temporality. I want to suggest that such an elision is possible only where thought is masculine.

In this context, Heidegger's work appears, on the surface, promising. The focus of his philosophical concern was, after all, the question of Being, a question which, he claims, has been "forgotten" by philosophy. This "forgotten" is a rejection of the question of Being as an empty one, as a question incapable of definition and clarification, far less of eliciting an answer. Heidegger believes that philosophy cannot continue to "forget" the question, and accepts as his philosophical task the clarification of Being. Being can only be understood even in a vague and indefinite way by beings who understand that such a question can be asked, beings for whom Being "is an issue."[2] That is to say, Being must involve the interrogation of one's own being. The human entity, which has its being in the temporal world and can interrogate itself as to what Being is, Heidegger calls *Dasein*.[3] Dasein is for Heidegger a living entity in the world, that *he* who is capable of understanding and questioning his own Being. Whether or not Dasein might be female is not "an issue" for Heidegger's Dasein. Like the notion of "mankind," the notion of Dasein does not deny the being of women: it simply judges sex/gender as irrelevant to being. Dasein in Heidegger's hands thus is existentially male, and interrogates masculinity without interrogating the partiality of this strategy. His analysis of Dasein is an analysis in which he endeavors to lay bare the structure of he-Dasein.[4] It is not my purpose here to try to explicate in detail this highly intricate analysis, but to try to grasp an understanding of some of its ontological presuppositions and existential and temporal consequences for women. On an existential level, Heidegger is trying to uncover what it is to be "human," an uncovering which he believes can be a matter of concern to "all" humans. This concern is not the exclusive prerogative of philosophers; Heidegger claims that "concern" is the existential meaning of *every* Dasein. In practice, he deals only with Dasein as male.

Heidegger insists that he is neither judging humanity, nor prescribing for it, but simply understanding it. Dasein simply exists. This existence, however, can be "authentic" or "inauthentic," and these words do have an evaluative ring. Dasein need not choose to be "concerned" about Being but not to so choose is inauthentic. I want to argue here that there can be no authenticity for a he-Dasein who does not recognize that temporality is a continuous *species* experience grounded actively and materially in birth processes, and not the passivity of simply "waiting" for Being to visit one's subjectivity.

Samuel Beckett's play *Waiting for Godot*[5] is dramatically concerned with this same question: what is the meaning of being human? In a play, however, abstractions cannot be rendered in timeless impassivity, as Beckett has shown satirically in *Breath*. Authenticity and inauthenticity must be characterized and staged, and this is just what Beckett does, even though authenticity never quite manages to tread the boards but exists only as a promise in time for which one must "wait." Nonetheless, Beckett is dealing with some of the most basic aspects of Heidegger's ontological analytic, and it is this aspect of the play which I hope to clarify. At the same time, I want to show that the play is also in a sense a dramatic critique of Heidegger's position, specifically with regard to the fundamental aspect of Being which Heidegger's male Dasein passes over--the aspect of being born of woman. Unborn Being is for Beckett both ludicrous and passive; his activities are restricted to the existential tedium of surviving and waiting.

Dasein for Heidegger has two aspects to his Being: one is transcendental (*B*eing) and the other is everyday (*b*eing). These modes are represented separately in *Godot*, where Vladimir the despairing thinker is at least potential Being, and hungry, sleepy Estragon is being. Both are "everyday," but for Estragon time is *now*, he has no future and he does not want to do anything, not even "wait." Vladimir wants to look to the future, but is constrained by his oppressive sense of the relation of time and death. What is this relation? It is unknown. For Heidegger, Being is Being-unto-death, radical finitude, the *Kehre* for *Das Man*, the releasement for which ultimately one must wait.[6] Waiting is the existential context, the fate of interrogative Dasein. In this sense, Godot cannot be Being, for Being's essence in Heidegger's model is composed of receptive thinking,[7] and we have no evidence that Godot will ever be received. Yet Dasein is not quite passive for Heidegger--he has to care, mostly about the Being for which he is waiting, but also for everyday being and for other beings. He has moods, he talks, he acts, he *discloses* his being to others. Such disclosure, however, is fundamentally a mode of waiting-in-the-world for the emergence of one's own authenticity. Authenticity is openness to Being, inauthenticity is a turning away from Being. Thrown into the world, fallen into everydayness, Dasein can easily forget the quest for authentic Being in his immersion in "facticity,"[8] in the trivia of being-in-time-and-world.

Beckett dramatizes facticity and throwness both visually and symbolically. In Heidegger's language, Vladimir and Estragon "find themselves" in the world, a formulation which completely negates the authentic woman's act of giving birth. Unborn, they have no clear past and are fearful of the future. Time itself is simply to be whiled away. The notion that separation from birth process may itself constitute a separation from existence in time from, for example, the reality of a culturally constructed and material, grounded species continuity, clearly does not occur to Heidegger. Instead, he chooses a strategy of interrogation of an everyday individual existence which is radically masculine. Unborn, men must seek authenticity--a real existence in time--in their minds. This is obviously a prescription for pessimism--if time is in the individual mind it is radically finite for it stops at individual death. There is a melancholy sense in which existential man can only be human in the act of dying wise. In this sense, the "essence" for which existentialists wait is simply a secular version of eternal spirit.[9] The notion of species continuity as a mode of a continuous time consciousness and as a necessary sub-structure of historical time is not rejected: the fact that the relation of individual and species continuity is mediated in women's reproductive labor is not even considered. In Heidegger's work, the "ontic," inauthentic world of being is radically opposed to the ontological, authentic world of thinking. The gap is to be closed by philosophical meditation on one's personal authenticity. All else is idle chatter. *Waiting for Godot* is full of idle chatter, but it also deals explicitly with the conceptual categories in which Heidegger's Dasein exists: care, with its existential fate in "throwness" and "falleness"; in the struggle for authenticity; others; the "ontic" everyday world and, of course, the passive act of "waiting."

Beckett's play is set in a stripped-down world which is nonetheless a composition of essentials. Here are men, situated in place and time: "A country road. Evening." Here is the productive world, represented by some old boots and hats and other manufactured artifacts. Here is the entrepreneurial Pozzo, controlling the accumulated knowledge of mankind toted by the enslaved Lucky in a couple of suitcases. Here are pointless activities and a great deal of chatter, a full range of mood and emotion, of sexuality and bodily pains and discomforts. Here are memories and promises and waking and sleeping and loving and hating and hoping and fearing. Brooding over all is a presence without definition, a possibility, a threat and a promise which Beckett names: Godot. The tragi-comedy is a remarkable evocation of is-ness without clutter, complete in the essentials of human life except for one. There are no women. Womanhood, however, is there in the same way as Godot is there. Femaleness is almost "named," in the ambiguous way in which Godot is also named: Estragon, a man, is almost the name of the female sex hormone, just as Godot is not quite the name of god. Further, there are children, a boy or perhaps two boys, who "come from" Godot as messengers of the fact that although Godot is rendered as invisible, Godot *must exist*, just as this Dasein in all his tortuous aspects, his divisions, must have been, as these boys also were, born of woman. But if Godot is woman, then all the interrogation in the world will not reveal a fecundity which is absolutely negated. There is no dialectic of birth and death, of subject and species, no tension of natural and historical time, no being and no Being.

In this tragi-comedy of Dasein, the dramatic ebb (never a flow, battling always a lugubrious stasis) is to show that the two tramps, Vladimir/Being and Estragon/being, must unite themselves if they are to be "authentic" existents. Heidegger says that Dasein must choose authenticity, confront his own b/Being, his own possibility.[10] But Dasein can also be, in his "fullest concretion . . . characterized by inauthenticity."[11] To avoid this, he must confront his average everydayness;[12] *Waiting for Godot* has its dramatic structure embedded in this confrontation, in which the two, Vladimir and Estragon, struggle to identify their authentic relation: they are aspects of one Dasein.[13] Vladimir constantly tries to bring Estragon in line but Estragon is ambivalent: "Don't touch me! Don't question me! Don't speak to me! Don't leave me" (p. 37). He is afraid of losing Vladimir, yet he resents Vladimir's uneven quest for authenticity:

> VLADIMIR: You'd rather be stuck there doing nothing?
> ESTRAGON: Yes. (p. 45)

Vladimir has to insist that Estragon must look at him before they can embrace: he (Estragon) cannot turn his face from Being. But Vladimir has his problems, too. He wants to free himself from the responsibility for authenticity, he is "happy" without Estragon (p. 38), yet at the same time he misses him: he is incomplete when the everyday aspect of his Dasein is *not there*. His Being needs Estragon; he cannot wait for authenticity without him. He wants to be happy, but his happiness, though real, is incomplete. He is responsible for making Estragon happy in his everydayness as well as showing him that the authenticity he rejects is a condition of happiness. The two aspects of b/Being must become one, but this is difficult.

> VLADIMIR: (Joyous.) There you are again . . .
> (Indifferent.) There we are again . . . (Gloomy.)
> There I am again (p. 38).

He feels that his mood must find a correspondence in Estragon:

> VLADIMIR: You must be happy, too, deep down, if
> you only knew it (p. 38).

Estragon is unconvinced. He says he is "happy" to oblige Vladimir and to be left in peace to escape from the world in dreams (p. 57). Vladimir recognizes the inauthenticity of this; he never lets Estragon sleep for long, and will not listen to his dreams willingly:

> VLADIMIR: Ah no, Gogo, the truth is there are
> things escape you that don't escape me, you must
> feel it yourself (p. 38).

Estragon is everyday in another important sense, the sense of the purely physical, the biological reality of Being. Unlike Heidegger, Beckett weaves into his existent a concern with the physical and some profound and moving commentary on life process, on birth and death, but in a very problematic way. Estragon eats, sleeps and cries, which Vladimir does not, but both laugh and hurt, though in different ways. Vladimir, however, takes on the nurturing function: he is responsible for meeting Estragon's physical needs, a sort of attenuated mother and breadwinner, except that within the complexity of the structure of this Dasein Estragon's needs are also Vladimir's own needs. Vladimir feeds Estragon; he decides, much to Estragon's annoyance, when Estragon can sleep. Estragon laughs really heartily, is "convulsed" with merriment (p. 23), only in Vladimir's absence. Vladimir cannot laugh, for it hurts him, and hurts him, significantly, in his pubis. Vladimir suffers from some kind of existential pelvic pain and inadequacy and longing. Estragon, the female sex hormone, has no female body: he is related to Vladimir as real children are related to their fathers, in terms of social responsibility rather than either ontological or biological certainty.[14] But Vladimir is a child, too; in foetal position (p. 45) he elicits a lullaby from Estragon. Then again:

> VLADIMIR: Come to my arms.
> ESTRAGON: Your arms?
> VLADIMIR: My breast! (p. 48-49).

This whole nexus of pubis-laughter-joy-pain-birth is enormously subtle, intensely compassionate. It is a compassion, I suggest, for men's separation from biological continuity, for the uncertainty of paternity, for the non-mediated relation of man to his species being which women mediate in the ontic existential act of giving birth. The play introduces "a boy," a messenger from Godot, in each of the two acts, but it is never clear where this child comes from: he is Godot's messenger, but is ignorant of just who or what Godot is. If Godot is the boy's father, the boy does not "know" him as such. Estragon denies the reproductive aspect of himself which his name asserts: he does not *care* that he is separated from time in the form of genetic continuity; the alienation of man from seed has no meaning for him. Indeed, he treats this alienation with a sort of stag bravado, refusing, for example, to differentiate between genital and urinary function. When Vladimir is taken short with the need to relieve himself and rushes off stage to the echo of Estragon's raucous laughter, Estragon thinks it is a great joke. Yet he is forced in his evasive way to recognize that there is more to Vladimir's pubic pain than merely this, for it makes him sad to discover that Vladimir pisses better without him (p. 38). Estragon is crudely concerned with his comfort as physical organism, but Vladimir, of course, is body too. Both are related to but separated from continuity, time is a day, a minute, an hour, a *present* with a vague past and an unknown future. Both are capable of physical suffering, but Vladimir wants to understand the meaning of his hurt, not just to accept the superficial explanation:

> VLADIMIR: There's man all over for you, blaming on his boots the faults of his feet (p. 8).

For Beckett, Dasein is doomed if he believes that "Man" is universal. If he searches for being only in aspects of himself, he will wait for Godot forever, not understanding that Man Alone, man without women, is doomed to sterility and impotence, to a systematic self-castration.[15]

Heidegger's perception of Dasein as "thrown" into the world is the patriarchal essence of his notion of existence and a total occlusion of women's reproductive labor. Beckett dramatizes throwness, but in a very oblique way. If one is simply thrown into the world, how can one do anything, except, perhaps, wait or fiddle around with the ontic and timeless trivia of mere survival. Estragon's first words in the play are: "Nothing to be done" (p. 7).

An assertion which Vladimir echoes twice (p. 8). Estragon is considering his boots and his feet, and it seems that what nothing can be done about is this everyday business of taking off and putting on boots:

VLADIMIR: Boots must be taken off everyday, I'm tired of telling you that (p. 7).

Yet, even while Vladimir is repeating "Nothing to be done," Estragon *does* take off his boots. Clearly, it is not this boot and foot business about which nothing can be done. Feet are facts, but to stand on them is to obscure the facticity of throwness. What is it, then, about which nothing can be done?

VLADIMIR: Suppose we repented?
ESTRAGON: Repented what?
VLADIMIR: Oh . . . (he reflects) We wouldn't have to go into details.
ESTRAGON: Our being born? (Vladimir breaks into a hearty laugh which he immediately stifles, his hand pressed to his pubis, his face contorted.)
VLADIMIR: One daren't laugh any more.
ESTRAGON: Dreadful privation.
VLADIMIR: Merely smile . . . It's not the same thing. Nothing can be done (p. 8).

They are factually thrown into the world, a throwness
from which Estragon constantly "turns away."[16] He lets the
fact of standing upright in his boots conceal the facticity of
his throwness while he escapes in his dreams. Vladimir sees
the necessity of turning towards the world and resists this
escapism:

> ESTRAGON: I had a dream.
> VLADIMIR: Don't tell me.
> ESTRAGON: I dreamt that . . .
> VLADIMIR: DON'T TELL ME!
> ESTRAGON: (gesture towards the universe) This
> one is enough for you? (p. 11).

Vladimir is enraged by Estragon's recurring sleepiness
almost to the end of the play (p. 57). Finally, he sees that in
fact sleep does not take him out of the world, does not abolish
facticity. Even in sleep, he stays in this world into which he
has been thrown:

> VLADIMIR: At me, too, someone is looking, of me
> too someone is saying, He is sleeping, he knows
> nothing, let him sleep on (p. 58).

Dasein exists in his throwness. This he understands pre-
logically and pre-cognitively. This understanding of his
existence is disclosed to him in his states-of-mind, his moods.
Mood, for Heidegger, is a "basic existential way in which
Dasein is its 'there'."[17] Mood makes it possible for Dasein to
"disclose things primordially . . . as it were, let Dasein
interpret itself."[18] Mood discloses to Dasein possible modes
of Being-in-the-world, "not as a psychological state but as an
intentional determinant."[19] Mood is that which reveals, it
has a revelatory function, it is a chosen path to meaning.

The tramps are given whole gamuts of moods, and a
skillful use of clothing imagery, boots and hats, body and
mind, allow these moods and their existential significance to
emerge dramatically. Likewise, the appearance of Lucky and
Pozzo allows symbolic extension of the world: to business,
science, academe; to power, oppression, blind arrogance, a
mechanization of time in which Pozzo is unmanned by the

loss of his watch. But it is not the case that nothing happens in the play. What happens is that Vladimir and Estragon, Being and being, become one: the structure of the two acts which compose the play represent the fusion of ontic and ontological. In a structural (ontic) sense, the two acts are the same--the scene, the characters, the waiting, the encounter with Pozzo and Lucky, the boots and hats, Vladimir's pelvic pain, Estragon's sleepiness, the encounter with Godot's boy. Yet there are several differences, the most notable of which is the fact that the tramps become united as "us" rather than divided as Being and being. Yet even this oneness is problematic. United, the pair are symbolically characterized as impotent: for Beckett, the music-hall lewdness of fallen pants will become the symbol of self-inflicted castration.

The unification of Dasein is very subtly done. It is in the first instance a discovery of the natural world, symbolized in "the tree." Vladimir struggles to grasp the meaning of the tree intellectually, while Estragon understands it in an intuitive way. In the first act Vladimir thinks the tree "must be dead" (p. 10); in the finale (p. 59) "Everything is dead but the tree." Yet the tree makes Vladimir happy, changes his mood, and he is puzzled by this:

> VLADIMIR: Wait . . . we embraced . . . we were happy . . . happy . . . what do we do now that we are happy . . .go on waiting . . . waiting . . . let me think . . . it's coming . . . go on waiting . . . now that we're happy . . . let me see . . . ah! The tree (p. 42).

Thus, Vladimir's mood projects him to the tree, which no doubt gives him a glimpse of the possible authenticity of his act of waiting; it affirms the mode of continuous time as over against the unilinear/fractional mode of time which makes men so unhappy. But why is it such a struggle? It is a struggle because men have chosen to define their relation with the natural world as one of struggle. This world of *anti-physis* which men have made intrudes between men and nature, separating them from the natural world as surely as the alienation of their seed in copulation separates them from genetic continuity. This ontic world comes between men and nature, men and the biological being which Beckett, unlike Heidegger, knows to be of profound significance to Being. I would argue that bereft of the integrative power of women in reproductive process, men stand alone, alienated from the natural world and from species continuity. There is in this play a small sense of natural renewal in the tree, the season, the rising and setting of the sun, which is quite absent from Heidegger's world without women. Yet there are no women to translate natural continuity into historic time in the act of birthing.

Vladimir cannot get himself together with Estragon as a "we" in an active historical way. He remains an isolated "I." In the second act, Vladimir and Estragon are together only in their "falleness" which they share with all mankind who understand themselves as thrown into the world rather than born of human labor. Vladimir chooses collective anonymity rather than an active relation of self and others, of being and nature, of life and time:

> VLADIMIR: Not indeed we personally are needed. Others would meet the case equally well, if not better. To all mankind they were addressed, these cries for help still ringing in our ears! But at this place, at this moment of time, all mankind is us, whether we like it or not (p. 51).

Vladimir here is still thinking as "we," and further trying to isolate this we in a "moment of time." So he poses the question the wrong way: "What are we doing here, *that* is the question" (p. 51) he says, and thinks he knows the answer: "And we are blessed in this, that we happen to know the answer. Yes, in the immense confusion one thing alone is clear. We are waiting for Godot to come."

Yet the waiting is passive. Godot does not come. Beckett, I think, intends the ambiguity of the moving and orgasmic meaning of "coming." Godot is ultimately *impotence*. Yet to understand this, Being and being must be united. This is foreshadowed when Pozzo and Lucky appear in the first act, and Pozzo suggests that waiting for Godot may be all right as long as it doesn't disrupt one's time schedule. Pozzo represents the view of time as commodity, as money. Vladimir breaks an unwonted silence to say: "Time has stopped" (p. 24).

Yet, when Pozzo and Lucky appear again in Act II, when he has failed to make Estragon "disappear" behind the tree, sink, as it were, back into nature, Vladimir is able to say: "Time flows again already. The sun will set, the moon will rise, and we away . . . from here" (p. 50). Estragon refuses Pozzo's orders, and reluctantly enters the search for authenticity: for the first and only time in the play he says: "I'm waiting for Godot" (p. 56).

So they are united in joint intention, but still left with the passive strategy of waiting. They are one, they have the freedom to choose to wait, yet authenticity is still a mystery. In both acts, Godot sends a boy messenger, an odd boy, perhaps two boys, perhaps any boy child. In the first act, Vladimir is still separate from his body-being, an inauthentic "us." His message to Godot is: "Tell him . . . (he hesitates) tell him you saw us. (Pause) You did see us, didn't you?" (p. 34).

In the second act:

> Tell him . . . (he hesitates) . . . tell him you saw me
> and that . . . (he hesitates) . . . that you saw me.
> (Pause. Vladimir advances, the boy recoils,
> Vladimir halts, the boy halts. With sudden
> violence.) You're sure you saw me, you won't come
> and tell me tomorrow that you never saw me!
> (Silence. Vladimir makes a sudden spring forward,
> the boy avoids him and exits running) (p. 59).

This leap forward into authenticity is exactly what Heidegger prescribes for Dasein, but Beckett knows that it is problematic. Estragon changes too: in his rough way he shows concern for Vladimir (p. 59). The tramps are liberated from each other in a bondedness of concern for being, for care. It sounds moral, but it is in fact merely mental. It is not in the world for Heidegger, it is neither active nor effective. This unity of ontic and ontological, of essence and existence, is still not complete. Godot hasn't come: if he doesn't come tomorrow, Vladimir says they'll hang themselves on the tree. There is none of the joy Heidegger promises to the individual.[20] We find this, too, in Hegel: "knowing that in his actual world he can find nothing else but its unity with himself, *can experience only joy in himself*" (original emphasis).[21] This joy relies on the extraordinary proposition that man makes himself, a radical subjectivism united with a radical isolationism which separates Dasein from community, from history, from interdependence with women, from biological birth. Heidegger's is a melancholy celebration of alienation, of passivity, of aloneness, overcome only in the orgasmic isolation of "coming," perceived in an abstract and ahistorical way. Self constituted as selfishness, a not owing existence to another, negates motherhood and renders the real alienation of men from reproduction as the universal rather than as the specifically male existential condition of being human, the condition of male but not female reproductive consciousness. Beckett, the poet, recognizes the tragic dimensions of separation, of dualism, of the cutting away of birth, of nature, and of community consumated in a sterile union with abstract mind, though it is less than clear that he understands the separation of masculine and feminine reproductive consciousness, and the systematic negation of the latter in sociohistorical terms as the ground of this sterility from dualist man's perspective, in any case. The result is impotence, a failure to "come" at all. His evocative use of clothing imagery, in which thought is a hat (Vladimir is wearing the intellectually impotent Lucky's hat as the play ends), and practical life is boots, sexuality symbolized in trousers. This most commonplace sartorial presentment of masculinity plays a significant part in the drama, and ultimately joins with the symbolic tree in a suggestion that man's alienation from the natural world is the material and existential root of a sterile passivity.

In the opening scene, Vladimir appears with his fly unbuttoned.

VLADIMIR: . . . (he buttons his fly) Never neglect
the little things of life.
ESTRAGON: What do you expect, you always wait
to the last moment.
VLADIMIR: (musingly) The last moment . . . (he
meditates) Hope deferred maketh the something
sick, who said that?
ESTRAGON: Why don't you help me?
VLADIMIR: Sometimes I feel it coming all the
same. Then I go all queer . . . Relieved and at the
same time appalled. AP-PALLED (p. 8).

Scripture says: Hope deferred maketh the heart sick, but
when the desire cometh, it is a tree of life.[22] So the tree is
introduced, very obliquely, and then is identified as the place
where they have to wait for Godot. To Vladimir, it is a place
of life and hope, quite specifically related to sexuality. To
Estragon, it is also death, a place to hang themselves (p. 12).
Vladimir demurs from the hanging:

VLADIMIR: . . . It'd give us an erection.
ESTRAGON: (highly excited) An erection!
VLADIMIR: With all that follows. Where it falls
mandrakes grow. That's why they shriek when you
pull them up (p. 8).

Birth and death are profoundly intermingled in these
exchanges. AP-PALLED, with its capitals and hyphen,
surely means pall-borne, dead. Yet, that speech of Vladimir's
(Sometimes I feel it coming all the same) is, in its terse
ambiguity, an announcement of the theme of the play. The
failure of Godot to "come" assumes a sexual dimension.
Godot is, indeed, the promise of some sort of ecstasy, some
sort of fulfillment. Beckett seems to me to be dramatizing
without analyzing the fact that it is a life-denying fulfillment
if we do not comprehend that the masculine separation of
sexuality and birth is the negation of the very foundation of
being-in-the-world, of being born. The mandrake plant is an
ancient symbol of birth, its root commonly supposed to
resemble a foetus.

It is notable, that whereas Estragon is physical organism in his everyday needs of eating and sleeping, it is Vladimir who has reserved for himself the sexual function. Estragon doesn't even understand it on a pre-creative level: he constantly confuses the genital and urinary functions, and has nothing to say of reproduction and birth. Vladimir, on the other hand, has bladder troubles: he hurts, it will be recalled, "in the pubis" when he laughs. Vladimir's bladder troubles are, in fact, rather more than that. He is perhaps slowly but surely castrating himself, for in a world where there are no women, Godot can never come and Dasein can never "be" in any aspect whatsoever. This may be faithful enough to Heidegger, who is a fitting heir to the oppressive and aggressive patriarchy of nineteenth-century German thought. Beckett seems to be at least aware of the limitations involved, in that he does give Estragon his life-giving name. But Estragon is not "female" in any separate sense. He is part of Vladimir. So it is that the breaking of the cord under the tree at the end of the play is essentially melancholy. Self-creation, Beckett seems to be saying, excludes procreation. Vladimir loves Estragon. This is a narcissistic love. Estragon *is* Vladimir. Vladimir, like the classic Narcissus, may, in loving himself, see things more clearly; see, as Narcissus did, a new depth in nature, in the trees of the forest. Yet he must eschew the hope of progeny, and without the continuity of the generations, time itself will soon cease to have human significance.

Vladimir can only wait. Godot is only possibility. He might be Being and ecstasy. He is probably Death, too, but Vladimir's death, like death for all of us, is not very important historically. It would be very important indeed if it was to be the Death of the human race. Yet perhaps Godot might even be just this. The form he will take is unknown. Thus the permeating anxiety of the play. Godot might be Christ, might be goodness incarnate. There is absolutely no evidence that this will be so. He might just as well be one of those who, in Estragon's phrase, "crucifies quick" (p. 34). Uneasily, we remember that Godot beat the boy who tended the sheep, another enigmatical/Christ-like allusion. Heidegger insists that authentic Dasein can "choose" his own heroes.[23] Beckett points poignantly to the dangers and terrible uncertainties of such a choice.

Without some attempt to interpret the sexuality and eventual dramatization of impotent man in the last lines, with the weird business of the trousers, the play becomes random and meaningless. In enacting a sad womanless parody of birth under the tree, Beckett has Estragon's trousers fall down. He stands, thus exposed, but he too must cover himself up, just as Vladimir had done when he buttoned his fly in the opening scene. Having his trousers down seems such an ordinary thing to Estragon that he does not even notice: Vladimir, though, is implacable. Three times he tells Estragon:

> Pull on your trousers.
> Pull on your trousers.
> Pull ON your trousers (p. 60).

This hiding of the genitals is pointless as anything other than symbolic castration. Vladimir has achieved some sort of reconciliation with his ordinary everydayness. The choice Beckett has had him make, though, is a very ambiguous one indeed. It seems almost as if he has gained his soul and lost the world. He has created a new self which is essentially impotent. Man has made himself, an objective which male-dominant society has always held as a dear dream, a dream of rebirth and auto-regeneration in which motherhood plays no part. Beckett's point seems not to be whether authenticity is achievable but whether it is a tragic and lifeless dream. Yet the specifically masculine intellectual habit of uniting birth and death in a crude biological continuum negates the possibility of grasping the notion of continuity embedded in the act of birth:

> Astride of a grave and a difficult birth. Down in the hole, lingeringly, the grave digger puts on the forceps. We have time to grow old. The air is full of our cries. (He listens.) But habit is a great deadener (p. 58).

Yet Beckett refuses to sink entirely into nihilism. Vladimir, not moving, denying energy itself, trousers in place, boots center stage, Estragon unhung: Vladimir stands in a state of total inaction. Yet all is not lost. He has Lucky's hat on. He can still think about it all. And it is not hopeless: there, in the world, frail but persistent, crying for cultivation, promising little except the keeping alive of possibility, there the tree still grows. And suppose Godot's a woman? Then the tree of life can flourish and the world be kept alive and time will not stop and authentic humanity can re-assert itself in the birth of women's children, of women children and men children, a birth in history, in continuity, in time understood as continuous and integrative, as in fact the essential grounding of any useful ontology.

NOTES

[1] Samuel Beckett, *Waiting for Godot*. (New York: Grove Press, 1954); Martin Heidegger, *Being and Time*. Trans. Macquerrie, John and Edward Robinson (New York: Harper and Row, 1962). Henceforth abbreviated: BT. I have followed the practice of giving section numbers rather than pagination, so that, if desired, the original German text can be referred to.

[2] BT 12.

[3] "This entity which each of us is himself [sic] and which includes inquiring as one of the possibilities of its Being, we shall denote by the term *Dasein*" (BT 7).

[4] BT 41.

[5] Samuel Beckett, *Waiting for Godot*, translation from the original French by the author (N.Y., Grove Press, 1954). All editions of the play have doubled pagination. Page references hereafter incorporated in the text.

[6] Calvin O. Schaag, "Phenomenology, Ontology and History in the Philosophy of Heidegger." In J. J. Kockelman (ed.), *Phenomenology* (New York, Doubleday Anchor, 1967) p. 289.

[7] E. G. Ballard, "Heidegger's View and Evaluation of Nature and Natural Science." In John Sallis (ed.), *Heidegger and the Path of Thinking* (Pittsburg, Duquesne U. P., 1970) p. 63.

[8] BT 191. I have followed Heidegger in capitalizing authentic Being and lower-casing everyday being (itself problematic!).

[9] "The thinker utters Being, the poet names what is holy." Heidegger, "What is Metaphysic?" I am indebted to Professor Christian Lenhardt of York University for this translated quotation.

[10] BT 43.

[11] BT 43-44.

[12] BT 44.

[13]"Relations are acts by which Dasein understands itself, a 'towards which' or 'for the sake of which' Dasein has concern" (BT 77).

[14]For an extensive analysis of the significance of paternal uncertainty within the dialectics of reproduction, see my *The Politics of Reproduction*, (London: Routledge & Kegan Paul, 1981) Chapter I.

[15]It is also true that Vladimir/Estragon must turn to the natural world, represented as the tree, and to the temporal world represented by the seasons. This is beautifully done, and I shall come back to these points.

[16]BT 135.

[17]BT 139.

[18]BT 140.

[19]Schaag, op.cit., p. 282.

[20]BT 310.

[21]F. Hegel, *Phenomenology of Spirit*, translation A. V. Miller (Oxford University Press, 1979) p. 242.

[22]St. James version of the *Bible*, "Proverbs 13, 12."

[23]BT 386.

8

The Root of the Mandrake: Machiavelli and Manliness

Despite Plato's celebrated dictum that poets represent a menace to a well-run polity, male political theorists, in significant number, have shown a yearning to give aesthetic expression to their philosophies. Plato's own work is not only structured dramatically but is widely considered to have claims to literary eminence. Many men who were primarily poets also wrote political treatises, most notably Dante and John Milton. In the work of Jean Jacques Rousseau, the line between philosophy and fable was a tenuous one, while in Friedrich Nietzsche it disappeared altogether. Samuel Taylor Coleridge fancied himself as a shrewd political commentator able to make sense of the Hegelian philosophy, and even the young Karl Marx wrote poetry. George Bernard Shaw, of course, wrote polemic in a number of prose forms, and in our own times, such diverse talents as Berthold Brecht and Norman Mailer attempt to render politics in both philosophical and artistic terms.

Niccolò Machiavelli, widely credited with having turned traditional political philosophy into a modern political science, wrote comedies: it is one of these, *La Mandragola*, which will be considered here.[1] It may be thought a little odd that feminist criticism should find it in any way useful to spend time on a rather drearily unfunny comedy which is, moreover, profoundly misogynist. There are, however resonances in the relation of Machiavelli's political theory and literary work which reflect on a question central to much contemporary feminist theory: the question of the separation of public and private life. This separation is not fanciful but is a concrete historical manifestation of both masculine subjective preoccupation with the dualism of human experience and the patriarchal practice which embodies this dualism in the political attempt to keep the private realm of necessity apart from the public domain of freedom. Hannah Arendt was perhaps the most eloquent modern apologist for this venerable dichotomy. She believed the separation to be under threat of extinction by the combined forces of the bourgeoisie and the proletariat and argued that only Machiavelli among the traditional greats of the discipline of political theory had a proper perception of the fact that the separation of the public and private realms is, in practice, the precondition of a rational and noble polity.[2] Arendt is correct in claiming Machiavelli as a staunch apostle of this ideological position. He never, however, spelled it out with the clarity which Arendt brings to her own phenomenology of the a priori dualism of the human condition. It must be said, moreover, that Machiavelli was a good deal more realistic than Arendt about the capacity of the public domain, properly constituted, to become the space in which fathers of families show forth their existential greatness. In fact, his major statements on the private realm and family life appear in his "literary" work, notably in *Mandragola*. I therefore propose to examine Machiavelli's political works with a view to uncovering his estimation of the relation of family and polity, particularly with regard to his symbolic positing of this relation in the ambiguous concepts of *virtu* and *fortuna*. The relation of domesticity and political praxis presented in *Mandragola* can then be analyzed in terms not only of dramatic irony but of the deeper irony embedded in the ideology of patriarchal politics.

A word first about the mandragola, a poisonous plant of the nightshade family known in English as the mandrake, or man-dragon. It appears to have been a favorite with alchemists and herbalists and was always girt with superstition. The root was said to resemble a fetus and the plant to cry when pulled from the earth. Poets have found it symbolic, as in John Donne's *Song*:[3]

> Go and catch a falling star,
> Get with child a mandrake root,
> Tell me where all past years are,
> Or who cleft the Devil's foot;
> Thou, when thou return'st can tell me
> All strange wonders that befell thee
> And swear nowhere
> Lives a woman true and fair.

The symbolism lives on in Samuel Beckett's work *Waiting for Godot*:[4]

> Estragon: What about hanging ourselves?
> Vladimir: Hmm. It'd give us an erection.
> Estragon: *(highly excited)* An erection!
> Vladimir: With all that follows. Where it falls mandrakes grow. That's why they shriek when you pull them up. Did you not know that?
> Estragon: Let's hang ourselves immediately.

This superstitious vision of a mysterious biological force threatening the integrity of man's sexual potency and reproductive power is part of Machiavelli's "pragmatic" politics. His political work attempts to describe the theoretical and practical dimensions of an autonomous polity: his ideal politicians are an austere priesthood of the singleminded, able to practice a doctrine of the justification of means by ends without flinching from its more harrowing implications.[5] I will argue that Machiavelli believes that the major obstacle in the path to this problematic glory is, in both practical and symbolic terms, Woman. I will also argue that, from the standpoint of feminist politics, Machiavelli is correct: women do indeed reject the neurosis which sees nature as a cunning and powerful foe. Resistance to this pernicious doctrine, in which the endless defense of public and private violence as "necessary evils" is posited as necessary to the common good, is an essential part of feminist struggle. Feminists believe that the separation of

the public and private realms does not merely institutionalize
the dreams and realities of patriarchy: it ensures that
politics *must* proceed from the violent exercise of power, an
activity to which men are apprenticed in the private realm,
inured to in popular culture, and practice as the dynamic of
public life.   Machiavelli's despair of overcoming and
controlling the natural world was realistic within a
patriarchal praxis.   It is not, however, this dimension of
"realism" in his thought to which male commentators have
given attention.   Machiavelli's "pragmatism" is generally
interpreted as resting in the reality of power relations,
perceived as immutable conditions of political life in general
rather than of patriarchal politics in particular.

Polity and Family

The family, in late Renaissance Italy, was not merely a
venerable social institution but was in the process of
undergoing the change associated with the vanishing kinship
relations which had underpinned the class structure of
feudalism. Jacob Burckhart doubtless exaggerates the extent
to which bloodlines yielded to individual experience and
performance.[6]   Humanism no doubt believed, with Poggio,
that there is no other nobility than that of personal merit,[7]
but in practice, families which achieved power, whether by
individual or collective endeavor, showed no tendency to
abandon their progeny to their own individual excellence but
kept the prerequisites of power in the family.   The Medici,
Sforza, and Visconti families, for example, showed a
hereditary durability which the Houses of Lancaster and
York might well have envied. These families, whatever their
origins, became and stayed powerful for long periods:
hereditary power is not the prerogative solely of monarchs.
Hereditary power remained the source of familial power and
personal potency until men discovered the potentiality and
potency of the "incorporation" (i.e., embodiment) of industrial
wealth.   Such wealth appears, happily for its possessors, to
reproduce itself in wombless fecundity.

The abrasive tendencies to factionalism in family-based
politics, examined and found tragic by Shakespeare in *Romeo*

and Juliet, were a reality of political life in Machiavelli's time (1469-1527). The desire to establish family power invaded and frequently corrupted political life. Nowhere was this tendency more clearly demonstrated than in the papal practice of nepotism. Popes in those days did not often maintain office for too long a time, and they generally hastened to establish relatives in lucrative and powerful spots before death or deposition deprived them of resource. Indeed, Machiavelli predicted gloomily that endeavors would be made to make the papacy hereditary.[8] As well as popes, merchant bankers and mercenaries became founding fathers of powerful families. Machiavelli did not care much for men in any of these occupational categories.[9]

In Florence, a long tradition of rendering the hereditary aristocracy politically impotent by "Ordinances of Justice" was undoubtedly a fine republican act and did much that was positive to widen the base of political life in the city state. The negative aspects, though, were formidable. The bourgeoisie were as patriarchal as the aristocracy. Family-based factions persisted in conflict for more than a century, and the hatred of the Ordinances themselves by still vocal and often rich aristocrats was a source of considerable strife.[10] Machiavelli was well aware of the dangers to which a dissident and defeated aristocracy exposed republics, but the replacement of noble families by rich families was not a solution especially relished by this "poor but patrician" secretary. Kinship seemed to Machiavelli to be a very destructive base for politics: he gave lip service to a norm of filial piety but rejected hereditary ties as the "most fallacious means of identifying the best men to rule."[11] Such was his dislike of the hereditary practice of leaving power--he is less specific about property--to "heirs and successors" that he advocated that the job of founding a republic, like the leadership of an army, was best done by "One man only."[12]

Machiavelli, steeped in the lore of republican Rome, considered that the longevity of a republic derived from its capacity to maintain the integrity of public life in the teeth of all the tests which *fortuna* could throw at it. He understood ideology and its workings, though he had no single word to describe it, and was appreciative of the political effectiveness of ideological hegemony. But in terms of the founding of republics, he quite specifically rejected Christian doctrines of original sin and pagan myths of primordial crime in favor of a practical and historical doctrine of political expediency, for which such notions as "sin" and "crime" are beside the point. His further rejection of kinship ties and heredity as grounds for the exercise of political power appears as a pragmatic response to realities of historical experience.

The domestic aspect of family life and its diverse social functions he viewed more ambivalently. He spoke briefly of "education," which he understood in quite broad terms encompassing what we now refer to as the socialization process.[13] He recognized some familial impact on the molding of character, but the main example he used--the insolence of the Appia--is a negative one and is contrasted unfavorably to "the goodness and gentleness displayed by an infinite number of *citizens*."[14] Private family life earns only a very brief chapter in *The Discourses*, and marriage arrangements introduce the chapter which expounds how women are liable to ruin states.[15] Machiavelli does not advise the Prince to leave his subjects' wives and property alone, which can be interpreted as recommending some form of protection for family life; the effect is somewhat muted, though, by being immediately followed by the observation that "men forget more easily the death of their father than the loss of their patrimony."[16] *The Discourses*, in the probably incomplete form in which we have them, end on the theme of the disorderly effect which new families had on Rome.[17]

Family life, then, emerges in Machiavelli's thought as it appears in his experience; it is a three-level affair, with a certain amount of ambivalence in each. The first level is Machiavelli's admiring interpretation of Roman family life, which he sees as separated from political life; this view, however, owes more to myth than to history, and the private realm was still responsible for the decline of the republic. The second level is founded on his observation and experience of the political machinations of the powerful families of his own time, whose activities corrupt public life by virtue of nepotism, factionalism, and self-interest. On the household level, education is useful, for it is "of great importance whether a youth in his tender years hears any act praised or censured; this necessarily makes a lasting impression upon his mind, and becomes afterwards the rule of his life for all time."[18]

All of this, despite some inconsistencies, seems relatively straightforward. Two centuries later, Oliver Cromwell would repeat Machiavelli's basic message when he argued against hereditary power on the grounds that "who knoweth whether he may beget a fool or a wise man?"[19] Cromwell, however, still named his own foolish Richard as his successor, but Machiavelli, a disgraced civil servant exiled to the privation of domestic life, did not have to face the problem of the legitimization of patriarchal power in personal terms. Yet the whole business cannot be understood simply as a response to actual events, historical and contemporary, for Machiavelli does not in fact let it rest there. He adds to the practical analysis a symbolic, indeed quite mystical conceptualization, which he expresses in terms of the existential struggle between two opposing forces that he calls *virtu* and *fortuna*. The politician must serve an apprenticeship in this struggle, and only those who succeed in conquering *fortuna* are fit to rule other men.

The exact meanings of *virtu* and *fortuna* are not clear. I believe they are best understood as male and female. The negative, bad acts which boys must be taught to abhor are those acts repeatedly characterized by Machiavelli as "effeminate."[20] Thus, I propose that the appropriate translation for *virtu* is "manliness," which is quite consistent with Machiavelli's conceptualization in a way which transcends the mere opposition to effeminate. There is something cosmic in man's struggle with *fortuna*, and something very familiar in the annals of the development of the theory and practice of male supremacy. Manliness is vigorous, thoughtful, prudent, passionate, aggressive, expansionary, and (regrettably), a scarce resource. Manliness is not self-seeking--and this is the ethical/mystical dimension--but is a transcendent service to the public weal. Effeminacy, on the other hand, is passive, unreasonable, unpredictable, given to luxuriousness and stay-at-home. Manliness can be explicated in terms not only of its *relation* to effeminacy, but also in terms of one of its own essential qualities: this is the ability for men to understand that "effeminacy" is but a pale personal reflection of a cosmic historical force called *fortuna*. *Fortuna* embraces the irrational contrariness and unpredictability of the natural world as embodied in her handmaidens, women, and if great care is not taken in childraising, will produce effeminate men.

Attempts to locate the imprecision of the concept of *virtu* within *virtu* itself are doomed to failure, for there can be no manliness and no *virtu* unless woman is actively overcome. Male commentators who struggle with the concept rarely put this in quite these terms and would no doubt deprecate their crudity. In fact, the failure to understand Machiavelli's treatment of the man/woman dialectic arises from the well-known tension which Machiavelli's admirers feel in justifying the tougher implications of his theory of politics. John Plamenatz, for example, separates *virtu* into the categories of "heroic" and "civic" virtue, arguing that the first, the nasty bit, creates the conditions for the second, the nice bit.[21] Such apologetics for the means and end dilemma cannot be supported textually in a consistent way, for the tension which Machiavelli himself sets up is not within *virtu* but *between virtu* and *fortuna*. Woman/nature/nurture challenges man/polity/violence in a primordial way which denies even the possibility of complementarity. *Fortuna*/woman challenges manliness to take her by force, to overcome and conquer her completely, to *control* her. The formulation of the encounter of manliness and femininity in Chapter XXV of *The Prince* is explicitly and aggressively sexual. She can only be "conquered by force," a force exerted more effectively by the bold than the cold. This is not merely the roughest of wooing nor the conventional prelude to holy matrimony: it is, quite simply, rape.

Machiavelli is working in one sense on a symbolic level, but the history of culture/nature, mind/body, public/private dualism suggests a strong relation of this conceptualization to the historical struggles to create and defend patriarchal institutions. Traditionally, the institution of marriage has as one of its stabilizing functions the direction of the sex drive into socially useful channels, though history does not suggest that social structures have always fulfilled this functional imperative with spectacular success.

Machiavelli perceives with admirable clarity the vital need for the state to find ways of channeling the energies of citizens. He sees with equal clarity that energy both creates, thrives on, and can overcome conflict.[22] He believes that conflict is that reality which makes politics necessary and necessarily utilitarian, but it is also that very necessity which sets up the potentiality for a man to be manly. Glory and utility are uneasy bedfellows, but manliness is both passionate and rational in Machiavelli's thinking. Prudent spontaneity and warm-blooded calculation are the apparent contradictions which pave the path to glory. This is why it is a path which, while it provides a backward perspective on history, cannot see where it is going. It cannot have an end, for an end would bring *stasis*, would cut off the possibility for action, and it is precisely in action that manliness shows itself forth. Manliness must constantly destroy and recreate its road to glory.

Manliness may create its own road, but it does not have to create its own obstacles. *Fortuna* does that; *fortuna* constantly drives man abroad. This is because woman's place, home, is the place for the effeminate, those who are happy with petty competition and who evade conflict, who elevate family over polity, and who are willing to pay others to fulfill not only their responsibility, but also their destiny. "At home" is precisely that place where manliness cannot be at home. The most it offers is the release of sexual energy and the continuity of generation. Says Pico: "The brutes bring from their mother's body what they will carry with them as long as they live; the higher spirits are from the beginning, or soon after, what they will be forever."[23]

Mere biological continuity, from a patriarchal perspective, means nothing, and not just because blood, as Machiavelli remarks, is "necessarily modified by marriage."[24] Necessity and *fortuna*, Felix Gilbert observes, are identical in Machiavelli's thinking.[25] The biological tie is a chain on manliness, but so, clearly, are the *social* relations of reproduction. Family life is a very problematic affair, with the necessity of *fortuna* and the contingency of paternity attendant on the cradle and the risk of women effeminizing the potentially manly. Paternity is therefore a duty to the polity and should aim to curb the dangerous seeds of *fortuna*. Machiavelli favored an increase in population, believing Rome to have been more sensible than Sparta in this matter;[26] he also understood the need for some social stability to permit the proper education of the young. These are not just necessary functions, but are also tremendously dangerous imperatives. Stability and tranquillity enervate, and enervation breeds corruption.[27] Family life is shot through with natural and biological reality, and also with the messiness of affection and concern for individuals; it is subject to the mindless whims of *fortuna* and her servant, Woman. In these circumstances, family and polity cannot be seen to stand opposed merely in an analytical or fatalistic way. "At home," the realm of women and their works, must be *actively* overcome, where necessary by force, as the precondition of the establishment of a public domain in which reason passionately prevails over necessity, unpredictability, and effeminacy. The separation of public and private exists historically in the development of Universal man, but the condition of that universality is the constant, violent maintenance of the rights of man and state to control the social relations of reproduction and the family, to overcome the soft seductiveness and passive destructiveness of women.

If this is a correct rendering of Machiavelli's view of the family, it must be noted that it bears significant relations to the realities of his times. Elected officers in Florence did not resign; they "went home" or, if disgraced, they were "sent home." Machiavelli himself was sent home in 1512, and his letters make it quite clear how unhappy this made him.[28] He was sent back to his marital family by a politically powerful family, the Medici. He appears to have been subjected to torture and then bored stiff, both of which were profoundly disquieting events. His vision of the relation of public and private life, however, is much more complex than a petulant complaint about his personal experiences. The contradictions involved transcend the psychological and personal realm and are perceived in the context of the existential and the historical. If in fact family life corrupts the very possibility of heroism, then this conflict may be presented in dramatic terms as, indeed, it has been since classical times. Dramatically, one may discover that the dilemma is ultimately insoluble, that it is ultimately impossible for men to be manly. This is the tragic vision, the bleak life in which Creon's strength is unequal to family customs and in which Godot never "comes." On the other hand, drama may illuminate the way in which men act absurdly in the mistaken pursuit of private rather than public ends. This is the comic vision. Triviality and glory share a vulnerability to folly which makes the dualism of human existence as problematic as the arbitrary separation of family and polity, manliness and effeminacy, tragedy and comedy. It is of such folly which *Mandragola* speaks, so it is worthwhile to discover what the play says.

The Private Realm as Comedy

Owing much to classical theater, the major debt of Italian Renaissance drama was to Rome. Shakespeare acknowledged this while poking fun at his over-awed and excessively imitative contemporaries. The words are given to Polonius: "the best actors in the world, either for tragedy, comedy, history, pastoral, pastoral-comical, tragical-historical, tragical-comical-historical-pastoral, scene indivisible, or poem unlimited: Seneca cannot be too heavy nor Plautus too light."[29]

Satirical though these words are, it is true, as Gilbert Highet points out, that drama cannot even be composed until its varieties and possibilities have been understood.[30] Only then can an age turn to creating something new within these forms. Machiavelli's contemporaries thought that he had created something new with *Mandragola*.[31]

From a literary perspective, *Mandragola* is a puzzling piece. Lord Thomas Babington Macaulay's famous accolade has been treated as a definitive judgment by many political writers.[32] Macaulay believed that had Machiavelli devoted himself to drama he would have produced a "salutary effect on the national taste." Given the sheer lewdness of the *Mandragola*, one might be forgiven for wondering about Macaulay's conception of the salutary and the tasteful.[33] What he is referring to is form and character; Macaulay's critical criteria are naturalism and believable characterization, and he finds the settings and characters of *Mandragola* suitably true to life, which, insofar as "life" is patriarchally defined, it is.

Other critics have been less adulatory. Highet believes that the early promise of Italian drama "went sour with the plays of Machiavelli and Aretino, who took the structure, plot line and characters of classical comedy, modernized them, and added dirt--dirt derived partly from their own minds and partly from medieval fablaux.[34] Most of the great theatrical innovations--flats, *periaktos*, and raised stages-- came after Machiavelli's time, and so the prologue of *Mandragola* indicates a classical street scene in the Renaissance fashion. The three classic scenes--street with palaces for tragedy, street with shops and houses for comedy, and a woodland scene for the satyr play which the Renaissance would develop as pastoral--all of these were known by the turn of the century. Machiavelli also uses his street setting to permit and accelerate action and movement in the comedy.

The plot, too, is conventional, demonstrating that the staples of the dirty joke are depressingly enduring. They are all here: cuckolded husband, the tricky seduction of the chaste woman, her rapturous discovery that she likes it, the venal mother-in-law, the confusion of the genital and excretory functions, four-letter word furbishings, and the general triumph of the Penis Rampant. All of this is given a touch of legendary magic by the superstition inherent in the symbolism of the mandrake. The plot turns on twin axes: sexuality and manliness; fecundity and the uncertainty of paternity. One can easily sympathize with Carlo Goldoni's initial disgust at the lubricity of the piece, which he records in his memoirs, adding that he was "enchanted" by the characterization.[35]

The plot, which Machiavelli himself knows to be "slight," (Prolog, p. 117) cannot be simply ignored while one praises the characterization, however aesthetically satisfying such a procedure might be. The relation of plot to character and situation is sufficiently deft and rather zanily believable to integrate form and content. To divide the two is to make of *Mandragola* an exercise in *imitatio* on the one hand and some kind of parable of *corruptio* on the other. *Mandragola* has artistic limitations. Comedy, said Aristotle, imitates men who are inferior but not altogether vicious.[36] In *Mandragola* the wolfishness of the comedy is overstressed, and the bitterness of the prologue colors the characterization. For Machiavelli's contemporaries, this vicious underlay was probably concealed by their keener appreciation of topical allusions and word play,[37] but these very limitations are more salient to the characters than to the plot. Despite them, *Mandragola* is a drama, not a smoking room anecdote nor a well-observed series of character sketches. Briefly, the plot concerns an old man, Nicia, whose wife, Lucretia, is a model of virtue, but childless.[38] Callimaco, a young merchant, develops an irresistible lust for Lucretia's body, but also a desire to destroy her integrity. He hires a shady character, Ligurio, to plan this overcoming of Lucretia, and suborns her mother and her confessor, both of whom join the plot. Siro, Callimaco's servant, is a general factotum.

The plot involves a cuckolding of Nicia made possible because he identifies his wife as the infertile partner. He is offered a magic potion to administer to Lucretia, who will become pregnant, Nicia is told, if she is serviced within twenty-four hours. Unfortunately, the conspirators say, the potion will kill her first impregnator, who will be, of course, Callimaco in disguise. Nicia swallows this yarn and agrees to the charade. Having tasted the pleasure of virile sexuality in this rape which her husband, mother, and priest all press upon her, Lucretia develops an insatiable, voluptuous lust for Callimaco, and her virtue sinks beyond trace.

Aristotle once remarked that what is right for a politician is not right for a poet.[39] "Right" or not, *Mandragola* has much in common with Machiavelli's political writing, though these latter are more poetical than the literary works are political. The first thing to be noticed about *Mandragola* is that the word "plot" can be taken quite literally. The whole piece is a well-structured and successful conspiracy. We know from *The Discourses* that Machiavelli regarded success in political conspiracy as rare: conspiracy "is understood to apply to a republic that is already partially corrupted; for in one not yet tainted by corruption such thoughts could never enter the mind of any citizen."[40]

The "comic" inversion in the play can be seen in the context of "Of Conspiracies," where Machiavelli warns that the prince who would guard himself against conspiracy must not harm his subjects' honor: "As to the attacking of men's honor, that of their wives is what they feel most, and after that their being themselves treated with indignity."[41]

Messer Nicia's foolishness tolerates both of these conditions. Yet he thinks that he is conspiring; he is too stupid to know that he is conspired against. The conspirators are performing in the play those very actions which, in *The Discourses*, cause conspiracies. This comic conspiracy, contrary to the fate foretold for most conspiracies in the *Discourses*, succeeds in the play. Cause and effect, as it were, are inverted in private affairs as opposed to public affairs.

This inversion gives form to the piece, but the political metaphor cannot be stretched too far: the real object of the conspiracy is Lucretia's chastity, a private realm virtue assaulted in terms of a metaphor which moves from conspiratorial to military activity. Lucretia's virtue is a fortress to be taken, and fortresses "may or may not be useful according to the times."[42] Lucretia has no friends, does not admit tradespeople to her house, and "has no maid or servant who's not afraid of her." The best fortress needs the love of the people, but Lucretia not only has servants who are afraid of her, but a husband and mother who dislike her.[43] She is thus vulnerable, but Callimaco still could not seize upon her without her husband's connivance, and Nicia's stupidity and lust for paternity are undoubtedly Callimaco's greatest assets. They are not, however, enough; fundamentally, Lucretia's vulnerability lies in her own virtue, as Timoteo, the priest, recognizes (3.9.800). The trouble with the marriage lies in its inversion: Lucretia dominates. Nicia not only stays "at home," he *wants* to stay at home: "I don't like to get off base" he says (1.2.782). Clearly this fortress has the wrong captain, but the "right" captain is impotent. The purpose of the play is to put manliness in command while *fortuna* is transformed to her proper state of purely sensual being.

The ostensible siege is made necessary by Callimaco's lust. His sexual desire is irrepressible, and he feels his whole being to be at stake. The exaggerated monologues in which Callimaco expresses his desire (4.1;4.4) are hyperbolic pastiches of great passion, which are rather well done. Callimaco is given the vocabulary of grand passion for the expression of mere lust. Yet for all this throbbing energy, his response is curiously oblique. He retains some prudence; no "off to storm the fortress" for him. He thinks at first to change Lucretia's nature (1.1.781) by removing her from her fortress. That scheme is quickly abandoned when Ligurio points out that he might have opposition then (1.3.784). Attacking and overcoming the fortress is a better risk, and he is prepared to try anything, "even if it's strange, risky, injurious, disgraceful" (1.2.784). These are Princely words, if applied to the Public Good. Callimaco the manly is inverting public and private life. This may be owing to his age or his calling; the dramatis personae lists him as a "young merchant." The first may explain his impetuosity. The second may explain his method, for what he does is hire a mercenary to organize the attack. Callimaco vaunts his versatility, but it is not quite a model of humanist eclecticism.[44] He passes his time in study, amusement, and business (1.1.779). Renaissance humanists, inexact though that term may be, were united in despising business. The result of Callimaco's activities was that he had peace, no enemies, and the favor of all classes. In Machiavelli's terms, he lived in an enervating state of tranquillity. But one fears that this Callimaco, despite his posturing, is basically "effeminate." This is why he needs a mercenary to organize his attack on *fortuna*. He is too lacking in manliness to perform this task himself. Here we have another public/private ambivalence. In his political writings,

Machiavelli never tires of pointing out the futility for employing mercenaries for manly tasks, yet what is almost always disastrous in public affairs becomes ludicrously successful in an assault on the private domain.[45]

The ascription of the role of mercenary to Ligurio does not rest on the fact that he is hired help. The whole of Act 4, scene 9 is a farcical battle, complete with a roster of phony troops, a friendly enemy, a simulated scuffle, surrendered "arms" ("Give that lute here") and military dialogue:

> Ligurio: Let's not lose any more time here. I'm going to be captain and draw up the army for battle. On the right horn Callimaco shall be in command, myself on the left, between the two horns will be the judge here; Siro will be the rearguard and reinforce any squadron that falls back. The battle cry will be St. Cuckoo (IV.9.813).

The classical symbols of cuckoldry--horns and cuckoo--are lost on Nicia. He is fighting for his own dishonor. Yet Callimaco is something of a mercenary, too. He is being paid to fulfill Nicia's manly responsibilities: the prize is Lucretia's body.

The conspiracy of Callimaco and Ligurio is a conspiracy of merchant and mercenary. "You and I have a natural affinity" Ligurio tells Callimaco (1.3.784). Indeed they have. By the end of the second act the conspiracy has been expanded to include Lucretia's priest and her mother. Who will recruit them? Ligurio tells Callimaco: "You, I, money, our rascality, theirs" (11.6.792). Merchant, mercenary, church, and family are united by their corruption and self-interest in a conspiracy of lust designed to overpower a virtuous woman.

By the end of the short first act, the natural affinity of Callimaco and Ligurio is established, and Ligurio is beginning to assert command. He has talked Callimaco out of his own scheme in favor of his own more dastardly plot. By the end of the second act, the web of conspiracy and deception has extended and Ligurio's authority is absolute:

Cal.: Where do you want me to go now?
Lig.: This way, that way, along this street, along
that one. Florence is a big town.
Cal.: (aside) This is killing me (11.6.793).

This last line may be simply contiguous with Callimaco's extravagantly romantic vapors. It might be more subtle. The dialogue is not distinguished by subtlety, but Machiavelli does rather contemptuously suggest in the *Prolog* that some of his audience will not understand what is being said. In any case, the plot structure realizes the subtle implication, whether it is or is not intentional, that what is "killed" is Callimaco's independence, his ability to act autonomously, his *manliness*. "Effeminately," he calls to Ligurio: "Oh, don't leave me alone" (11.6.793).

This development constitutes the first ironic axis of the comedy:[46] I do not want to make equivocal distinctions between tragic and comic irony, as I agree with Northrop Frye that irony has its own movement and form. By the phrase "ironic axis" I want to convey the sense of *acted* inversion, the contradiction of intended end and experienced means which emerges visibly in the structure of the play but which is invisible to the protagonists. To this quite ordinary meaning, I wish to add the sense I am attempting to explicate between the play and the political writings. The "comic" inversion, the "funniness," is derived from Nicia as inverted citizen, Callimaco as inverted soldier, and Lucretia as a chaste woman to be inverted to a harlot in the process of the action. Callimaco desires to show forth his manliness in the course of sexuality, but he can do so only by destroying his manliness. This is worked out dramatically in the first two acts. The second ironic axis is worked out in Acts 3 and 4. Here, Lucretia surrenders her claim to virtue. Lucretia is a strong woman. The overcoming of a strong position by brute strength or guile is not particularly ironic, and in Machiavelli's terms, is manly. It was a favorite ploy of the Romans for taking fortresses.[47] What is ironic is that those conventional bulwarks of family virtue, the parent and the priest, should be the agents of transforming family virtue to the rejection of family virtue. The only activity left to

Callimaco is that of the stud, and Lucretia's lack of effeminacy is remedied by her transformation to a whore, a true daughter of *fortuna*.

These twin axes meld into one, formally and boisterously, in Act 5. A new, contemptuous conspiracy is formed, not against any individual but against the state of matrimony itself. Lucretia has forgotten her desire for children in her desire for Callimaco. Instead of educating children in honor, she is educating Callimaco in ever more corrupt intrigue, teaching him "how we can be together at anytime without suspicion" (5.4.819). Callimaco has entered the fortress by a trick, but Lucretia is still in command.[48] Lucretia's transformation is complete, and her husband, ever ready with a curiously acute cliché, says to her that it is "as though you were born a second time" (5.5.819). Indeed, she has been; her biological birth has been transcended--she has no father--and redefined by masculine desire.

As for Callimaco, it is left to Fra Timoteo to define him with *double entendre*. "They are bringing out the prisoner" (5.1.815). Callimaco is the prisoner of his own desire, now controlled by the transformed Lucretia, but he is also in a very real sense hopelessly in thrall to Ligurio. The latter will share with Callimaco the key to the downstairs loggia, courtesy of Nicia, "because they don't have women at home and live like animals" (5.6.820). This spavined lion and scruffy fox, one suspects, are going to be much more beastly at home with the Nicia family than anywhere else. Callimaco is patently in trouble with his mercenary. In any case, there is nothing to stop Ligurio from rejecting his *condotta* for a better one. Nicia is acting paymaster as the comedy closes, and Ligurio is already jogging his arm, telling him to remember to pay Siro (5.6.820).

Siro is an interesting and not entirely minor character, who does all the running about and finally runs off altogether (5.2.816). His master, Callimaco, knows him to be faithful but believes him to be something of a rascal (4.3.808). In fact, Siro is just as much of a rascal as his master desires him to be, and he has a well-articulated notion of good service: "I'm your servant, and servants ought never to ask their masters questions about anything or pry into their business, but when the masters themselves tell them, they ought to serve them faithfully; and so I've done and so I'm going to do" (1.1.779).

One may judge a Prince by his ministers, Machiavelli tells us, and where a minister is "competent and faithful" one can know his master to be wise.[49] So unwise is Callimaco that he does not know his own servant, spurns his advice (1.1.780), and never quite enlightens him as to the details of the plan (2.4.789). The more astute Ligurio spots Siro as "capable" and, with the connivance of Callimaco, takes him over, demonstrating again the identity of Callimaco and Ligurio: "When he gives you orders" says Callimaco, speaking to Siro and referring to Ligurio, "imagine that I am speaking" (4.5.809). Callimaco has handed over his manliness to a mercenary captain, and Siro obeys, although he has warned his master that Ligurio is "not reliable." Siro has also suggested that had Callimaco confided in him before they left France, he would have known how to advise him (1.1.). Presumably, he would have advised him not to get involved in the absurd affair at all. Callimaco is a failed prince who does not know a good servant when he sees one. Machiavelli, the rejected secretary, has an axe to grind here.

Perhaps it is to read too much into the text to suggest this affinity between prince and adviser and master and servant, though a comparison between Chapter XXII of *The Prince* and the relations of Callimaco and Siro is suggestive. It may be even more unlikely that Machiavelli put himself into his play as a member of the lower classes, but the difference Siro points out between the risk he takes and that of his master is wry enough: "I'll be in danger of my life and my master of his life and property" (2.4.789).

Machiavelli does plead "poverty" in the *Prolog*, and says he "plays the servant to such as can wear a better cloak than he can." Further, Siro is the only character not on stage at the end of the play, having "run away" (5.2.816). He escapes the final corruption, and the sharp Ligurio sounds his epitaph: "Doesn't anyone remember Siro?" (5.6.821).

Ligurio himself had dismissed Siro with a quite gratuitous threat to "cut his throat." Siro is the good man who does the dirty work, keeps his mouth shut, and is humiliatingly rejected (and unpaid) for his pains. His is an invocative characterization.

The fact that the literary and political works of Machiavelli show thematic consistency is not, of course, remarkable. Nor is it surprising that this consistency is expressed in terms of paradox and irony. What is interesting from a feminist perspective is the fact that Machiavelli's dualism, expressed in terms of technique by the two different disciplines of theory and literature, is based upon a radical separation of public and private life which is perceived as quite fundamentally problematic. Whether the fairly persistent relationship of politics and literature reflects the problematics of patriarchal "overcoming" of nature, family, and women is a matter for further critical work. Machiavelli, an exceptional theorist in many ways, is almost unique in the annals of male-stream thought in his understanding of the fact that gender struggle is an essential substructure of history and that this fact has hard, cold consequences for the theory and practice of patriarchal politics. This dilemma cannot be seen merely as a result of Machiavelli's lack of economic sophistication, a sort of poetic substitute for a lack of understanding of class struggle. Marxist aesthetics could find in both the literary and political work sufficient evidence of the "degraded hero": Lukács' symbol of the ethical tensions between art and capitalism which appear in bourgeois literature.[50] Machiavelli's distrust of mercantilist families and the portrayal of Nicia and Callimaco as "merchants" might be interpreted as an early and acute comprehension of the process of transformation of merchants' capital to capital proper. Imaginative Marxists might see the servant Siro as a working-class consciousness antithetically posed against mercantilist corruption. However suggestive class analysis may be, however, it would have to be done inferentially, for Machiavelli's economics, derived from Sallust, are somewhat rudimentary.[51] But if the relations of production do not particularly excite Machiavelli, there can be no doubt that the social relations of reproduction are central to his political analysis. The struggle for an autonomous and scientific politics is a struggle in which political man, by whatever means he can devise, breaks free from the chains which bind him to biological and affective life. The fact that this precondition of polity tends to be dealt with on a literary rather than a theoretical level is a fact which, at the very least, presents feminist scholarship with a key to understanding one level of the ideological nature of male supremacy. It is only from a feminist standpoint and through a serious theoretical analysis of the process and relations of reproduction that the dialectic of Machiavelli's work can be uncovered.

I have argued elsewhere that the material base of the persistent dualism in patriarchal thought lies in the dialectical structure of human reproduction and the consequent differentiation of male and female reproductive consciousness.[52] The birth of a child is a double alienation: for women, a concrete experienced alienation mediated in living labor. For men, the alienation of the seed is a separation from nature, and from species continuity, an alienation which can only be sublated *culturally*; in Machiavelli's terminology, it is an alienation which must be "actively overcome." Paternity is fundamentally ideal; it is knowledge of process in general which cannot be particularized in the context of individual experience. Men are existentially passive toward and detached from the moment of birth: they participate only *potentially*, a participation which they have culturally defined as *potency*, yet potency is radically contingent. Male participation in reproduction is therefore understood *politically*; that is to say, in terms of a *right* to the child rather than in the value-creating reality of laboring to produce a child. This argument is supported by Machiavelli's transcendent realism, and my own analysis of the dialectics of reproduction in fact owes much to a careful reading of Machiavelli.

The dilemma which sends Machiavelli, the pragmatist, off to the physical/meta-physical confrontation of *fortuna* and *virtu* may be stated thus:

I. Manliness is the crucial individual quality demanded by the tension between biological and civil society. Biological necessity, which takes as its cultural form the family, constantly threatens polity in several ways:

1. A tendency to effeminize young men in the course of a female directed socialization process.
2. A tendency to fall back into the irrationality of biological reality, the natural world embedded in necessity, which creates the need for the family in the first place. Reproduction embodies a lack of certainty for all men, while sexuality and the *libido dominandi* undermine the certainties of rational lives: both reproduction and sexuality are resistant to control, by reason of their fundamental lack of reason.
3. Men cannot, indeed must not, fall for the obvious trap in the simple solution presented in the notion of staying home and helping to socialize the children. Such a procedure would effeminize them further on the individual level; but they also must be free to create a public, collective realm in which necessity may be superseded and its embodiment, the family, be firmly controlled by various politico/legal/militaristic processes which do not shrink from violence.

II.   Polity is the crucial social structure required to produce and defend manliness as reasonable and just and therefore legitimately entitled to *control nature by the exercise of reason*. The strategy is to separate the realm of control-- polity--from the realm of necessity--family. This cannot be a merely theoretical separation, for necessity/*fortuna*/woman is as cunning as she is persistent, and children must keep on getting born. Constant vigilance is therefore necessary, a constant heroic fortitude which never lets up for a moment, constantly and aggressively undertaking a life of angst and conquest. Pico's "higher spirits" must constantly remake themselves in action, be reborn continuously in a struggle which they are certain they have created for themselves and in which they are certain that they "make" themselves.

The irony of the first formulation is that the remedy must lie with the father, but he cannot attain exemplary manliness unless he leaves the battlefield of the domestic realm, where his male children need him, and fights his battles from "abroad." The primeval uncertainty embedded in his manliness destines him to a life of warfare. He can never wholly escape from the nature which is his mother's problematic gift to him; from the children whose paternity is in doubt if he leaves home; and from the sexual desire that lies ever in wait to trap and sap his manhood in uxoriousness.

The irony of the second formulation is that political man, having separated public and private, reason and passion, is left with little but undirected libido and a norm of aggression. He exchanges the integrative warmth of the hearth, with its intransigent contingency, for the cold but ironclad certainties of the Temple of Mars, where the rational drill of ends and means is clear but means must constantly bend to the enemy of chance which man never quite overcomes.

Isolated in this crude schematic way from its historical reality, the dilemma is so absurd that it cannot be expressed in anything but ideological or imaginative terms. In practice, men move from one realm to the other, and even Lorenzo the Magnificent, Machiavelli tells us, loved to play with his children. Yet *Mandragola*, despite its earthiness, rests finally on the writer's sense of the irony of the iron men, who can ultimately deal with uncertainty only by the exercise of violence, while much vaunted "reason" rusts.

Reason, however, can also spawn intrigue, intricacy, and the general moral debilitation we see in the play, where Fortune and Nature are personified in fear and hope: "It's true that Fortune and Nature keep their account balanced. The more my hope has grown the more my fear has grown" (4.1.804).

One gives him courage, the other hope. *Fortuna* and nature are identical in their nonrationality. Necessity traditionally governs the domestic realm, and the domestic realm is traditionally the setting for comedy, and of course, it is the women's realm. But for Machiavelli, necessity is precisely that contingency which challenges and creates opportunities for manliness. The rules which govern the action in the play are general rules of human behavior. They are, however inadequately, institutionalized and, however inadequately, assert an exemplary moral code.   For an autonomous politics transcending conventional morality, it would have to be demonstrated that experience and authority in the political realm differ substantively from that in the social realm, and patriarchy has defended political authority in this way. *Mandragola*, if its relation to the political works has any validity at all, demonstrates exactly the opposite case.   In neither literary nor political writings does the objective goal of the action provide the thrust of the action. "Objective goals"--Lucretia's virtue or the good republic--are not goals but accidental foundations.[53]   The goal is an abstraction--manliness--that can only be rendered concrete by social definition but, ironically, is inseparable from the family which it must transcend.

This, of course, is not to insist that known forms of family are the only possible means of regulating the social relations of reproduction, any more than mercantilism or capitalism are the only alternatives in regulating the relations of production.   It is to insist, though, that political activity which seeks autonomy over and against the diversity of these relations is doomed to a self-destructive impotence, a pathos of manliness.   Manliness, however understood, is radically one-sided and contingent in terms of human life-process. Machiavelli, whatever his status in a humanistic tradition, realized a peculiarly antihuman conception of politics in which manliness, divorced from humanity, finds its most apt expression in compulsive masculine militarism.   The ultimate irony of the Man of Iron is that he cannot reproduce himself. He can only rust.

NOTES

[1]The translation by Allan Gilbert (*Works*, vol. 2) of the *Mandragola* has been used throughout this chapter, and references are placed in parentheses in the text, giving act and scene of the play and the pagination in this edition. Niccolò Machiavelli. *The Chief Works and Others*. 3 vols, translated by Allan Gilbert, Durham (North Carolina: Duke University, 1965). For a discussion of the dating of *Mandragola*, see Sergio Bertelli, "When Did Machiavelli Write Mandragola?" *Renaissance Quarterly* 24, no. 3 (Autumn 1972), pp. 317-326. The edition used for *The Prince and the Discourses* is Niccolò Machiavelli, *The Prince and the Discourses*, translated by Liugi Ricci (New York: Modern Library, 1950).

[2]Hannah Arendt, *The Human Condition* (New York: Doubleday, 1959), p. 33.

[3]Arthur Quiller-Couch, ed., *The Oxford Book of English Verse* (Oxford: Clarendon Press, 1939), pp. 231-232.

[4]Samuel Beckett, *Waiting for Godot* (New York: Grove Press, 1954), p. 8.

[5]The most commonly quoted formulation is that of the Italian idealist philosopher, Benedetto Croce, who talked of Machiavelli's "austere and painful moral awareness" of the implications of such autonomy. Quoted by Frederico Chabod in *Machiavelli and the renaissance* (London: Bowes and Bowes, 1958), p. xii.

[6]Jacob Burckhardt, *The Civilization of the Renaissance in Italy* (New York: Washington Square Press, Inc., 1966).

[7]Ibid., p. 218.

[8]"History of Florence," in *Works*, vol. 1, p. 1063.

[9]One of the most hasty and thorough practitioners of nepotism was Sixtus IV, whose activities demonstrate both the self-interested cooperation and distrustful factionalism of the papal, mercenary, and mercantile families. Sixtus, himself of low social origin, elevated his Rovere-Riarao

nephews to princedoms, including the marriage of one nephew to an obscure illegitimate daughter of the Sforza family, none other than Machiavelli's antagonist, Caterina. She later remarried into the Medici connection. For an account of these devious and very complex relationships, see Ernst Breisach, *Caterina Sforza, A Renaissance Virago* (Chicago: University of Chicago Press, 1967).

[10]In one year (1393) Rinald opened the electoral rolls to the *grandi* because he needed their help and a few months later closed them again so that he could pronounce Cosimo d'Medici a member of the *grandi* and incapable of holding office, Cosimo was not neutralized, neither by this device, nor by his subsequent imprisonment and exile. As a contemporary remarked, the same golden bag which bought him out of prison would buy him in from exile. See C. C. Bagley, *War and society in Renaissance Florence* (Toronto: University of Toronto Press, 1961), p. 127.

[11]*Disc.*, 3, XXXIV,, pp. 509-510.

[12]Ibid., 1, IX, p. 138; 11, XXIII, pp. 394-396. See also *Prince*, X, p. 37.

[13]*Disc.*, 4, XLVI, p. 535.

[14]Ibid., p. 536 (my italics).

[15]Ibid., 3, LXXVI, p. 488.

[16]*Prince*, XVII, p. 62.

[17]*Disc*, 4, XLIV.

[18]*Disc.*, 4, XLVI, p. 535. The importance which Machiavelli also ascribed to the militia as a socializing agency is noted by Neal Wood in his Introduction to *The Art of War* (Indianapolis: Bobbs-Merrill, 1965), p. xxvii.

[19]Quoted by Antonia Fraser in *Cromwell: The Great Protector* (New York: Dell Publishing Co., 1975), p. 664.

[20]Examples are too numerous to be listed. See Wood on *ozio* in *The Art of War*, p.iv. In *Disc.*, 1, XIX, p. 172, Machiavelli unites the themes of heredity and effeminacy: a hereditary monarchy can lead to a city which is "effeminate and a prey to her neighbors." Chapter II of *The Prince* notes that hereditary monarchies are often stable, but as Rome can furnish no examples, Machiavelli notes only the House of Ferrarra. It was this same house which played perhaps the leading role in the development of theater in Renaissance Italy.

[21]John Plamenatz, ed., *Machiavelli* (London: Fontana/Collins, 1972), p. 19.

[22]For an account of the development of the concept of conflict as dynamic, see Neal Wood, "The Value of Asocial Sociability: Contributions of Machiavelli, Sidney and Montesquieu," in Martin Fleisher, ed., *Machiavelli and the Nature of Political Thought* (New York: Atheneum, 1972), pp. 282-307.

[23]Quoted by Burckhart, *The Civilization of the Renaissance in Italy*, p. 216.

[24]*Disc.*, 4, XLVI, p. 535.

[25]Felix Gilbert, *Machiavelli and Guicciardini* (Princeton: Princeton University Press, 1965), pp. 40-41.

[26]Machiavelli approved the Roman custom of admitting strangers to citizenship. See *Disc.*, 2, III.

[27]*Disc.*, 1, VI, pp. 127-129.

[28]See especially letter No. 120: "I must discuss public affairs or be silent;" No. 225: "I love my native city more than my own soul"; and, of course, the justly famous and quite marvelous lived theater of No. 137 in which Machiavelli transports himself to Rome. *Letters*, pp. 103, 249, 139-144.

[29]*Hamlet*, 2.2.424. A reference to a proposed production of *Mandragola* occurs in a letter to Guicciardini in 1525, which is signed "Niccolo Machiavelli, *Istorico, Comico et Tragico.*" Quoted by J. R. Hale, *Machiavelli and Renaissance Italy* (Harmondsworth: Penguin Books, 1972).

[30]Gilbert Highet, *The Classical Tradition* (Oxford: Oxford University Press, 1970), p. 128.

[31]Hale, *Machiavelli*, p. 138.

[32]"Superior to the best of Goldini and inferior only to the best of Moliere." Macaulay, Preface to *Mandragola*, p. 48. Macaulay thinks Messer Nicia "the glory of the piece," comparing him with Shallow, Falstaff, Slender, Sir Andrew Aguecheek, Cloten, Osric, Patroclus, Calandrino, and Simon de Vila. Although Nicia is characterized as a crude typification in this analysis, this does not mean that he is presented without wit. To compare him with this list, however, is excessive.

[33]Ibid., p. 50.

[34]Highet, *The Classical Tradition*, p. 136.

[35]Lewdness was popular not least among the clergy, who were fond of the bawdy tales of Plautus. Pius II is reported to have written a grossly indecent play before his elevation.

[36]Aristotle, *On Poetry and Style*, trans by G. M. A. Grube, (New York: The Liberal Arts Press, Inc., 1958), p. 10.

[37]Jokes, Aristotle also notes, are "pleasant to those in the know: but do not seem felicitous" to those who are not. Ibid., p. 94.

[38]This paper was written before publication of Hanna Pitken's *Fortune is a Woman* (London, University of California Press, 1986). Pitken's fine analysis places *Mandragola* firmly in the context of Machiavelli's dread of effeminacy.

[39]Ibid., p. 55.

[40]*Disc.*, 3, VI, p. 431. "On Conspiracy"; see also *The Prince*, XVII, XVIII, XIX. Allan Gilbert notes in his translation how Ligurio guards against the revelation of this "comic conspiracy" at the end of Act 1: "The shortness of time and the business itself will keep him from discussing it, and there'll not be time to spoil our plan even if he does discuss it" (1.3,785). He could have added the testing out of Timoteo (3.4), the throwing off-balance which Callimaco suffers from the unexpected complication (4.2,816), and the general keeping of Siro in the dark.

[41]*Disc.*, III, 3, 6, p. 412.

[42]*Prince*, XX, p. 86.

[43]*Prince*, XX, p. 80. "Therefore the best fortress is to be found in the love of the people."

[44]Levi-Strauss has argued that humanism as an ideology actually paves the way for dehumanization by virtue of its intransigent dualism (C. Levi-Strauss, *Structural Anthropology*, vol. II, Monique Layton, trans. New York: Basic Books, 1976), p. 41. For a feminist critique, see Geraldine M. Finn, "Understanding Social Reality: Sartre, Marx and Levi-Strauss," unpublished doctoral dissertation, University of Ottawa, 1981, pp. 67-71.

[45]An account of Machiavelli's view on mercenaries with its historical grounds is provided by C. C. Bayley. Mercenaries had and still have admirers. The two most famous equestrian statues of the Renaissance were erected in honor of *condotteri*. For a lavishly illustrated and circumspectly sympathetic account, see Geoffrey Trease, *The Condotteri: soldiers of fortune* (London: Thames & Hudson, 1970).

[46]There is considerable conflict of opinion in literary circles about the nature and form of irony. See, e.g., the notion of irony as an essentially temporal dimension in Northrop Frye, *The Anatomy of Criticism* (New York: Atheneum, 1968).

[47]*Disc.*, 2, XXXII.

[48]Machiavelli may have in mind here the Countess of Sforza, a redoubtable woman said to have been prepared to sacrifice her children to avenge her husband (*Disc.*, 3, VI, p. 430). Machiavelli in his diplomatic career encountered this formidable woman. See also, Ernst Breisach, *Caterina Sforza*. See also *Disc.*, 3, VI, p. 430. "History of Florence," VII, *Works*, p. 1149.

[49]*Prince*, XXII. It is instructive to read the whole chapter with an eye to Callimaco and Siro.

[50]Marx's notion of form emerging from content is the basis of the aesthetic theory which George Lukács develops in *The Historical Novel*, trans. by Hannah and Stanley Mitchell, (Harmondsworth: Penguin Books, 1969). The distinction between "realized" and vulgar types used here owes much to Lukács, in the first case, and to Stalinist realism and Lucian Goldmann, in the second. However, Lukács's notion of "universal type" is not transferable to Renaissance comedy without a much more elaborate treatment than can be given here. He himself remarks, rather tantalizingly: "In comedy, the problem is somewhat different for reasons which cannot be explained here" (p. 104). One of the reasons might be the encapsulation of time, which tends to deprive comedy of a historical dimension; another, the need for the inversion of reality to create the comic effect. The suggestion of "more adequate" typification relates to the placing of these characters outside of their "symbolic" context of trade,

family, servant, and mercenary into a wider and therefore more adequate context.

[51]Felix Gilbert points out that Machiavelli uncritically inherited from Sallust the notion of money as the root of all evil (pp. 174-175). The notion is not, of course, absent from the Christian tradition either.

[52]Mary O'Brien, *The Politics of Reproduction* (London: Routledge & Kegan Paul, 1981), Chapter 1.

[53]*Disc.* 2, II, p. 112; "Chance has given birth to these different kind of governments among men."

9

The Art of Falling Upwards:
Milton on Marriage

Until quite recently, feminist theory has largely been a
critique. In the first couple of decades of the contemporary
movement, feminist scholars were properly concerned with
the important task of uncovering sexism and patriarchal
ideology in theory and research in general. Methodologically,
such work has been burdened with the ironic need to derive
an *apparatus criticus* from that body of work to be criticized,
the tradition of mainstream thought. In terms of political
studies, one result of this trend has been the development of
hyphenated feminist scholarship: socialist-feminist, liberal-
feminism, and so forth. This phase has, however,
strengthened the feminist critical enterprise, for the process
has clarified the dimensions and realized content of theory
which are crucial to the understanding of women's
oppression. However, it has also led to an appreciation of a
need to theorize autonomously from the standpoint of women,
a realization currently producing a sudden nervous rash of
"taking feminism seriously" on the Left. The Right, of
course, has taken feminism seriously for a long time.

Central to the development of autonomous feminism is a
recognition of the intransigent dualism of male-stream
thought and a particular interest in the social structure of
the traditional separation of public and private life.
Feminism poses the question as to whether this venerable

dichotomy represents a "real" separation or merely an ideological one and answers that, in some sense, it is both. The historical materialist task is to ground patriarchal perceptions of dualism in general and of the misogynist form of dualism in particular in concrete social praxis. If the relation of public and private life is in fact a dialectical one, why is it that Marxism does not deal with it? Leftist preoccupation with structural models and economic reductionism has found no room for consideration of the fact that, while women are oppressed by the social relations of production, they are also concretely oppressed by men of all classes. More generally, the question of why politics is a man's world is either arbitrarily rooted in the given, rooted in ontological determinations such as those of Hannah Arendt,[1] shrugged off as natural law, or praised as the enduring legacy of classicism.

In earlier work, I have argued that the ground of gender oppression lies in the dialectical structure of the *process* of reproduction itself, a material and historical process from which emerge forms of reproductive consciousness and the social relations of reproduction.[2] The analysis of reproductive consciousness is a totally neglected epistemology--what does it mean to speak of knowledge of reproduction or of reproductive praxis? The gist of this theory is summarized elsewhere in this volume; it posits a differentiation of gender *consciousness*, arguing that the act of birthing is "work" which integrates women and children, whereas men experience paternity as alienation. John Milton's work in political theory tells us much about this alienated consciousness.

Briefly then, the reproductive process is dialectical in that it mediates in the first instance between the human world and the natural world and does so in terms of the dialectic of reproduction of the individual and of the species, a classical confrontation of particular and universal. Female reproductive knowledge is *mediated* in the classical mode of mediation of the human world and the natural world: that is, by *labor* and practical knowledge. Male reproductive consciousness is mediated by abstract knowledge, the historical discovery of the relation of copulation and birth.

The knowledge of paternity therefore remains ideal and uncertain, for the alienation of man from his seed is an alienation from nature, from continuity over time and from species. The radical uncertainty of paternity is the unspoken ground of male reproductive consciousness. At the same time, paternal consciousness is a consciousness of alienation and freedom: freedom from labor of course, but also freedom to "acknowledge" nonimmediate paternity and in so doing to project and create the social strategies for the mediation of alienation and freedom. The most elemental of these social mediations has been the appropriation of children together with the female reproductive labor embedded in children, an exploitive appropriation which demands cooperation between possible fathers and a social apparatus of definition and legitimation. What feminists call patriarchy is the sociohistorical constitution by men of the relations of men and species, men and women, men and time, in short, the social relations of reproduction. Patriarchy constitutes itself as a "universal" concept, but its monogenderic structure conceals the fact that it is grounded in the dialectics of reproduction. The condition of this universality is the negation of mothering. Motherhood is not, in fact, a conceptually barren, mindless, immediate, contingent natural phenomenon. The "product" of reproductive labor is helpless, and the labor itself dangerous and difficult. Cultural formations must be--and have been--created to deal with these exigencies, but they must also deal with an intransigent involuntarism within female reproductive experience. It is precisely this component of nonfreedom which is radically transformed in the development of generalized contraceptive technology.

Patriarchy and ejaculative male alienation from birth process cannot be understood simply as neurosis: some of the manifestations of male supremacy in action have, to be sure, pathological overtones, but the main question is an epistemological one: paternity is essentially ideal, a question of belief rather than experience. The mediations of contradictions within productive process and between productive and reproductive substructures must be mediated in praxis: paternity must be constructed historically. The

need for such a strategy was understood by Hegel but
distorted by his misogyny:[3] it was not understood at all by
Marx or Engels.

While the forms and theoretical formulations emergent
from the dialectics of reproductive process are complex, I
want here to discuss an aspect which is significant for
political theory. The separation of public and private life has
historically required men to have two natures, and the
discussion of man's "second nature" has created a
substantial but often quite spiritual body of male-stream
thought. Like women, men have "natural" needs which are
met in the private realm. Unlike women, men also have
claimed to have "natural" needs as "polis animals." Man is
perceived by the thinkers who have universalized him as
creating a political space in which he can construct,
reconstruct and more recently, deconstruct the duality of his
experience.   This "experience" involves, of course, the
uncertainty of paternity.   Men invoke and transcend the
contingency of the "natural," transforming nature into more
manageable notions of law and legitimacy. This process has
been a long one, and its grounds and mediations are encoded
in a language of "body politic" and of "constitution," of
equality (any man, after all, can have fathered this child), of
freedom, of natural law, of *arete* and of *virtu*. I do not, of
course, claim that these concepts may be reduced to male
reproductive experience, rather, I claim that the dialectics of
reproduction not only constitute significant and neglected
aspects of polity and political theory but also form material
grounds for male dualistic thinking. Such perceptions are
particularly important in periods of radical social change. At
such times, gender relations are restructured, and women are
even allowed occasionally on the barricades, though they are
more often thought to be responsible for chaos. For
Augustine, the birth of great cities was rendered hopelessly
mundane by the harlotry of its midwives; for Juvenal, women
were the evil force which emerged from privation to bring
great cities to perdition.[4] Men have understood themselves
as engaged in an endless struggle to conserve the separation
of the public and private realms--a struggle perceived as that
between masculine rationality and the mindless forces of first

nature, of which women are the handmaidens. These are of course the forces which Niccolò Machiavelli called *virtu* and *fortuna*. Machiavelli understood quite clearly that the condition of arbitrary separation of public and private life was the commitment of universal man to violence. Milton was much more ambivalent,[5] and his notion of the sperm as spiritual (holy seed) is one which Machiavelli would have found ludicrous.

The old saw, then, that behind every theory of politics lurks a theory of human nature is more inaccurate than most clichés: political theories are theories of *second* nature. Theory is rarely discussed in these terms: "universal" man does not usually understand his universality as derived from the social practice required to mediate the material separation of himself from his species. He prefers to express the intransigent dualism of his experience in the world in more recondite antimonies. Milton was exceptional in this case: as we shall see, he found it necessary, in the era when "natural law" was adduced as the legitimation of freedom, to posit not one but *two* natural laws.[6] He gave men separate natural laws for both first and second natures. To be sure, Milton did not recognize man's reproductive alienation overtly; he regarded alienation, or "divorcement," as a "natural" part of his experience. He also, though, understood the consequent need to *mediate* man's separation from nature. The primordial alienation for Milton, however, was not man's material alienation from his seed but his spiritual separation from his natural wholeness in his Fall. Milton could not bear to think of man as fallen, but could not deny scripture: he had to deal with man's Fall in justifying male supremacy. He therefore sought some transcendent mode of moving from an uxorious prelapsarian condition to a postlapsarian rationalistic, rather bleak, but still quite uxorious heroism. In falling, Miltonic man actually created the conditions of his superiority. The historical means by which he did this, Milton argued, were the inventions of the marriage contract and the "office" of husband. Man in general may have fallen, but as *individual husbands* men were able to fall back upwards.

One may note that locating the superiority and authority of man in his role as husband rather than as father not only evades the question of the uncertainty of paternity: it also mediates men's alienation from *continuous time.* The continuity women constitute materially in the labor of childbirth not only reproduces the species but also produces an individual. For Milton, however, continuity must be claimed as the product of men's "holy seed," but to historicize this uncertain continuity men had to be given authority over the bearers of the holy seed. Women were to be kept in line by a combination of love and preaching: Milton's husband is a preacher with a captive congregation of one, a benevolent despot with a single subject, and a messenger of God carrying the principle of the continuity of the species in his holy but tiresomely alienable sperms.

The point at issue is not that man has strayed from first nature to second nature and that this is the source of his triumphs and his tragedies and his oppression of women.[7] What is at issue is the question of the continuity of the body politic and male supremacist efforts to lend legitimacy to the privatization and oppression of women by transcending rather than mediating the relation of culture and biology, of history and reproduction. Theories of man's "second nature" obscure the epistemological and social significance of the relations of reproduction and must be submitted to careful scrutiny. They are the stuff of the ideology of patriarchy but are materially grounded in men's concrete alienation from natural continuity. Seventeenth-century England is an important time and place for examining what might be called the modernization of male supremacy. The Marxist account of these changes is correct but incomplete. The relation between mode of production and forms of family relations is usually perceived as a hard rock of causal connection in the tempestuous tide of historical dialectic. Patriarchal theory has ignored the relation of the everyday economic reproduction of the individual and the everyday regenerative reproduction of the species as dialectically opposed material substructures of historical process, a classical confrontation of particular and universal process. It will not do to define one as creative history and the other as brute determinism, for both are the material substructures of social activity and historical struggles.

Thus, when seventeenth-century thinkers sought to legitimize historical struggle and political change in the doctrine of "natural" freedom grounded in "natural" law, they had to do more than simply show that monarchy was not a "natural" form of political organization. They had also to deal with the delegitimation of patriarchy objectified in the King as Father: the monarchy, unlike the legendary Leviathan, was not autoregenerative but hereditary and highly sensitive to the issue of the uncertainty of paternity. The claim that all men had equal rights and powers in the private realm was much easier to concede than claims about rights in the public realm. Crucial at the time, John Locke's rejection of the continuity of private and public life in *The First Treatise* is now considered as quaint as Sir Robert Filmers' defense of biological paternity as the source of legitimacy and continuity. Nonetheless, the relation of public and private realms was confused by efforts to root the legitimacy of men's familial and political power in "natural law," for the postulates of natural law are never self-evident. The law of nature, as Ernest Sirluck observes, "is one of those concepts whose origin is obscure because *man*kind never seems to have been without some form of it."[8] It does not occur to Sirluck that this concept may have as much to do with the nature of masculinity as it has with the definition of power and "legitimacy."

The notion of a "Charter of Nature" handed down over generations and entitling "all subjects and all Countries whatsoever to safetie by its supreame Law," as William Barker put it, created many practical and theoretical problems.[9] One of the most knotty of these pertained to the impact of the Fall on the continuity of natural law over time and, indeed, on the whole notion of "Genesis." This notion sounds like a rather esoteric anguish from a contemporary standpoint, but the prospect of embedding continuity in political institutions in some less problematic form than biological continuity has clearly been an important ideological task for male supremacists. In medieval Christian thinking, God's gifts of grace and reason could bridge man's Fall and give divine sanction to the positive law made necessary by that Fall, thus lending legitimation to both canon and civil law. For the Puritan, the Fall was absolute, so that the embarrassing lack of definition which attends "fundamental" theories of constitution and contract becomes more acute. To express it somewhat crudely, human access to knowledge of the original legitimation of all law was cut off by a punitive, vengeful but, of course, lawful act of God in his resolution of the debacle in Eden. The bridge created by divinely sanctioned civil law was God's somewhat enigmatic way of conserving guilt while permitting species survival and ordaining patriarchal power. This archetypal separation of man from God, with the proviso that the separation can be mediated by forms of social action, is, it may be noted, similar to the separation of real live men from the certainty of paternity, and the role of women in the drama suggests that creation myths are in fact grounded in biological necessity and human experience. Women, mediating their alienation of infants in human labor, have no need of these kinds of myths. Nonetheless, the ancient and modern concern with the question of whether man is sociable "by nature" was an important premise of theories of political power and questions of war and peace. In the seventeenth century, Thomas Hobbes took the lead in denying a determinist postulate about sociability which flew so clearly in the face of the historical evidence, and only Hobbes has had the intellectual courage to write a chapter "On Religion" which simply disregards the Fall.[10] Hobbes saw clearly the difficulty of deriving either sociability or reason from isolated postulates of matter in motion; and C. B. Macpherson's argument that the additional postulates derived socially rather than naturally is well-taken.[11] Hobbes, however, did concede one human characteristic to "first nature": "And first, it is peculiar to the nature of Man to be inquisitive into the events they see."

Thus, curiosity rather than reason and grace took its place in Hobbes' ontology as the bridge from first nature to second. This mundane ontology clearly cannot afford to linger in the Garden of Eden, where inquisitiveness, rather than being the essence of Adam, was the sin of Eve. The point is, however, that the relation between man's first and second nature was important to an age exploring the ideology of the free man. Nature was adduced as legitimate progenitor, as indeed it had been in antiquity. This question of whether "man" is "naturally" free has clear political implications which have been debated for centuries. What was never publicly doubted was man's "natural" superiority to women. Women's views on the question were not often conserved nor published. Hobbes and Locke were both careful to point out that male superiority could not rest on man's status as father, important though that status may be in property relations.[12] The fact is that the basic dualism of masculine thought and the doctrine of male supremacy went virtually unexamined for centuries, for such considerations were not perceived as constituting any kind of problem for universal man except for the occasional heretic like Milton. Milton wanted to argue that "divorce" is creative and just: he also had an urgent desire to unload an incompatible wife.

A religious man less devoted to logic than to the poetic expression of archetypes, Milton accepted the Fall as historical but found little residue of man's sinfulness in his own proud self. Milton's ontology was of the existential-subjectivist brand, and in his self-explorations he found "within" himself not only reason and spirit but a powerful and creative will and a driving sexuality. Furthermore, within that tradition of English humanism reaching back to John of Salisbury, Milton saw reason as an adequate mediator between pre-Prelapsarian and fallen man. In the synthesis of "nature" and "grace" which gives birth to men of reason, however, Milton defines nature in generous terms: nature *is* society, thus society is "carnality" in the broadest sense. For Milton, that which was neither spiritual nor personal was natural and social, therefore fundamentally mundane. God said, "It is not good that the man should be alone" (Genesis 2:18), and this text was paradigmatic for Milton: it says that men are sociable both by nature and divine command. By reason of his natural sexuality and his first "social contract," which is the contract of marriage, man is sensually sociable and sociably rational. Unlike Hobbes, for whom sociability was at best latent in the state of nature and realized only in enforced social contract, Milton believed that sociability was realized *before* the Fall when God installed Adam in the "office" of husband. Historical sociability is realized in the obedience to God's will that man be married. "Natural" marriage expressed concretely man's prelapsarian sociability, while civil marriage bridges the divorcement of fallen man from his natural and spiritual essence. This marital redefinition confirmed man as free by first nature but compelled by his postlapsarian second nature to create and defend the conditions of liberty in the context of legal restraints. The institution of marriage was not lost with paradise but rather had to be toughened up. It follows in Milton's logic that there must be two conditions embedded in this institutional reorganization: the duty of man to marry lawfully and the legal right to break that bond if it does not further his duty to express his prelapsarian natural freedom in his postlapsarian civil libertarianism.

Ernest Sirluck, the erudite editor of Milton's prose works, argues that Milton's struggle with the ontology of the free married man reflects changes in his thought related to the ideological and political turbulence of the times.[13] The orthodox Presbyterian positions adopted in his anti-Episcopal tracts are quite different from his radical views on divorce. However, it has to be noted that Milton wanted a divorce for personal reasons, and his strong desire to present divorce as a moral imperative and a politically free choice is consistent with his moral liberalism. This, after all, is the man who could think God's thought on the general notion on separation and "divorce" with eloquent equanimity. What he would later do for heaven he had vested interest in doing on earth, which was to extend the notion of freedom to its existential limits. This is an early pronouncement of the doctrine that the personal is political--for men. Particularly for husbands.

What Milton is actually dealing with is the real dualism of patriarchal ontology. The discontinuity in Milton's thought that Sirluck notes comes, I would argue, from Milton's ability to face up to the implications of dualism. He was one of the few thinkers in the male supremacist tradition to do so. "Divorcements" is his word for dualisms, and he saw some of the implications of this ideology of contradiction in mundane terms: the separation of public and private life, for example, as well as personal and political realms. To be sure, he rooted these dualisms in the myth of the Fall, but he also believed that the poetry which read God's mind had to be supplemented by political and personal practice. He thus tried to heal the breach in continuity as it related to marriage and reproduction by insisting that marriage is logically inseparable from divorce, just as the Fall is logically inseparable from man's morality.

The possibility of a material basis for men's reproductive experience in the actual separation of men from paternal certitude would not have occurred to Milton: he regarded sperm as holy. Miltonic marriage was a spiritual, affective, and uxorious haven, enhanced by a moderate quantum of restrained copulation. But Milton saw clearly that marriage has a political dimension, not only as a power relation but in its contribution to the stability of the polity. An uppity wife was therefore more than a tiresome mistake: she was a threat to man's freedom. Further, the dualism of personal and political life, he thought, was yet another primordial separation which women could not understand. The Fall itself, after all, was a sort of divorce, God throwing out disobedient man and not accepting wifely turpitude as an excuse for disobedience.

Milton constantly reminded his readers that marriage and the family are the foundations of the Commonwealth, but he argued that in both family and polity, liberty means the capacity to redefine or even break apart historical formation, political or domestic. If a spiritual paradise can be lost, why should not domestic bliss be rent asunder? In a very fundamental sense Miltonic marriage historicizes the relation of the personal and the political *for men*: "as a whole people is in proportion to an ill government, so is one man to an ill marriage."[14] This position is not entirely novel: notions of paternity as a paradigm, analogy, or rationalization of political authority are ancient.[15] Milton goes further than this, though: marriage, as the mediating force between individual and polity, private and public, obedience and liberty, and a whole host of traditional dualisms, becomes an institution in which free man may be rendered unfree. He must therefore be allowed to revolt. Further, marriage is not only the bridge from natural to historical law and from pre- to postlapsarian ethics, but is precisely a moral force which makes it possible for fallen man to be good. In marriage, fallen man can acquire the art of falling back upwards, being, as husband, moral and free. Marriage is a precondition of true understanding of liberty at the individual level, and this understanding is a precondition of public religious and political liberty. Such understanding is possible because marriage is also didactic, not only in the crude sense of husband as teacher, but in the sense that the institution itself is able to teach political lessons in "how far the territory and dominion extends of just and honest liberty."[16] Clearly, it extends across spiritual, political, familial, and sexual life.

The lesson of marriage and divorce, then, is fundamentally a lesson in individual governance and morality. Miltonic husbands are office-holders, and marriage is their training school: they also have a "calling," and only those who are called to govern may do so. The politician, the Presbyterian, and the husband are all "called" to perform their manly offices. Further, they each have at least one subject. As subject, woman is taught her proper place, but radical liberalism cannot deny her right to rebel, and such rebellion may take the negative form of refusing to perform her function of keeping the domestic domain peaceful and being a help "meet for man." Such rebellion does not go unpunished, of course, and as it is a rebellion rooted in her woeful contribution to the Fall, the proper punishment is divorce and expulsion. Just as Satan is expelled from paradise, uncompliant wives are to be expelled from marriage. This notion of the ontological inevitability of rebellion as an inherent condition of liberty will, of course, be the theme of *Paradise Lost*, on both sacred and profane levels. Only God, however, could "divorce" princes who disturbed the peace of heaven; only husbands, in Milton's view, can divorce for incompatibility. Wives may initiate divorce proceedings only for the conventional reasons which Martin Bucer had already identified.[17] Milton's major contribution to the discussion of divorce was to introduce the notion of divorce for incompatibility, but this is not quite divorce by mutual consent, as some of Milton's contemporaries supposed. The religious parallel is clearly excommunication; the political one is more complex, though it is notable that when Milton comes to write the regicide tracts of justification, he makes the king sound like a guilty wife succumbing to "temptation" and changing from father to tyrant.[18] Like Eve, he abandoned sweet reason for the tyranny of lust.[19] Milton seems to suggest that reason is originally a natural quality, which is lost and has to be restored by God as a law rather than a gift. In any case, the grounds for regicide clearly had something in common with the grounds for divorce. The "common equity" which maintains "the good of the family, Church or Commonwealth"[20] must provide a mechanism of disengagement for each of these spheres, for a social institution may not defeat its own purpose. Milton saw estrangement, separation, dualism, and divorcement as rational and creative forces, tools in the development of liberty without license and in the management of the primordial alienations rooted in and growing from the Fall.[21]

It would be wrong to make too much of Milton's primitive dialectics of family, church, and state, which are profoundly self-interested, or of the analogy of tyrannous king and erring wife. Nonetheless, it is interesting that this bitter misogynist shared a concern with contemporary feminism in restoring the unity and canceling the contradictions of public and private spheres, although his aim was to allow the imperial patriarch the right of abdication. His three spheres of social life are understood first of all as *necessities*, responses to "natural" first nature needs with the additional function of mediating the second nature separation from these needs brought about by the Fall. Politics, family, and religion are all grounded in first nature, and, in the sense which George Armstrong Kelly invokes in his discussion of Rousseau, the state had to become a "surrogate mother," looking after all the needs of first nature but guided by the rational and historically wrought rules of second nature.[22] But rationality appears to have been for Milton a first nature gift of intuitive and discursive reason which has the same status as biological needs, and which therefore makes it possible for Milton to posit education, free discourse, and intellectual needs as *necessities*.

Reason, sociability, and biological needs all survived the Fall. What was lost was moral nature, but in Milton's ideology morality and sexuality were still unified. His major intellectual quest was in fact the creation of the historical conditions for the recovery of moral nature, starting once more with an understanding of the meaning of marriage. If morality was irrevocably lost and the Fall precluded morality, then absolutism in politics was the only possible course for men rendered unethical by second nature. If the divorcement from natural goodness can be transcended, men, or at least good men, can be reunited with their first natures and thus be whole. Men must, however, *learn* this wholeness in marriage and must have the right to separate from a marriage which does not achieve these moral ends. Women, having no public role, do not need to learn how to fall upwards, for their husbands will, if they are totally obedient, defend them from their immersion in first nature. Milton, renegade Puritan, had a theory of election, but he does seem to have understood it as an autoregenerative act of will rather than as random election of the Calvinist kind. The elected elite must recover their first nature subjectively, *within themselves*. Society therefore has a dual function, in ethical terms: to control the majority of men whose underdeveloped second natures cannot transcend postlapsarian defects, but also to provide the conditions in which the free and moral few may fall upwards and regenerate themselves.

All this would be pretty mystical were it not that Milton sees these problems in concrete social terms. People and things are sufficiently alike to make society possible, but they must also be radically unlike, for in divorcement alone lies liberty. First nature, the Fall, second nature: this is a historical sequence in which each stage is subsumed and sustained. The historical evidence and the empirical indication that men are to be wielders of moral and political authority, however, lie in men's relations to women. It is no small glory for man, Milton tells us, that a creature so like him should be made subject to him. The question of continuity as a component of political stability is therefore resolved for Milton in the execution of the office of husband. As Milton has much less to say about fatherhood, the appropriation of women's reproductive labor and women's children is not addressed. Biological discontinuity compels men to mediate his separation from species continuity in the alienation of his sperm. Marriage affirms man's authority over women, his reproductive powers, and her freedom cannot be defined by the right to rebel. The office of husband does many things for Miltonic man, but the poet is not concerned with the "legitimacy" of children but with the legitimation of men's freedom. Marriage also happily liberates him from attending to mundane and tedious manifestations of necessity. Marriage has as its reason and essence man's irreversible separation from his species, his first nature, his God, and his reason. Separation is the necessary condition of freedom, and freedom to divorce is quite simply a natural right for men. Creation is always by separation, which is assumed in the origins of the universe itself: "God and nature signifies and lectures to us not only by those recited decrees, but ev'n by the first and last of all his visible works; when by his divorcing command the world first rose out of chaos, nor can be renew'd again out of confusion but by the separating of unmeet consorts."[23]

Divorced from cosmology, it may well be that Milton's struggle with the antithesis of social and conjugal man, of public good and individual conscience, is in fact a reflection of the fundamental antithesis of the developing mode of production of Milton's time, the antithesis of private ownership and social labor. Nonetheless, Milton's problematic is not expressed in terms of production but in terms of the social relations of reproduction, and, bizarre though these appear, they also address a material reality, that of species continuity. Yet Milton has almost nothing to say about children: he recognizes that the claim to dominance over women must rest ultimately in sexuality rather than paternity, that the sex act is, for man, a divorcement. It cannot be denied that Milton was a radically alienated man; that he made an "unfortunate" marriage;

that he was, in terms of religious, civil, and domestic notions, a heretic. His main doctrinal heresies can be found in *De Doctrina Christiana*[24] where he rejects predestination but retains the universality of the Fall and retains election but modifies its arbitrariness with the possibility of autoregeneration. He also maintains that the Son is of a different essence from the Father and did not exist in the beginning. He holds the materialist view that God cannot create ex nihilo, and also asserts that the soul, being inseparable from corporeality, dies with the body. All of the doctrines he promulgated would have made much trouble for Milton in an earlier era, but then, Catholic hegemonists never did feel the Protestant need to "justify the ways of God to man." In terms of civil society, Milton's justification of regicide would also have been deemed heretical. These are later developments in Milton's thought, but their foundations are clearly laid out in the divorce tracts and in the notion of separation as creative. In the midst of distracting theological arguments, Milton holds firm to the notion that man's destiny is to have the courage to define necessity, to have the will to be free and the legal capacity to cast off constraints on this destiny.

Milton's view of incompatibility as the major ground for divorce horrified his contemporaries, for whom the argument that Christian liberty can only be rendered practical by the divorcement of all things unmeet was not persuasive. The notion that divorce is a moral condition of marriage was not popular with Puritan men, though there is some evidence that it excited support among Puritan women, who did not understand that the right to dispense with a spouse was confined to men.[25] Milton believed that the creative poet could educate these doubters: the poet is to accept the challenge of Jesus of Nazareth: "from the beginning it was not so" (Matthew 19:8). The creative poet will discover how in fact it was in the beginning and then reveal this truth to the elect who will then bridge the gap between first and second nature. He has scriptural authority for the elitist aspect of this. "All men cannot receive this saying," said Jesus, apropos of his rather oblique reference to how it was in the beginning, "save they to whom it is given. . . . He that is able to receive it, let him receive it." Milton, having presumably received it, relies on didactic poetry to promulgate the word that the Fall is reversible for the tough-minded, that divorcement is the condition of wholeness. He leans heavily on the education of the many by the few as a means of ensuring social stability and moral continuity.

The disappearance of "the beginning" behind the Fall is therefore not simply embarrassing but a necessary truth of the relation of wholeness to separation. The concrete testing ground for a true elect is marriage, where the elect can show their fitness to govern: he who rules with love need never fear rebellion for he is armed with right reason and, handily, a "divorcing command." Contrary to general opinion, the purpose of marriage is not the generation of the race, for "generation is . . . a secondary institution in dignity though not in necessity."[26] The task of biological species generation has to yield priority to the task of individual moral regeneration: to put this notion in another form, generation and marriage are civil phenomena, whereas divorce is moral. Obviously, the male act of autoregeneration transcends the female act of species reproduction. Milton's whole understanding of marriage hinges on a fine distinction between marriage and divorce on the one hand matched with civil and moral law on the other. To be sure, the notion of marriage as a sacrament was yielding at that time to a more secular perception, but few saw the intricacies of the social relations of reproduction in such transcendental terms. Marriage and civil law make children; divorce and moral law create the commonwealth; and mediating these fine distinctions is he who understands his office as husband as that of a true self fit to make moral choices. Milton was really much closer to modern existentialism than early liberalism. For him, regeneration is a process which isolates while it individuates. Such doctrines tend to pessimism, and it is not surprising that resignation is the keynote of Milton's last great poem. The lesson of *Samson Agonistes* is that *agon*, or contest, is ultimately absurd, for, "none daring to appear antagonist" (1628), Samson is forced to compete with stone pillars. These pillars--acting as combatants--carelessly destroy "the best" (aristocratic men and poets) while "the vulgar" stand outside the struggle and escape (1659). Samson, "all passion spent," is forced into this absurd contest for a now predictable reason: "His lot unfortunate in nuptial choice" (1743). Presumably had he been allowed to cut off his wife and keep his hair, Samson could have stayed in the moral world which men create.

What is suggested here is that dualism, the interpretation of being and time as a series of antimonies, is a peculiarly and specifically masculine mode of understanding materially rooted in the particularity of male reproductive consciousness. The refusal to recognize the significance of the ideal character of paternity and the concrete social forms of mediation of male alienation and uncertainty is, I contend, a specific and neglected area of theoretical understanding. To be sure, this contention cannot be proven, any more than the relation of class formation to mode of production or of the ego to the id can be expressed as self-evident causal relations. A dialectical logic based on transcendence of biological necessity can make these connections persuasively but is one-sided if it insists on a single or predominant realm of necessity. Economic production reproduces, basically, individual lives; biological reproduction reproduces the species. Of course, neither of these may be strictly "necessary," and the species is currently behaving as if this may not in fact be the case. Nonetheless, the need to think seriously about species survival in political terms is now acute. We are confronted with a situation in which natural resource potential is diminishing, population is increasing, and random genetic and reproductive adventurism is having a major impact on the social relations of reproduction. It is therefore useful to examine the struggle of those dominant males who seek to resolve the discontinuity of patriarchal consciousness, such as Milton, in all its complexity, vision, and absurdity. Indeed, such an activity is essential to the development of feminist theories of historical praxis.

Milton, of course, regarded dualism as historical, but this view was premised on his perception of the Fall as a historical event. In fact, the myth of the Fall makes much more sense if it is seen in the context of the historical discovery of paternity, symbolized in the access to and separation from the tree of life. The divine power of paternity is translated into secular terms, and the question of continuity over time requires male dominion over the natural world. For Milton, continuity was finally a question of law, for here the concepts of continuity and legitimacy link up. The seventeenth century debates offer an immense "portfolio" of legal terms:[27] common, statutory, canon, divine, positive law, the law of nations, the law of conquest, and such misogynist particularities as surviving Salic Law. Law may evidently have letter, spirit, intention, power, and restitutive and retributive functions. None of these terms were particularly exact, and on their flanks lurked two equally ambiguous notions. One maintained that one man, the sovereign, was above all law but God's; the other, the revolutionary notion, asserted that every individual made his own law. However its terms vary, it can be noted that law does provide an asexual principle of continuity. Like the family, law is a precondition of polity, and the English language maintains the familial and legal sense of continuity in the word "legitimacy." Milton's attempt to render coherent the dualistic implications of the Fall with an ideal continuity from prelapsarian first nature to the lost morality of second nature leads him to the famous poetic effort to justify and elucidate all this as God's rather obscure purpose for man. The loss of morality emergent from God's separation from man in the Fall is to be healed by love. Love is the reason in divorcement, in separation, in alienation. Children are made legitimate not by the breakable contract of marriage but by love, which also is the force which blesses man's "Holy Seed."[28] Love is, for Milton, the fulfilling of the Law (Romans 13.10) and the absence of love is, by definition, unlawful.[29]

This axiom of the fulfillment of law in love is integral to the justification of divorce for incompatibility, as defined by the husband. No law, he claimed, "should bind against the prime and principal scope of its own institution."[30] As marriage was instituted for the comfort of men, and the end of marriage is love, then he who ceases to love must resign his office of husband: this is clearly the only moral course. All this, given the premises, is clear enough, but what

remains unclear is the status of the law, for Milton insists
that ultimately the law is what men say it is, an antinomian
view of a rather radical sort.   Yet Milton's Royalist
contemporaries were quite wrong to accuse Milton of
anarchism, for what Milton asserted was a new view of the
traditional dualistic relation of reason and passion.   Man is
necessarily sexual, and sexual love is therefore good, not only
nor even importantly in terms of the necessity of
reproduction but, to use a later term, in and for itself.
Sexual needs can in fact spawn rational choice, namely,
divorce.   This doctrine clearly divorces Milton from the
Platonic tradition, and he quite specifically rejects the
distaste for sexuality which accompanies spiritual and
theological theories of continuity.   God's edict that *they must
be one flesh* "will be found to import no more but to make
legitimate the carnal act which else might seem to have
something of pollution in it."   Sex means nothing without
love, for without love there is no transcendence: rather than
"one flesh" they are but "two carkasses chained unnaturally
together."[31]

The difficulty with love as God's legitimate end for man is
not that it is carnal and passionate but that it is
unfortunately prelapsarian, and its post-Fall status
ambiguous.   God had to correct this unfortunate loss, and the
Fall, first great historical event in Milton's epic history of the
race, makes inevitable the second great event: the
Incarnation of the Son of the Father.   God does not give the
law; he gives his Son: the prelapsarian man was perfect and
had no need of law, just as there was "no decree
necessitating his free will."[32]   Lawlessness cannot survive
the loss of morality, but the Fall does affirm the free will of
the individual who chose to disobey, and only a free will can
know what justice is.   The political problem for Milton is how
the lapsed sinner can make just laws.   Milton solved this
problem by theorizing that man's dualist nature is subject to
a Second Law of Nature.

As the notion of a Second Law of Nature clearly restores
the inevitability of dualistic perceptions of man in a way
which claims to have first resolved the dualism symbolized by
the Fall, it is very important in the feminist analysis of

patriarchal ideology. It is developed by Milton in *Tetrachordon*. We must try to free it a little from the ancillary batteries of expostulation with which Milton defended his doctrine, for the problems of legitimacy and continuity emerged in a quite practical way in this effort of Milton's.

Milton's discovery that Man's second nature is fallen, yet that in his falleness lies, as it were, the chance to rise again, to annul his divorce from natural morality with his subjective discovery of natural freedom, is heady stuff. The vehicle for this existential leap is individual man's reason, which does not so much provide continuity from first to second nature but reveals the truth of the first and the healing power of divorcement to process in general. "The paradox of the Fortunate Fall," Christopher Hill remarks, "is as old as Christianity, but for Milton it was breathlessly new and immediate."[33] Hill believes that Milton's version of reason was basically the rationality of bourgeois society, which was busy defining man's second nature as that of the moral exploiter. Hill does not explain why Milton expresses his economic sensibilities in terms of marriage. There is some indication that Milton was at least dimly aware of the dialectical structure of economic relations. He claims, for example, that a free commonwealth is the form of government most conducive to trade. But all of this is marginal to his great desire to cure man's alienation from his prelapsarian perfection. As a proponent of divorce, he tends to play down the notion of the importance of "lineal descent."[34] However, the hereditary principle remained as important to bourgeois property relations as it was to patriarchal monarchy and class hegemony. James Harrington defined a gentleman as "one of known descent": these "naturally" make superior magistrates and soldiers.[35] The affirmation of paternity in the teeth of material alienation is still important in terms of property disposition. Milton's concern went beyond this. What he proposed was a radical reformation of the family, not only as a school for peace and rational solutions to strife, the teaching of doctrine, and the model of discipline, all of which are useful to the state, but also as the proving ground of men's will to unify his dual nature in the unity of responsibility, freedom, and dissolvable marriage: "Mark then, Judges and Lawgivers, and ye whose office is to be our teachers, for I will utter a doctrine, if ever any other, though neglected or misunderstood, Yet of great and powerful importance to the governing of mankind."[36]

This is of course the promulgation of the art of falling upwards.   It is not true, as Hill maintains, that Milton, though a practicing politician, offered only a doctrine of grace and faith to account for his prelapsarian goodness. Milton in fact quite specifically dealt with the social conditions in which men can be reintegrated with nature yet maintain their social superiority over women and asserted that men have the right to cast wives aside if they refuse to pander to men's desires and comforts.   He understood that the *form of the social relations of reproduction can be changed historically.*   Less obviously, Milton also attempted to deal with men's "divorcement" from nature and from continuity over time, a result of uncertain paternity, but he did so in a very abstract and problematic way which is both ethereal and earthy.   Marriage is civil, divorce is moral.   The soul is material, the male seed spiritual.   Society is carnal, government is natural.   Woman makes man comfortable but man makes himself.   To be sure, there are mutual grounds for divorce--adultery, desertion and so forth--and these are shared by fallen men and women.   Divorce for incompatibility is exclusively a male choice and a right, in conformity with the end of marriage given before the Fall.   Moreover, the moral law of divorce was never denied by Christ himself. This latter contention comes from Milton's very convoluted attempt to maintain the ancient permission to divorce given in Deuteronomy despite Jesus of Nazareth's contention that such a permission was given only to Pharisees because of their hardness of heart.   Milton wanted to legitimate the putting away of wives for just men, not merely for hard-hearted sinners.   He therefore identified hardness of heart not with individual sin but with universal falleness.   The first law of nature is that all are fallen. The second law of nature is that some can rise again by divorcing themselves from any condition which stands in the way of so doing, including, of course, unsuitable wives.

Is this, then, simply a poetic vision? Are the hidden premises in fact derived from socioeconomic realities, as Macpherson argues in the case with Hobbes, or is there indeed a direct relation between Miltonic ontology and burgeoning bourgeois ideology? Certainly, Milton's struggle with the notion of continuity over time, bizarre though it may be, is more interesting and subtle than the reliance of Whig history on the ancient constitution. Milton's effort to bring the hot passions back into the cool arms of respectability might simply be an aesthetic gloss on the new ideological industry which was busy claiming respectability for the passion of greed. Adam Smith, coming later, will be quite comfortable in conjoining the greedy, hard of heart capitalist with the progressive rationality of the marketplace. Yet ultimately these questions are not the ones that Milton cared about. His overt concern was the legitimacy of male supremacy, which may be why his prose writings are as disregarded as those of Filmer, who had similar goals. His profound misogyny is something more primitive yet infinitely more sophisticated than despair in having married the wrong woman. It is in fact primordial, first nature stuff and one of the least justifiable to man of God's works:

> Oh why did God
> Creator wise, that peopled highest Heaven
> With Spirits masculine, create at last
> This novelty on Earth, this fair defect
> Of nature, and not fill the World at once
> With men, as Angels, without feminine;
> Or find some other way to generate
> Mankind?[37]

Milton's theory of second nature is much closer to that other literary theorist, Jean-Jacques Rousseau, than it is to English natural law theory. Both of these literary politicians are convinced of the power and the problematics of the notion of "natural" male supremacy and seek to define legitimacy in terms of political rather than familial authority. Both also recognize that the dualism of public and private life is a

problematic affair. Hobbes and Locke were also conscious of
the unsatisfactory nature of paternity as an authority
paradigm. Hobbes is characteristically pragmatic: "For in
the condition of meer Nature, where there are no
Matrimoniall lawes, it cannot be known who is the Father,
unlesse it be declared by the Mother: and therefore the right
of Dominion over the Child dependeth on her will, and is
consequently hers."[38] He adds that the sentence in civil law
is, however, in favor of fathers, for the pragmatic reason that
"for the most part Commonwealths have been erected by the
Fathers, not the Mothers of families." Locke, in the *Second
Treatise* warns his readers that the hereditary principle
makes women equal to men, a position he clearly felt to be
important for he had devoted the *First Treatise* to it.[39]
Rousseau believed both Hobbes and Locke were simply
unreliable on the question of human sexuality.[40] Like
Milton, he was much concerned with the regulation of
sexuality, and it is not very helpful to think that this
concern was a product of the individual psychology of the two
men. The political problem of "divorcing" the disobedient is
a difficult one, and one remembers that the "divorcement" of
the king who behaved in a way which perverted the ends of
the commonwealth was lethal. Adam and Eve received a
suspended sentence of death for their sin in the garden,
provided they understood the hazards of continuity over time:
"Know thy birth, For dust thou art, and shalt to dust
return."

The concerns of Milton were not wholly esoteric or
irrelevant to dialectical materialism. They are not, though,
obviously related to the economic forces of seventeenth
century England. Yet Milton's concerns were grounded in
social reality and raise important issues for dialectical
materialism. Critics of E. J. Hobsbawn and
C. B. MacPherson have argued that capitalism was
insufficiently developed in the early seventeenth century for
thinkers of that era to be able to deduce the social structure
of mature bourgeois society. Milton, nonetheless, was able to
deduce a radically enucleated family, reduced to man with
wife. That world of the extended family which Peter Laslett
so monotonously mourns was still well established in the

1640s. Laslett's London baker was master of his extended family in 1619, but Sir Richard Newdigate's household was thriving still in 1684.[41] It is therefore of some interest to students of social consciousness that Milton not only described the enucleated family prior to its historical generalization but also justified it and made social and political deductions from it. He also saw the need for change in family structure created for a rearticulation of the ideology and practice of male supremacy.

More important, Milton's perception of the *structural* significance of the social relations of reproduction was far more acute than that of contemporary Left structuralists. In the raging arguments over determinism, reductionism, and incipient idealism, the protagonists do not appear to have considered that the question of why the proletariat have not rebelled pales historically beside the much older, wider question of why women have accepted the dominion of the male sex. The separation of public and private life is to the social relations of reproduction what the separation of capital and labor is to the social relations of production. This is the message which feminism brings to Marxism. The refusal to understand that the material dialectics of production and reproduction are the necessary substructures of history has dire consequences in the age of contraceptive technology: individual men would do well to remember Milton's suspended sentence on universal man who rejects biological realities:

...so death becomes
His final remedy.[42]

NOTES

[1]The modern defense of the separation of public and private is, of course, that of Hannah Arendt in *The Human Condition* (New York: Doubleday, 1959). For a critique see Mary O'Brien, *The Politics of Reproduction* (Boston: Routledge & Kegan Paul, 1981), pp.116-139. See also Jill Vickers, "Memoirs of an Ontological Exile: The Methodological Rebellions of Feminist Research," in Angela Miles and Geraldine Finn, eds., *Feminism in Canada: From Pressure to Politics* (Montreal: Black Rose, 1982), pp. 22-46. For an attempt to reintegrate public and private within the parameters of particular modes of production, see Wally Seccombe, "The Reproduction of Labor Power: A Comparative Study" unpublished Ph.D. thesis, Ontario Institute for Studies in Education, 1981.

[2]O'Brien, *The Politics of Reproduction*, Chapter 1.

[3]Hegel saw the need for this strategy very early in his pursuit of absolute knowledge. It is integral to his philosophy of nature, but appears in an early fragment "On Love," in *Early Theological Writings*, T. M. Knox, trans. (Philadelphia: University of Pennsylvania Press, 1971).

[4]Juvenal, *City of God*, XVI; "Sixth Satire, The Legend of Bad Women" in *The Satires of Juvenal* (Ann Arbor, 1965) and commentary in Dolvnii Luvanalis Satvrae XIV (Cambridge, 1955).

[5]Which, of course, commends him to Arendt. See Arendt, *The Human Condition*, p. 33.

[6]The promulgation of the Second Law of Nature is to be found in *Tetrachordon*. Milton's "divorce" pamphlets are to be found in *The Complete Prose Works of John Milton*, vol. 2, with introduction by Ernest Sirluck, ed. (New Haven: Yale University Press, 1953). They are abbreviated here thus: *CPW*: editorial and introductory materials; *D & D*: "The Doctrine and Discipline of Divorce"; *M.B.*: "The Judgment of Martin Bucer Concerning Divorce"; *Tet.*: "Tetrachordon";

Col: "Colasterian."   The pamphlets were published
1643-1645.   *P.L.*: *Paradise Lost and Selected Poetry and
Prose*, Northrop Frye, ed., (New York: Holt, Rinehart &
Winston, 1967).

[7]As Milton remarked: "it can be but a sorry and ignoble
society of life whose inseparable injunction depends on flesh
and bones" (*D & D*, p. 309).   Substituting holy seed for
biological determinism, however, is hardly an adequate
solution.

[8]Ernest Sirluck, *Complete Prose Works*, p. 25. My italics.

[9]William   Barker,   "Observations   upon   Some   of   his
Majesties late Answers and Expresses," in William Haller,
ed. *Tracts on Liberty in the Puritan Revolution*, vol. 2, p. 3
(New York: Columbia Press, 1934). Michael Waltzer, in *The
Revolution of the Saints* (New York: Atheneum, 1969), pp.
30-34, discusses the "second nature" created by the Fall in
the context of Calvin's belief that first nature was so nearly
dead that it had little political significance.   In fact, Puritan
versions of pre-Prelapsarian nature are already "second
nature theories" for they generally posit an "instinct" for
religion.   Milton is not alone in believing marriage to be of
pre-Prelapsarian nature.   Christopher Marlowe also lends
weight to the notion of marriage as both natural and
historical: "in violating marriage sacred law You break an
honor greater than yourself: To be a King is of a younger
house Than to be married; your progenitor Sole-reigning
Adam on the universe, By God was honored as a married
man But not by him annointed for a King" (*Edward III*,
2.1,260).

[10]Thomas   Hobbes,   *Leviathan*,   C.   B.   Macpherson,   ed.
(Harmondsworth: Pengujin Books, 1961), Ch. XXII, p. 168 ff.

[11]C. B. Macpherson, *The Political Theory of Possessive
Individualism* (Oxford: Oxford University Press, 1962), pp.
68 ff., 265.

[12]For an excellent discussion of patriarchy and politics,
see Gordon J. Schochet, *Patriarchalism in Political Thought*
(New York: Basic Books, 1975).

[13]Ibid., p. 2.

[14]*D & D*, p. 229.

[15]Schochet, *Patriarchalism.*

[16]*D & D*, p. 47.

[17]*D & D*, p. 324, *M.B.*, p. 462-463.

[18]"The Tenure of Kings and Magistrates" (1649), in K. M. Burton, ed., *John Milton's Prose Writings* (London: Everyman's Library, J. M. Dent & Sons Ltd., 1970), pp. 190-197.

[19]*P. L.*, Book IX, lines 270, 532, 568, 1130.

[20]*D. & D.*, p. 318.

[21]For example, see *D. & D.*, pp. 347-348. Milton was mildly ashamed of his adducement of sovereign authority for husband and turned it quickly to an attack on the Papal church for making women's sexuality public, which is not in women's best interests.

[22]George Armstrong Kelly, *Idealism, Politics and History*, (Cambridge: Cambridge University Press, 1969), p. 11 ff.

[23]*D & D*, p. 273. See also *Genesis*, 1:4 and *P.L.* 1.10.

[24]Milton did not acknowledge his heresies: "I adhere to the Holy Scriptures alone--I follow no other heresy or sect," he wrote in his dedication. See E. M. W. Tillyard, *Milton* (Harmondsworth: Penguin, 1968), p. 182.

[25]The redoubtable Baptist, Mistress Chidley, seems to have been well aware of the political implications of the Doctrine of Toleration; (Barker, "Observations," p. 94). See also Keith Thomas, "Women in the Civil War Sects" in Trevor Aston, ed., *Crisis in Europe 1560-1660* (New York: Doubleday, 1967).

[26]*D & D*, p. 235.

[27]See Sirluck's discussion of law as the inheritance of the people, *Complete Prose Works*, pp. 11 ff.

[28]*D & D*, p. 259.

[29]*D & D*, p. 258.

[30]*D & D*, p. 225.

[31]*D & D*, p. 326.

[32]*D & D*, p. 293.

[33]Christopher Hill, *Reformation to Industrial Revolution* (Harmondsworth: Penguin Books, 1969), p. 202.

[34]*Tet.*, p. 594.

[35]Charles Blitzer, ed., *An immortal commonwealth, the political thought of James Harrington* (New Haven: Yale University Press, 1960), p. 74.

[36]*D & D*, p. 318.

[37]*P.L.*, X 890.

[38]*Leviathan*, p. 254.

[39]*Second Treatise*, Bk. IV.

[40]See Jean-Jacques Rousseau, "The First Part" of "A Discourse on the Origin of Inequality," *The Social Contract and Discourses*, G. D. H. Cole, trans., (New York: Dutton, 1968).

[41]See Peter Laslett, *The World We Have Lost* (London: Charles Scribner's Sons, 1971), pp. 1-7.

[42]*P.L.*, XI 61-62.

10

Hegel: Man, Physiology, and Fate[1]

There have been few intellects in the history of Western thought quite so subtle and sapient as that of Hegel. The general problems associated with critique and exegesis of the man's work are notorious. On the most superficial level, the effort to simply understand what he is saying, to come to terms with a formidable syntax and his neological language demands quite a bit of concentrated attention: one must cope with the deadly serious glecfulness with which he cossets the ambiguities of language, for this is an integral methodological component of his attempt to uncover the ultimate moving complexities of Reason. Wrestling with these preliminaries constitutes only a sort of dry run at the most accessible rung of the Hegelian ladder which mounts dizzily downwards to the living, moving heart of what may well be the most ambitious philosophical system the Western world has produced.

Hegel has been accused, among other things, of thinking God's thoughts. This man claims to have grasped the significance of Absolute Knowledge in a dialectical unity of thought and action, and in so doing to have lowered the curtain on the historical development of Reason. In so doing, he excites about equally the wrath of traditional metaphysicians and the indifference of modern empiricists. Hegel is not, however, an intellectual megalomaniac nor an unrepentant gnostic. He is a man attempting to correct the empiricist fallacies of the Enlightenment, with its crude and unconsciously abstract notion of History as Progress, and in so doing to restore to philosophy the difficult but vital task of resolving the problems uncovered by the metaphysical pioneers of Classical antiquity.

The systematic and formal wholeness of Hegel's work presents a further bedevilment for critical analysis. This raises the question of the relation of parts to whole, which is an absurd question if viewed from Hegel's own totally unified perspective.

He irritated his friends by what they saw as his dilatoriness in publishing, a tardiness which even in 1807 evidently had serious effects on academic careers. It does not appear to have been the case that Hegel did not want to publish until he had *something* to say, but that he did not want to publish until he could say *everything*.[2] It is an interesting historical coincidence that not so far away in place and time, though aeons away in philosophical understanding, Jeremy Bentham was driving his friends to distraction with the same sort of tardiness. Bentham had an adequate private income, however, which Hegel did not. Both men seem to have felt that language was no longer capable of expressing clearly what they wanted to say. Bentham tackled this problem by writing--execrably--in French, Hegel by torturing language into an oddly ebullient submissiveness. The resultant systems cannot be approached critically, however, in the same way. Effective critique of Bentham's inductive/synthetic Principle of Utility is effective critique of the Utilitarian system. To attack Hegel's fundamental postulate that Reason is real is to do more than criticize Hegel: it is to undermine the possibility of philosophical knowledge itself.

Despite Hegel's own insistence on wholeness, it is possible and perhaps even necessary to isolate parts of his system for critical analysis, and such partial endeavors are legion in the stormy history of Hegelian interpretation. For example, Hegel's parable of the struggle for Mastery, the famous "Master and Slave" episode, has by itself generated a great deal of exegetical heat. On the conceptual, or, as some would claim, the ideological level, the battles between young and Old Hegelians, Left and Right Hegelians are a matter of record. Members of these schools have variously retained Hegel's metaphysics but rejected his dialectics, launched desperate tirades against the Universality of Reason itself, or retained the dialectics and rejected the idealism. The position of Hegel's greatest successor, Karl Marx, does not fit into any of these schools. Engels is a straightforward member of the anti-idealism school, but Marx did much more than simply privilege Hegel's sense of the historical significance of human labor and the confrontation of Master and Slave as an idealized paradigm of class struggle. Marx's own rather ambiguous claim to have turned Hegel upside down confuses rather than clarifies the relationship between the two thinkers. This turning upside down is usually construed in a simplistic way. Crudely, it is argued that Hegel says the world is constituted by Ideas and Marx says that Ideas are constituted by the world. This chicken and egg view vulgarizes the dialectical enterprise of both thinkers, an enterprise which attempts to comprehend theoretically the human struggle to synthesize rational thought about the world with the course of actual, active human history. Perhaps we can grasp more adequately the fundamental unity and cleavage between the two men if we consider the turning upside down in terms of the major preoccupation of both thinkers, *history itself*. For Hegel, history is complete. For Marx, truly human history has not yet started.

It is precisely at this point that a specifically feminist critique of Hegel can enter the interpretive fray. Such a critique certainly encounters all the difficulties which have been sketched above, plus a few peculiar to the feminist perspective. It is not proposed here to offer a critique of the whole system, but it is not proposed either to suggest that the shooting down of a part triumphantly entails the destruction of the whole. In fact, it is argued that there is one important sense in which Hegel's system is a "whole," a sense in which it does mark a break in history's hitherto unfaltering stride. The system is the most ambitious attempt ever made to define humanity as masculine, to celebrate the transformation of real people to the abstract concept of Universal Man. From this perspective, Hegel and Marx are *both* correct in a very important dialectical sense. History *has* stopped insofar as the long tenure of male dominance is crumbling. Truly *human* history has not yet started, and can start only in a rational and free association of men and women.[3]

This perspective on the Hegelian System still does not solve the operational problem of a critical approach, but it does suggest that Hegel's thought is of great importance to feminist thought. We shall be dealing here, in a preliminary way, with what Hegel actually has to say about reproductive relations and the family, not in the congealed prejudice of his mature work but in the struggle for generic understanding in his early works. A critique of Hegel from a feminist perspective cannot consist merely of an anthology of proofs that Hegel is a male chauvinist. This would be a simple task: a skip through Part III of *The Philosophy of Right* would provide an arsenal of polemical ammunition. What we shall do is attempt to approach Hegel more constructively, for we can in fact derive from his work a dynamic model of generic antagonisms which is both dialectical and potentially historical, a model which can in turn serve as a theoretical base for an understanding of generic history which transcends Hegel's own particularist vision. Thus, we shall be partial critics, leaving out any consideration of huge and important tracts of the Absolute system. At the same time, we can demonstrate that the unity of the Absolute in Hegel is *not* complete, and that one important reason for this is that he never does resolve the opposition male/female except in "spirit." We shall, however, still be obliged to offer, for purposes of clarification, a few interpretive abstracts of some of Hegel's more general propositions. This is a daunting task, and anathema to all Hegelians, but one cannot assume that all of one's readers are Hegelian partisans, for Hegel is a representative of that kind of male-stressing thought which many feminists feel is dickied up patriarchal ideology. Further, Hegel is peculiarly resistant to digestion and translation into a less esoteric vocabulary, and to any enraged Hegelian purists I can only say that I am not concerned with Hegel so that I may offer another "interpretation." Rather, I look at his work as a serious building block in Western ideologies of patriarchy which has to be understood if the *universal* fact of patriarchal theory and practice is to be negated.

As far as his analyses of reproduction and racial regeneration are concerned, Hegel stopped the clock of history, but he stopped it at the dawn of history rather than the end where his "completion" of philosophy is immodestly asserted. He understood that the *process* of human reproduction is dialectical, and that the social relations of reproduction (i.e., forms of family) change historically. He did not understand that the *reproductive process itself* is not reducible to "nature." The reasons why the clock has to be stopped are twofold: Hegel negated the conscious constitutive powers of women's real reproductive labor in favor of the reflective prowess of the *Idea* of paternity. Yet he did not grasp quite fully the implications of the fact that paternity fundamentally and intransigently is a *conceptualized* experience, a claim inherent in the interesting old "concept" of carnal *knowledge*. The second consideration is itself historical: Hegel could not, any more than Malthus or Marx, or millions of unwilling mothers, anticipate a rational ordering of the social relations of reproduction: such a notion had to await the highly problematic transformation of human reproductive experience by contraceptive technology. This contemporary technology materially transforms the *process* of human reproduction, for within that process the crude materiality of the biological event is inseparable from human consciousness, as Hegel showed in only a one-sided way in that the forms of consciousness he analyzes are crudely sexist in their understanding of who knows what is going on. The ideology of male supremacy has generally insisted on the absolute contingency of reproduction, perceived as an uninteresting animal affair which somehow obliterates human consciousness in anything but a crude reflexive sense. Hegel was more perceptive: he not only recognized a synthesizing parental consciousness of the child as responsibility and potentiality, but also he was, at least in his youth, much concerned about the relation of self-consciousness and sexuality. His perspective on the consciousness question is nonetheless one-sidedly masculine and thus itself still only an *abstract* consciousness.

As a young thinker, Hegel pondered very seriously upon the emotionally and physically synthetic powers of sexuality. In 1797-1798 he held the view that human love was a miraculous and ultimately incomprehensible affair. This view may well have been derived from his reverent study of Classical Antiquity, where it is present, for example, in Plato's obscure discussion of "the nuptial number," and evidently formed an important aspect of the doings of the male Mystery cults.[4] As Hegel's synthesizing ambitions developed, it became quite clear to him that the aspirant to the goal of unification of all contradiction could not bow before the most commonplace opposition of all, the generic differentiation of the species. In an early paper, evidently developed from his 1802-1803 lectures, Hegel attempts to deal systematically with the anthropological foundations of history, "anthropological" meaning to Hegel the pre-conscious, pre-rational and therefore pre-historical forms of human spirit.[5] For an Idealist history of Reason, objective biology offers a very balky starting point, yet without the biological person there is no mundane mansion in which Reason can be at home. Hegel must therefore discover the nature of a movement from biological being to rational, ethical and spiritual being, from unawakened non-differentiation to self-awareness. He must chart the necessary alienation of rational humanity from its own organic origins while preserving these origins. Self-awareness is, in its awakening form, the potential mediation of rational being and brute world, which in due course will transform abstract naturalness to concrete social history. The biological, prehistorical opposition of male/female, is never an Absolute but merely a relative opposition, and as such is indifferent to the mediative prowess of Reason. There is clearly some kind of synthesis at work in the creation of a new life, but life itself, prior to consciousness, is mere negativity, devoid of the ethical reality which marks Reason's debut in the world. Mere life *knows* no opposition, though it will come to grasp death's significance, and has only the dimmest and most negative conception of the reality of the Other:

> The other . . . [is] Evil, a being-in-itself, the
> subterranean principle, the thing which knows
> what lies in daylight and witnesses how it brings
> about its own decline, or is in such active
> opposition that, on the contrary, it substitutes
> negativity for its own being, for its own
> self-preservation.[6]

This rather Romantic notion of a "dark principle" haunting the struggling consciousness of primordial humanity owes much to Schelling, but for both men it also clearly owes quite a bit to the arboreal antics of Eve and her serpentine paramour. More importantly, it is this principle of mere life which Hegel, abandoning poesy for a more rigorous philosophical vocabulary, calls "natural" *Particularity*.

Hegel's dialectic always involves an opposition between a Universal and a Particular, and it is therefore important to know what in general Hegel means by these terms if we are to understand the significance of woman's Particularity. For Hegel, a Universal is a unity of conceptualization and reality in which the Concept is the creative essence. The forms which Reason takes in the course of history vary, but the importance of the Concept and the source of its universality and wholeness is that, unlike ordinary understanding, which is of particular knowledge, the Concept is universal in the sense that it creates itself, it determines what it is, generates its own rational reality and wholeness. Its reality is Reason so that each of its particular creations becomes both rational and real. The Concept is not an empty abstraction, but a living and active reality which determines its own content and its own being.[7] When the Concept has synthesized itself with itself, as it were, unified its universal form and the particular content which it has itself generated, it becomes *Idea*,[8] a synthesis of the object of thought and the creative thinker which Hegel likes to call "concrete." This is a confusing use of "concrete," for it does not only mean objectively present, but embraces an empirical content which remains essentially "abstract" if it is not enfolded and unified with thought. Mind therefore is in constant motion; it is creating and recreating itself in a world which it is thus actually "making" in its own image. The analogy Hegel frequently uses for the objectification of the Concept in the world is an organic one; the tree is potential in the seed. We may note that he shares with male-stream thought in general a tremendous yearning to create a form of auto-regeneration which is superior to biological *procreation*, but unlike many of his predecessors and successors he does not propose a principle of continuity which is independent from biology and therefore "abstracted" from the real.

The important thing about the Concept, for us, is that it *creates* the particular, in fact it creates a whole series of particulars which stand in contrast as *content* of the Concept, which is a *form*. The Idea is the synthesis of form and content. The Concept becomes in effect the core of reality and the inner life of anything which is real. As woman remains particular and man is the "tool" of the Concept, the logical conclusion is that *man makes woman* in a sense which transcends the merely biological mode in which women indubitably "make" men. Hegel never says this in a forthright way, but Hegel has no interest in the forthright, which lies in the realm of the particular as opposed to universal knowledge. It is, however, something a little more implicit in his analysis, for we find in *The Phenomenology* that man's need to invert biological reproduction to spiritual regeneration entails the constant "suppression" of women. Male supremacy is not established, as it were, in a "one-shot" deal. It has to be worked at. Clearly, men *have* historically "made" women. This is the basic premise of Simone de Beauvoir's analysis of feminine Otherness.[9] De Beauvoir herself, who shares an intellectual indebtedness to Hegel with existentialism in general, accepts without reservation the masculine ontological denigration of biological reproduction in a way rather more absolute than Hegel's own.

Hegel's dialectic of thought and reality is something more than a new epistemological model to solve the ancient dualism of subject and object, and Universality is something more than the unity of Reason and History. This is because, for Hegel, Reason itself is something more than the sum of the workings of particular human minds. It is a little difficult to say quite what this "something more" is. It has distinctly theological overtones, and the traditional notion of God comes nearest to Hegel's concept of the Idea. But the parallel is misleading, for Reason objectifies itself in the world, *continuously* concretizing itself in history in all that has been created in and by history. God's objectification of himself in his Son *was* a "one-shot" affair.[10]

In this mobile dialectical model, Universal and Particular stand opposed to one another, and Universal strives at all times to annul and absorb the Particular which it has realized so that it might in turn be transformed to a "higher" (i.e., more rational) reality: this model of process is retained by Marx in a more practical and more easily understood way. For Marx, the important particular/universal opposition is that of the active individual and historically created society. The internal tension of the capitalist mode of production is both creative and doomed by virtue of the opposition of *individual* ownership and *social* labor, an opposition concretized in class struggle. For both Marx and Hegel, Particularity is given a negative evaluation, for of itself it is both abstract and irrational. It is scheduled for negation, by self-universalizing Reason for Hegel, by historical class action for Marx. Marx's prediction of the burial of the individual bourgeois capitalist, or rather the capitalist's self-interment in his self-dug grave, is not a prospect which necessarily disturbs the majority of people, who don't happen to own the means of production. Those who do give no public credence to the analysis, but work hard to ameliorate the nastier aspects of capitalism in the hopes of affecting the dialectic. Hegel's position is more important for feminists. While the Concept creates and annuls a long series of Particularities, women are the *Principle* of Particularity from Hegel's early work right through to the *Philosophy of Right*. Similarly, we remain objectively affixed in the domestic sphere of Particularity (the private realm) from pre-history until the arrival of the universal and homogeneous State, which Hegel

sees as Reason's ultimate social arrangement. The argument
that this is actually what happens, that men have "negated"
women and recreated them to suit their needs, is *not* Hegel's
argument.   His woman is *infinitely* particular precisely
because there *can be no absolute "negation"* of her necessary
reproductive function. We are, as it were, a practically non-
negatable reproductive function. As negation is the process
by which history becomes rational, we are clearly unable to
"make history."

Woman is Particular because she represents mere .life as
opposed to creative life. Here, Hegel has not advanced much
beyond Plato's *Symposium*, where the rejection of the vitality
of procreation in favor of the greater creativity of male
intellectual intercourse is put into the mouth of a woman,
Diotima.   However, neither Plato nor Hegel, for obvious
reasons, are proposing an all-male universe. The male desire
for an all-male universe is not often expressed out loud, but
John Milton, who some misguided feminists in his own time
and ours have thought of as a friend of woman because of his
early advocacy of divorce by consent, gives the yearning to
Adam:

> Oh! why did God Creator wise, that peopled
>   highest heaven
> With spirits masculine, create at last
> This novelty on earth, this fair defect
> Of nature, and not fill the world at once
> With men as angels without feminine,
> Or find some other way to generate Mankind?

> *Paradise Lost*, Book X, 888-895

For Hegel, women are rescued from pre-history (as indeed
are men) by the development of a moral sense, a limited
ethical life which involves, in its natural manifestation, the
conscious sacrifice of one's own desires in the interests of
dependent infants. This is a genderically shared task, with
the crucial difference being that women are arrested at this
level.   Men, for reasons which Hegel never quite clarifies,

develop also a *social* consciousness, and in doing so start
upon their real history, though not, as we shall see, without
a struggle. *Before* men embark on their history, the family is
established as the first "natural" moral institution, and it is
a *patriarchal* family, a circumstance Hegel appears at first
glance to have thoughtlessly deduced from the *subsequent*
course of patriarchal history. The important point is that
the family, while it is established pre-historically, changes
and reforms and in fact is eroded in the course of history, but
in all these transformations one aspect of the family is
curiously resistant to the revolutionary potential of the
Concept in action. Patriarchy remains constant, and women
remain satisfied (with a few distressing historical aberrations
and the happily natural guidance of brothers) within the
non-conflictual, loving and spiritual ambience of the family.

Men, on the other hand, transcend the particularist
limitations of family, for they must constitute their own self-
consciousness, in effect create themselves. The conditions of
the birth of the self-constituted self, the self-made man, are
the *recognition* of death and of other men. However, other
men too desire to be recognized, and this conflict of desires,
which is a desire of each for the desire of the Other, must be
fought out in mortal combat. The risk of life necessary to
this combat comes about because male consciousness has
recognized the nature of the Universal Negative, death itself.
For men, the actualization of the self is at the same time the
recognition of the Negative within and inseparable from the
self, hence the desire for external recognition of one's
actuality. The price of recognition is a willingness to
confront Negation, namely, to risk one's life in struggle with
an Other's similar desire for a recognition of self-negation.
Hegel's protagonists do not in fact fight to the lethal finish,
for one man decides that he values mere life above the
struggle for self-conscious life and its chilling embracement of
finitude. This Other (though Hegel does *not* say this
specifically) becomes *effeminate*, in that he values mere life,
his particular life, and eschews the Universalizing
potentiality of the struggle to overcome and master Nature.

This epic confrontation is Hegel's celebrated myth of the
Master and Slave, for he who chooses Particularity is

enslaved by he who confronts death in a free act of potential self-alienation.[11] Neither Hegel nor de Beauvoir notice the crucial form of *immediate recognition* which biology denies to man, namely recognition of his particular paternity. Neither do they note that women do not need to create a *principle* of continuity, for they create continuity *concretely* by reproductive labor. But then, neither even addresses the possibility of a *reproductive consciousness*. The myth is essential to Hegel's view of history, for it moves mankind from non-differentiation, heretofore present only in a relative and abstract way in generic opposition, to a differentiated reality, a new Particularity, a creative and potent particularity which is already reaching out to the negation of its own finitude, and the negation of mere death in creative history. In effect, human continuity is removed from *biological continuity*, which women actively affirm in reproductive labor but from which men are alienated, to an *artificial continuity* in which men who have succeeded in "making themselves" proceed to make historical continuity. Hegel's great merit is to see and acknowledge that the condition of man-made history is to suppress without actual negation the reality of reproductive process. Birth therefore remains privatized and takes place within time but outside of history, which of course goes public. The separation of public and private life becomes a condition of *history*, rather than, as it actually is, a working structure of patriarchal hegemony.

Hegel's Master and Slave parable has many implications, but our interest is a limited one, which is no doubt symptomatic of the particularism of feminist consciousness. Hegel's myth is spun in support of the very reasonable claim that human history is the history of human mastery of the world by means of a unification of rational consciousness and creative activity. This mastery is not, however, simple mastery of the natural environment: Adam the patriarch had already started this process with his little spade. It is mastery of other men, and is the root of the *inevitability* of class divisions which persist up to and beyond the end of history, which Hegel ultimately realizes in the modern State. But at least general class antagonism in its primordial

particularity is established *historically*.   Male supremacy
over women is established *prior* to the dawn of history, and is
therefore presumably "natural."   It is also rational, for
Nature for Hegel is rational.   Unfortunately for woman,
Nature is also *impotent (Ohnmacht)* in Hegel's system, and is
capable of rational and transformative vitality only when she
is synthesized with thought in the Concept. The Concept and
the sperm appear to have functional similarities, with the
sperm's swim outside of history into the cavernous womb
made inevitable by its impotence.   Having detached this
tiresome artifact, men can achieve potency in the making of
history.

What Hegel is doing is creating a form of continuity which
transcends genetic continuity.   There is, of course, nothing
wrong with such an enterprise. We are not launching a plea
for the regression of life to the biological level. The effort of
humanity to come to terms with the natural environment is
and has been a struggle, a struggle in which indeed
humanity has shaped and defined itself in concrete ways. It
is futile to complain to history for being what it has been. It
is imperative, though, as Hegel sees so clearly, to *understand*
what it has been, and for women that understanding must
embrace the historical phenomenon of actual male
supremacy.   For Hegel, the non-historicity of women rests
squarely on her Particularity, which in turn rests on the fact
that as the bearers of life, women are principles *only* of life,
and are hostile to the risk of the lives which they have so
hardly borne.   They will not risk their lives like those who
master slaves. The fact that women do risk life in childbirth
does not interest Hegel, perhaps because childbearing was
not a rational choice in the pre-contraceptive age.[12] As the
bearers of life, women have no contradiction between
themselves and Nature to negate and recreate, and just as
Nature is impotent in terms of the creation of concepts,
women are impotent in terms of the active creation of
history.   Women's actuality in its unity with birth is of
course negated by death, but this is a negation which they do
not and evidently need not negate by creating for themselves,
as men do, a *second* and transcendent nature. The "second"
nature which women create is a *new* life, not their own life,

and a life, moreover, which by virtue of its own self-creative powers, will break away from dependence to independence.

Ironically, this transformation from dependence to independence makes women occasionally resistant to their natural impotence. Women, for example, are credited by Hegel with the destruction of the pagan world, an uppityness which presumably justifies their suppression by and incarceration in the domestic realm as rigorous as that practiced in the Athenian *polis*.[13] These ancient women asserted the primacy of life in opposition to man's first Universalizing task force, the death-dealing Homeric heroes. In effeminizing these splendid creatures, women destroyed them. Likewise, Hegel becomes cross with the Romans for permitting women to own property, setting up a dialectical relation with the objective world which permitted women to take action in that created world, thus further eroding the natural ethical functions of the family. Despite these historical outbreaks, women remain for Hegel limited creatures who do not share the thrust to Universality. Hegelian Universality is essentially a *Brotherhood*, united in the creation of a community and in the annulment of the natural, in whose sphere women may chafe only impotently. Hegel never gets around to the historical persecution of witches, a very masterful chunk of negation indeed.

What happened in prehistory, like the drama in the Garden, thus required a woman concerned only with carnal reality and abstract species continuity, which she couldn't comprehend beyond one small baby. It also required a man with at least a flickering sense of a wider ethical and rational mission. The mastery of beasts and women, which God gave to Adam, Hegel bestows on pre-self-conscious man: it is a precondition of his awakening to self-consciousness and his coincident discovery of his finitude. This is all very biblical, except that Cain does not slay Abel but enslaves him. In effect, too, patriarchy becomes man's first political office, political not only in the crude sense of power over others, but in the human sense of being able to *rationalize* that power. Hegel nowhere argues, as might well be argued within his theoretical scenario, that this control over women, which he does not in fact see as control but as a relation of unity, constitutes a primordial taste of mastery for prehistoric man which dictates that his subsequent relations with nature and other men will necessarily take the form of power relations, relations of *force*. This is because of his ahistorical and non-dialectical belief that the essence of the relation of men to women, unlike the mastery of men over men, does not entail an act of will which lays existence itself on the line. In terms of consciousness, paternity appears for Hegel to be immediately apprehended. Mastery over nature for productive purposes must be mediated in thought and action, for man's separation from nature is here *absolute*, as is his differentiation from other men. In reproductive process, the only separation is *relative*, the male/female opposition. It does not need to be mediated by individual consciousness, but is mediated by a *potential* consciousness, that of the child.

Hegel sees that the child is a human product in the objective sense, but the labor which produces the child is not unified with rational thought and it is not, strangely, the authentic parturitional sweat of the mother. It is the joint "labor" of copulation.[14] This odd view of sexual intercourse as an aspect of human work in general arises from Hegel's view of the baby as a "tool" of Reason, for Reason must have a living carrier in biological man before it can objectify its metaphysical destiny in human history. The making of the child is not itself a particularly rational business and, indeed, Hegel owns that "it is more rational to make a tool than a child."[15] Further, the baby itself is only pure intuition, a bundle of needs absolute only in its dependent Identity with "life." This "Identity" is complete, for the baby in its primordial being annuls distinction between desire and reason and also annuls the sexual differentiation of the parents, a point to which we shall return in a moment. In a limited sense, the baby is the *Concept* of biological reproduction, created and *potentially* self-creating, but in its first appearance able only to manage a particular, abstract and pre-rational self-actualization.

The baby, however, is conceptually related as a tool of Reason to all of Adam's other tool-making activities, and in this sense the "making" of this tool in the "work" of copulation is related to the general tool-making activity which Adam takes on to serve his Divine sentence of perpetual labor, but this particular activity he shares equally with his woman. Here, of course, young Hegel is developing one of his most brilliant insights, the fact that human labor is the creative alienation which mediates between man and his world. Labor is the activity which in *The Phenomenology* will eventually negate the negation of the slave's freedom, and the factor which will become the lynchpin of Marx's creative Materialism. At this moment, however, we are still contemplating Adam's baby and his role in his father's struggle to raise himself from the merely emotional universality of sexuality and reproduction of the human wherewithal to meet Reason's need for worldly continuity. For Adam, this is a "satisfaction" without as yet the conceptualization of non-immediate gratification, which he develops in the *productive* realm where, like Prometheus, he discovers foresight. At this stage, man has not yet developed the specifically human tool of mediation, which he will create in language. We need not go on to this higher state, for somewhere in the lower state woman has been left behind in the practical realm of dumb intuitive intelligence whose only claim to Universality is the sentimentality of family relations, with one side of her reality in indifference and the other in Particularity. In one sense, men and women are equal, for each has intelligence and each "works" at the creation of the child, but this is undifferentiated equality:

> Labor, subsumed under this intuition, is a one-sided subsumption, since in this very process the subsumption itself is superseded.

(This supersession is the objective unification of intuitions and parental intelligence . . . the child.)[16]

> The labor [which produces intelligence] is a totality and with this totality the first and second levels are now posited together.

(These first two levels are the inorganic and the organic, now being completed with the addition of intelligence.)

> Man is a power-level, universality, for his other,
> but so is his other for him.

(At this point, men and women are alike and equal in having
the power to create and the intelligence to know they are
creating a new intelligence.   However, this unity and
equality cannot persist, for it returns the protagonists to
non-differentiation, albeit on a higher level.)

> and so *he* makes *his* reality, *his* own particular
> being, *his* effectiveness in reality into an adoption
> into indifference, and *he* is now the universal in
> contrast to the first level (my italics).[17]

Thus people are, in the work of creating a child, capable of
knowing themselves as both Particular individual and
Universal, sensuous as well as sentient, singular as well as
social.   The man and the woman "desire" one another but
this desire itself is not self-determining, it remains the
intuitive desire of each for the other's body:

> This supreme organic polarity in the most complete
> individuality of each pole is the supreme unity
> which nature can produce.   For it cannot get past
> this point: that difference is not real but is
> absolutely ideal.

(By this Hegel appears to mean that it can only be felt, not
thought, and in any case its middle term, the child, is a
separate intelligence, at least potentially.)

> The *sexes* are plainly in a relation to one another,
> one the universal, the other the particular: they
> are not absolutely equal.   Thus their union is not
> that of the absolute concept but, because it is
> perfect, that of undifferentiated feeling.[18]

What Hegel is saying here is that in the first instance men
and women are each to the other and for each self both
universal and particular, and thus in danger of collapsing
into absolute non-differentiation.   This non-differentiation is
"Love," but it is emotional rather than consciously ethical,

and it cannot become ethical until a new opposition develops out of this indeterminacy. That "opposition" is the child's potential intelligence, mediated in the first place by the child's absolute dependence. What Hegel is *not* saying is why this new but old differentiation into opposition posits the male as Universal and the female as Particular.[19] He never does tell us this, and it can, of course, be written off as mere masculine prejudice. Nonetheless, we can hardly ignore the fact that men have constituted themselves as universal: this is underscored in the linguistic affirmation of pseudo-generic "Man," to say nothing of the historical record of male dominance. We shall therefore pursue Hegel's conceptualization of reproduction a little further, to see if any more light can be shed on the matter of man's *primordial* Universality, already present in biological paternity.

In an earlier fragment, *On Love*, Hegel had addressed the question of sexuality with a little less composure, for the piece was written amidst the political excitements of the 1790s and, presumably, Hegel's own maturing sexuality. Sexuality, which young Hegel decorously refers to as "love," is clearly a problematic and still somewhat mysterious affair. Nonetheless, Hegel recognizes the dialectical form of reproductive process, though the Negation at work here is not the Absolute of death but the partiality of passion. Sexual feeling sweeps the lover into a unity with an Other, a unity which negates the sense ("his" sense, but perhaps hers too) of individuality and annuls the consciousness of self: "the individual cannot bear to think of himself in this nullity." Hegel is here giving expression to a proposition central to his own epistemology and also to that of Marx: human consciousness *resists alienation* and is *forced* into mediative action. Oddly enough, Hegel probably is being *generic* in this part of his analysis when in fact a little more rigor would require a *genderic* differentiation. Both lovers may indeed "lose" their sense of identity, but the male loses something much more concrete. He loses his seed. Hegel does not go into this: "Nothing carries the root of its own being in itself. . . . True union consists only between living things which are alike in power."[20] This idea of "alikeness in power" will be modified by Hegel and by history as the years pass. Here, Hegel is concerned with the simple reality that these objects each carry a seed, and the "root of being" is the unity of these seeds from separate entities unified in the act of copulation. Love, that is, sexual love, annuls not only the distinction between the two lovers, but the further distinction between the lover as lover and the lover as physical organism. In Hegel's view, then, sexuality not only negates lovers as distinct individuals, but annuls the distinction between emotional and physical life: "All distinction is annulled."[21] This state of universal non-differentiation is not apparently negated by its mere transience, at least at this stage of Hegel's development.[22] The lover is submerged in the brute and undifferentiated biological unity and continuity of the race: "The mortal element, the body, has lost the character of separability, and a living child, a seed of immortality, of the eternal self-developing and self-generative race . . . [is] this unity . . . [but] is only an undifferentiated unity."[23]

The process of human regeneration, then, is a process of "unity, separated opposites, re-union."[24] In other words, it is a *dialectical* process at its most fundamental level, though it is clearly not at this point a Universal, for the Concept is not operative, and only an external and as yet merely potentially intelligent mediation is available, the promise of the living child. Hegel is correct: the process of reproduction *is* dialectical. What is less convincing is, in the first instance, the absolute bodily separation from the process, for this is simply not true for women. Further, this important dialectical perspicacity on Hegel's part is tied to an opposing *historical* opacity. This is because Hegel cannot break out of an emotionalized organic shell: there is no *struggle for recognition* going on here, with all its creative potential. In fact, the whole analysis presents a problem for an idealist theory of consciousness rooted in the primacy of the Concept, for reproductive process is *formally dialectical prior to its conception in thought*; it has however nothing concrete to contribute to the expansion of self-consciousness, but only to the creation of the potential consciousness embedded in the child. The dialectical moments are going on, as it were, behind the back of the beast with two backs.

Hegel appears to have been dissatisfied with his analysis. At some unknown moment he added to his manuscript the words: "The child is the parents themselves." Perhaps seeing the problem created then in the constitution of a self-consciousness for the living "tool" of Reason without a conflict with both parents, Hegel scores out this phrase and lets his original youthful statement stand: the child is the embodied unity of separated parents.[25]

The consciousness which attends reproduction is finally a reflexive consciousness, not a creative consciousness, in Hegel's analysis. Both parents recognize their child, but the child is ultimately the product of action without thought. The fact that the process of reproduction is dialectical in form prior to the bestowal of the formal blessing of the Concept may be the reason why Hegel creates the family prehistorically, but this still cannot explain why this form of the family is already patriarchal.

The family cannot ultimately further the ethical development of Man, for its unity with the organic is fixed in a mute and unchangeable historical presence. The form--family--persists in time, indeed its *essence* is in a sense temporal. It provides the formal biological continuity of the tools of Reason, but is in its Particular content constantly negated. As the children grow, each particular family duly decays. Historically, the expansion of needs and desires created by the Universalizing advance of Reason in its objective manifestations erodes the family, which is incapable of responding to the needs and desires as they become ethical projects of man as *citizen*, striving for the common good of the community.

Man's heroic task of shouldering the burdens of historical process does not go unrewarded. He has "satisfaction," the true creative satisfaction dug up like treasure by Adam's shovel, and he has Mastery, of which more in a moment. On a more prosaic level, he becomes the guardian of the family property. He also has recognition, the respect of his neighbors and the *persona* awarded by the legal systems he develops. When Hegel first talks of ownership in his *System* he speaks of "abstract" ownership, in the sense of the need for means of production still undifferentiated from the preservation of the laborer and his immediate family. Concrete ownership appears with the development of a social surplus and the possibility of exchange. Exchange is motion and action, a motion which takes man beyond the family into relations with others, relations which negate the pure abstract freedom enjoyed by man at work in providing for his own self-maintenance. Ownership now moves from the abstract Universal of kin-shared property to particular ownership, with all the consequent panoply of Law which realizes the otherwise abstract "right" to property.[26]

Hegel's development of the property theme interests us here for its influence on the young lover coping with his self-annulment. The romantic ardor of the sexual engagement is somewhat mitigated by the lovers' sense of bourgeois propriety, in both senses of the word. A "dead world of external objects" intrudes upon the consciousness of the young lovers, in the form of the families' property holdings. In opposing a lover, each lover is opposed also to his or her possessions and those of the other lover. Clearly, things would be simpler if only one lover was a property owner, which may account for Hegel's dislike of Roman activities in the field of property law. Thanks to this ancient resistance to the rational, the women of Hegel's time evidently appeared to him to have travelled a long way from the propertyless perfection of Antigone, even though their position in relation to property looks grim enough to contemporary feminists. Women could have property willed to them by testamentary disposition, an ownership limited to their own life span. Even this limited ownership of property comes between the lovers for, according to Hegel, the possibility of sharing property is not a practical one. The embodied unity which the child represents in the process of reproduction is evidently not accessible to the parents' property relations. Property embodies the alienated labor of the individual superseded by the "pure infinity" of legal right invested in the thing--Hegel's way of expressing the idea of *value*.[27] For "things," in this case property, no relation is possible, according to Hegel, except mastery of the object. Clearly with Plato in mind, Hegel argues that the possibility of shared goods is illusory, for "community of goods is still only

the right of one or the other to the thing."[28] There seems to
be little doubt in Hegel's mind as to *which* one: "Since
possession and property make up an important part of *men's*
lives even lovers cannot refrain from reflection on this aspect
of their relations"[29] (my italics).

Now we must ask, what is the meaning of all this? There
is no doubt at all that Hegel is defending male supremacy,
and that the categorization of Female as Particular and Male
as Universal has arbitrary (i.e., non-dialectical) components.
The effects upon Hegel in his maturity are predictable. The
creation of communities emergent from the Concept of
exchange, itself made possible by the labor of the mastered
slave, depends upon the race's capacity to overcome
particularity. This is correct in an important sense. The
question is why only male particularity is negated, because of
course this is the apologist root for the identification of our
species as "mankind." Particularity is not of course
destroyed, but merely annulled, negated in one form to
reappear in another which subsumes but does not obliterate
it. Nothing is obliterated in Hegel's view of history. The
negation of the individual will is the condition of the ethical
community, but the life-giving particularity of women is also
necessary to the community, for children are determinate
moments in the advance of Reason. The transformed, higher
form of community spirit which transcends family is Law, a
developed concrete Universal, and Hegel says of law that it
"in its efficient operation in general is the manhood of the
community."[30] Among these Laws, of course, are those
which realize what Hegel understands as the "spiritual
essence" of marriage, but they also "realize" the *abstract*
nature of paternity, a point which Hegel seems to be hinting
at obliquely. The notion of a spiritual essence for marriage
neatly evades the actuality of the uncertainty of paternity,
which Hegel does not name as a "determinant moment" in
reproductive process. His analyses of reproductive process as
resistant to constitutive conceptualization pussyfoots around
man's efforts to mediate his estrangement from his seed.
Knowledge of paternity in general stands opposed to the
uncertainty of particular paternity. Thus Law is indeed the

efficient objectification of "manhood." Hegel at times seems to come close to this underlying reality only to shy away again. Thus, it is production and exchange which become the only basis for the necessary move to sociability beyond kinship. Hegel does not see, or does not consider important, the fact that the uncertainty of paternity *commands* co-operation between men as a class: lay off my woman and I'll lay off of yours.

Hegel's opposition of life and livelihood is a profound and original understanding of the fact that relation between the social forms of reproduction and the social forms of production is a dialectical opposition, a point which rather generally eludes Marx's understanding. Yet even this more complex opposition within and between the processes of production and reproduction is for Hegel curiously non-creative: it is *irritant* squabble rather than heroic confrontation, and is dealt with in a most curious way. Men deal with the tension of life and livelihood, of individual and society, not by struggling with women, but by becoming soldiers:

> Since the community gets itself subsistence only by breaking in upon family happiness, and dissolving [individual] self-consciousness into the universal, it creates its enemy for itself within its own gates, creates it in what it suppresses, and what is at the same time essential to it--womankind in general. Womankind--the everlasting irony in the life of the community--changes by intrigue the universal purpose of government into a private end.[31]

Women "ridicule the grave wisdom of maturity . . . make this wisdom a laughing stock" and thus teach their children a lack of respect for men and their philosophies. She cares only, Hegel says, for the "force of youth" and elevates her personal relationships with son, husband, brother to a position which disregards the wider good of the community. The community deals with this, as both Plato and Machiavelli dealt with it, by turning this high-spirited individualist youth into a soldier. This is not simply an

expedient way of correcting the baleful effects of feminine
influence on young men; the community *must* have soldiers
anyway: "War is the spirit and form in which the essential
moment of ethical substance, the absolute freedom of ethical
self-consciousness from all and every kind of existence, is
manifestly confirmed and realized."[32]

War destroys property and even the lives of individuals,
but this destructive force "stands out as that which preserves
the community." At the same time, it keeps "the individual
who provides pleasure to women" employed.[33] War in its
destructive aspect, dependent as it is upon *physical* strength,
is, like women, immediately related to nature. Yet there is
clearly a difference between women and soldiers, for the
soldier is serving Universality, even though he does not know
he is doing this. This may be a fair example of what Hegel
means when he talks of the *cunning* of Reason. Women do
not even do this sort of ignorant service. The Universal
component of their Being is simply the continuity of the race,
and the care of the individual keeps them "constantly
dissolved in the fluent continuum of their own nature."[34]
War is clearly the universal version of the master and slave
dialectic, the ethics of life-risking writ large, but there is no
need for this kind of battle between men and women. To be
sure, the community must suppress "the spirit of
individualism," and "suppress it as a hostile principle."[35]
The objective form of this principle, woman, must clearly
simply be tolerated as a necessary irritant for the sake of
creating a concrete community at all.

We may be angry at this show of prejudice or we may
even, as Hegel accuses us of doing, mock the comic overtones
in this version of ourselves. More constructively, we may
look systematically at the moments of Hegel's analysis of
reproductive process, which, whatever it does to objective
idealism, makes an important contribution to a materialist
epistemology; and a feminist epistemology must be
materialist, for women *have* a material relationship with
nature which is particularly feminine. Male denigration of
this relationship has left some women intolerant of it, and
left in some feminine hearts a yearning to escape from their
involvement in reproduction, which is as one-sided and

pathetic as the male urge to get back in. In general terms, we may note that the most primitive human functions-- eating and giving birth--are dialectically structured. Marx has shown us that this is also the case with "pure" labor.[36] This being so, it may be argued that the structure of human consciousness is dialectical, and that this structure guarantees that humanity will remain restless, creative, and struggling. The structure, however, does not emerge from some metaphysical essence in the Ideal Form of Reason, but it does not emerge solely from material productive relations either. It emerges from humanity's early and immediate experience of *necessity*, and necessity has *two* poles, eating and production on the one hand, copulating and reproducing on the other. A feminist epistemology must take both into account, for male-stream thought has not overtly done so.[37] Of course, the two are only formally similar. In the most obvious case, the *relation* between production and eating is clear and immediate while that between copulating and giving birth is not: it is precisely here that Hegel first goes a little astray. Producing and eating are not *necessarily* social: even where physiological paternity is not understood, reproduction involves at the very least a dyad, mother and child. Women are in fact fundamentally cut off from mere particularity rather than enmeshed in it amorphously and infinitely. We need no act of derring-do to develop a sense of the unity and separation of another human. We recognize our own children.

What Hegel does not ever come right out and say is that *paternity is necessarily a Concept*. This is the unwritten reality underlying his analysis and distorting it. Paternity must be conceptualized because it is not immediate, but is shot through with an intransigent uncertainty, an uncertainty contingent upon the alienation of the male seed. For men, physiology is fate. It is as the custodian of his estranged seed that man experiences woman as oppressive. When Hegel tells us that in the raptures of love the body loses its character of separability, he does not note that the character of separability itself is generically differentiated. The seed separates from the father, while the "undifferentiated" unity embodied in the child separates only from the mother. Further, this undifferentiated unity which "breaks free" from the original unity does not simply break free; it is not, as Hegel claims, "a self-generating entity." It is brought into the world by the mother's *labor.* Hegel's bizarre attempt to give to copulation rather than to parturition the character of labor consciously or unconsciously turns the gestational clock back to a constitutive moment *prior* to the alienation of the male seed, thus evading the very real separation of men from genetic continuity. Man in fact has a double finitude: the individual finitude which he shares with all living creatures, and the general finitude in which his participation in the race is abrupted at the moment of ejaculation. This is why he sees the race as "self-developing and self-generative." It is nothing of the kind. It is developed and sustained by women's labor, a labor, moreover, of which women are *conscious.* Consciousness is an integral part of reproduction, though it has been customary to imply that because women cannot help what they are doing in childbirth they do not know what they are doing. What woman is doing as she labors is mediating her separation from the child, canceling by life-risking activity the self-alienation of *her* seed in the certain conceptualization of the child who is born as hers. She is establishing a living *continuity* which men must establish *artificially.*

Hegel does not pay attention to the fact that the male alienation of the seed and the female alienation of the child are *temporally* separated, which does more than exacerbate the uncertainty of paternity. The poets are wiser: "Between the conception and the creation" writes T. S. Eliot, "falls the shadow." This is the shadow of uncertainty inseparable from lapsed and discontinuous time. The significance of this for male and female time consciousness is considerable and almost totally unstudied in an age when temporality and finitude are acute and often melancholy concerns of philosophical thought. Time is not only an enemy of man because of his particular death, but because he "dies" genetically with the alienation of his seed.[38]

Hegel's Idealist conception of history, like all such conceptions, takes off from the world of reality, but at least

Hegel tries to get back. Nonetheless, the demonstrable male partiality for separating thought from reality and imputing "reality" to somewhere other than the world has a material base in male reproductive experience, for men are naturally abrupted from *genetic time*, which has its necessary substructure in the process of reproduction and its human objectification in history. Hegel is concerned to make thought temporal and reproduction ahistorical. Yet reproductive process, as soon as the relation between copulation and childbirth is discovered (and we simply do not know when that happened--there are those who consider it part of man's innate equipment, gifted, no doubt, by a patriarchal deity); as soon as this connection is made man is forced to conceptualize paternity, for the relation is susceptible only to rational comprehension. It is not as *lover* that man is annulled; it is as *parent*. If he is to restore himself to genetic unity, indeed, if he is ever to make any sense at all of the notion of a Universality for men, a species-being, he *must* act to negate nature's negation of his temporal unity with his species.

It is this nullity, the negation of paternity which stands in absolute opposition to the concept of paternity, which history shows us very clearly that men *cannot bear*. Despite Hegel's spiritualization of marriage, it simply does not make sense to say that man is concerned about the loss of himself in sexual rapture, for rapture is *always* transitory, for the married or unmarried, for men and for women. Nature cares not at all for orgasmic or conjugal bliss. *Men* have constructed historically a huge institutional edifice designed to ameliorate the uncertainty of paternity, an edifice which is a true *Idee*, embracing the ideological and actual aspects of men's response to what is perceived as a natural injustice. But the fundamental response, the paradigmatic mediation on which this edifice is constructed, is man's relation to the child. Hegel is correct *for men*; the separated child is the middle term between himself and biological universality, but the middle term *for women* is their active labor.

The relation between male subjective preoccupation with death and man's objective history of wanton killing is not easy to establish. Men do murder and destroy the children of women but this is not because philosophers have said that death is the ultimate human reality. Thomas Hobbes perceived the capacity to kill as the only true equality, and an important causal factor in the urge to create contractual limitations which would transform the equality of the killing capacity to the fragile legal obligation not to exercise this equal capacity haphazardly.[39] Hegel is much concerned with death, and in his *System* spends quite some time in the analysis of the differentiated moral content of different kinds of killing.[40]

Men do kill for many reasons, or for no discernible reason at all. A feminist perspective, however, cannot indulge in the abstract contemplation of Death as the Universal Negative. Nor can we dismiss the historical record which shows a dialectical unity between a consistent mesmerized philosophical infatuation with death and an objective record of the irrational destruction of life. Women must show that their particularity, far from being a dehumanizing and pre-ethical preoccupation with "mere" life, is both more rational and more ethical than the unholy conventicles of those masculine angels of death who have hitherto appropriated "their" particular children while they slaughtered young and old "Tools of Reason" with universal abandon. Men have seen the heroic defiance of the reality of death as their most momentous triumph over Nature, a conceptual, spiritual ideological triumph touted as a real one. Its relation to the actual "triumph" over nature's perceived injustice in the realm of birth has not been even contemplated in a serious way by anyone but Hegel. Yet for Hegel, too, it is not by birth that man acquires a historical reality, but by death, an inversion which women must find in the first instance simply weird. Death is, for Hegel, the Great Negation, the negative within life which is, in Harris' words, "the link between the natural and ethical level of the rational individual's existence."[41] Thus, while the discovery of physiological paternity is ignored as a historical event, rational man discovers death "historically." The reason that this event signals the transcendence of the natural by the ethical is presumably that having discovered his potentiality as killer, men may choose not to exercise it, or to exercise it "impersonally," as in war, or as a tool in the development of the Concept of Legality, as in the trial by combat.[42] We have already seen that killing in defense of the community is supremely ethical, and presumably the threat to the community in the first place is an aspect of the essential drive to cancel alienation in mastery. Murder, on the other hand, is in the first instance pre-ethical for it is fixed in the negative aspect of mere life and hence in Particularity. It is the taking of a particular life, and as such, is the essence of *family* killing, the *lex talionis* of the natural justice of revenge. Family killing is not so much unethical as simply insignificant in ethical terms. Murder is not that important to the family, Hegel argues, for family life goes on despite the death of one individual who has only a "formal" as opposed to an ethical existence to negate, and can be satisfactorily balanced by another death taken in exchange. Life itself continues. The important death for Hegel is the "personal" death, the death inflicted on a *known* other in single combat over a point of "honor." This is important because here "justice" is involved, and Justice is an ethical concept. "Honor" is the urge to subsume, to gain mastery, as Hegel says bluntly, and in family war (that is, between, not within, families) the only question is "Who is to dominate?" or, "Who is to seize the ethical honor of dominating?"

Hegel's analysis is extremely difficult to follow. For our present purposes, while it is not quite clear how Hegel gets where he is going, it is quite clear where the terminus of his journey lies. It lies in the *polis*, in political life, which Hegel sees as the realization of the "absolute ethical life," which subsumes the natural ethical life, which is the best that the family can do. The mediation of this transcendent move lies in negativity, the negation of the individual and his rebirth as citizen, but also negativity which transforms the particularist notion of death by the creation of negotiated rules of war.[43] As Harris remarks, Hegel's analysis is worked out more logically at the Conceptual level, where an orderly transition of the Concept of ethical relations from one stage to another is relatively clear and continuous.[44] There is less continuity between actual family life and political life, where there is no mediation, but simply a play of non-defined "negativity," and the abrupt replacement of family by polity. Despite the opacities, it is quite clear that Hegel is saying that there is no place in the orbit of family life for the exercise of man's need to master. Here, as we have seen, Hegel is simply wrong, but the result is a very curious one. Man's lust to conquer, to overcome negation, to be willing to die and to kill--all of these leave the family, heretofore limited in its preoccupation with the regeneration and sustenance of *life*, hermetically sealed in the eternal flow of death. Women, the agents of life, become the passive servants of the gods of death whom men transcend.

Women won't kill, and thereby deprive themselves of the creative power of negation and conscious self-alienation. This refusal to risk life, one's own or another's, means that women have no need of a higher ethical system, a timorousness for which Hegel clearly despises us. This lack is also a lack of the desire to command the desire for recognition which the Other flourishes in challenging opposition to self-consciousness. The result is that women can have meaningful relations only with the dead, who have in their negativity presumably universalized the passive life.[45] This necromantic dalliance means that the woman's status as daughter and sister, the genealogical line with dead ancestors, is ethically more important than her status as wife or mother, in which her particularity is invaded without resistance and the genealogical purity of the ancestors is continually diluted. The household of *The Phenomenology*, as opposed to the now developed political realm, exists primarily as the arena of death, a conclusion which is cogent enough if, like Hegel, one draws one's historical data primarily from the Classical drama. Death is the "Lord and Master" of family life. This inversion of the existence of women in the continuity of reproductive and productive life to existential immersion in passive death is dialectical of course, for it moves from the particularity of individual life to the universal inevitability of death, but the dialectical logic in question, however impeccable, owes more to the real life activities of male supremacists than to the unfolding of Reason. The inversion leads to yet another travesty of biological reality, subsumed with a vengeance in a particular

Concept of paternity: "In a household of the ethical kind [i.e., patriarchal marriage] a woman's relationships are not based on a reference to this particular husband, this particular child, but to *a* husband, to children in *general*."[46] This is not dialectical opposition but ideological inversion, for it is, of course, *men* who are related to "children in general" and to a particular woman--the legal wife--a truly dialectical opposition mediated by marriage. The freedoms to sire and seduce are not the rewards for ethical effort, but an artificial superstructure mounted on a substructure of biological reality and sexual incontinence. Men are compelled to mediate their "freedom" of choice in paternity (whether or not to "own" the child) with the uncertainty of actual paternity. The inversion of women from the agents of life to the custodianship of the dead is matched by Hegel's inversion of the mediated synthesis of each particular woman with her particular child to a general relationship with undifferentiated children. To be sure, parturitive labor does synthesize women with the genetic reality of the species, but not in her non-laboring particularity as some man's daughter and some man's son's sister, but specifically as mother.

It is at this point that Hegel has nothing more to teach us on the subject of generic opposition, except, perhaps, what we already suspect: that even the most exalted male intellects cannot make male dominance a *rational* phenomenon. Hegel held among his philosophical aims that of abolishing the Kantian distinction between phenomena and noumena, and his objective idealism is an important step in the vital task of demythologizing worldly reality. But the noumenal Concept of paternity escapes ultimately from his analytical rigor. Though it would be extravagant to claim that the necessarily *abstract* male reproductive experience at the biological root of history guarantees the ultimate metaphysical form of the Hegelian and, indeed, all Idealist systems, it would be fair to claim that any system of thought which grounds itself in an ahistorical and idealized version of human reproduction is doomed to go through its most elaborate conceptual hoops somewhere beyond the reality of actual human experience. Hegel finally gives up on the puzzle of sexuality and regresses to the Antigone fetish, a cult of Sisterhood so extravagant and absurd that it embarrasses his most committed devotees:

> The brother . . . is in the eyes of the sister a being whose nature is unperturbed by desire and is ethically like her own. . . . The brother is the member of the family in whom its spirit becomes individualized, and enabled thereby to turn towards another sphere. . . . The brother leaves this immediate, rudimentary, and, therefore, strictly speaking, negative ethical life of the family, in order to acquire and produce the concrete ethical order which is conscious of itself.[47]

The sister stays home to mind the household gods. She is not, of course, separate from her brother's lawmaking activities; indeed, they include arrangements to stop her falling into the destructive and chaotic behavior patterns by which she had put an end to the ancient world. She is not *conscious*, however, of this role being hacked out for her in the real world by her loving brother; she only *feels love*, and as a mother will provide the feeling of love for her children. The brother, meanwhile, is acquiring in the public realm the "rights of desire," which apparently serve to keep his sexual ardor in check, for in acquiring these rights, "he keeps himself at the same time in detachment from [desire]."[48]

One cannot help reflecting that in the same year that Hegel published this affirmation of man's capacity to transcend sexual desire in the pursuit of the ethics of Universality, his own illegitimate son was born. In fairness to Hegel, it should be added that he brought the boy into the "natural ethical community" of his own household with, he claimed, the full acquiescence of his wife.[49] The fact that Hegel's own relationship with desire was less detached than his analytical intelligence suggests is less important, however, than the realities which he inverts rather than mediates. Male consciousness, however certain of itself as Man, is uncertain of itself as father, and no amount of ethical sincerity can annul this uncertainty in spiritual rectitude. In an oblique way, Hegel perhaps recognizes this, though he still directs the lack of recognition to the female parent:

> Just as the individual divine man [the historical Christ] has an implied father and only an actual mother, in like manner the universal divine man, the spiritual communion, has as its father its own proper action and knowledge, while its mother is eternal Love, which it merely *feels*, but does not behold in its consciousness as an actual immediate object.[50]

Thus the mother is etherialized and the father objectified, and the struggle against nature's tiresome negation of paternal certitude is complete.

Hegel's development as a thinker and as a man is an increasingly conservative one, a drift which starts with his admiration for Napoleon and his movement from youthful revolutionary and sexual ardor to total immersion in the higher intoxication of the Bacchanalian whirl of philosophy. By the time he writes *Philosophy of Right* he has become a rather tetchy old party committed to Law, Order, a doctrinal decency of admittedly dubious orthodoxy, and an encrusted view of the eternal reality of class and genderic inequality. The heroic figures of Napoleon the activist and Hegel the prophet of the realized Idea have yielded up their youthful vitality: on the one hand to the staid symbolism of the particular father of the people embedded in the bourgeois Constitutional Monarch; on the other hand, Universal Man, born into the world in the heady intercourse of the man of action and the man of thought and comprehended in his totality by the philosopher, has been neatly, facelessly and somewhat disappointingly realized in the new universal man, the detachedly ethical bureaucrat.

This conservative Hegel, painting grey on grey in a rather Olympian detachment, has little to offer to feminist understanding. He is a bit of a drag on the Hegelian Left, too, but parts of the Hegelian Left have, in an interesting way, sensed the erotic and reproductive undercurrents in Hegel's work. W. Thomas Darby, in a paper on the Koyre-

Kojève interpretation of Hegel, has noted the persistence with
which the image of the mythic Androgyne underlies this
particular post-Hegelian current.[51] She/he is present in the
dynamic structure of the Napoleon/Hegel ego complex and the
objectification of that unity in the universal and
homogeneous state. In this state, an existent and not a
Utopian one, Napoleon/Hegel has (have?) transcended desire
and resolved all traditional antagonisms: "active and
passive, *praxis* and theory, time and eternity, Man and God,
male and female."[52] Darby says that the sexual polarity is
"the most glaringly concrete"[53] of these, but in fact it is the
only concrete opposition in the sense of a non-abstract
polarity. The others are concrete only in the Hegelian sense
of completion by the Concept in its elaboration of itself.
Their objective content, unlike real men and women, remains
ideal. Further, one might be permitted to wonder how
generic opposition can be resolved in the unity of
interlocking *male* egos. Darby appears to recognize this
absurdity, but backs off in a suitably Hegelian way:

> To take the term [Androgyne] at face value is,
> however, too fundamentalist[!] since the term
> possesses a multi-dimensional infrastructure. The
> androgyne, the perfect being, is not one in whom
> the mere (bio-psychological) tension between the
> sexes is reconciled. Among the male principles are
> reason and action and among the female intuition
> and passivity. Too, the male presents the
> principles of destroying and creating and the
> female those of conserving and nurturing.[54]

We have argued of course that these oppositions are not at
all spiritual, but have a material base in the process of
reproduction. Male yearning for the seductive peace of
bisexuality is not creative synthesis but a cop-out, a
weariness with the costs of maintaining the desire for
dominance which is burdened by the endless expense of spirit
demanded by the maintenance of the artificial in the guise of
the natural. One wonders if these seekers after the
androgynous synthesis are aware that modern biology is

quietly eroding their symbol. It is now generally agreed that the male is an androgynized female, and that only a quite late infusion of those hormones which men have chosen to call androgens into particular female fetuses creates the masculine. Early forms of life appear to be exclusively bodies feminine.

As Hegel grows old like Time itself, his Universal man tires a little of his apocalyptic quest and lapses into a rather tremulous particularity in his quest to "count as a man by virtue of his manhood alone."[55] Further, as Darby notes, the ultimate unity of Hegel and Napoleon is a sterile unity.[56] Hegel has "recognized" Napoleon, but Napoleon never did recognize Hegel, and perhaps Hegel senses that indeed the recognized conquerors of the world will enslave also those who comprehend them in thought. In any case, the ultimate unity of all opposition in the union of Napoleon and Hegel has a much more commonsense sterility than that implied in the notion of the end of *history*. That particular union cannot make any more little tools of Reason, and not history but the *race* which is its material base will perish.

Hegel's is probably the greatest and most sustained attempt to rationalize and perfect the tradition of male-stream thought and to justify the definition of creative humanity as "Man." Yet even Hegel cannot resolve men's reproductive dilemma, and he only abstractly resolves their existential one, created by the definition of the human historical task as being that of mastering and possessing Nature rather than rationally and lovingly nurturing a balanced unity with "Her." Nonetheless, Hegel is not just a historical monument or a stuffed Owl. He has taught us that reproductive process is dialectical. He has shown us, sometimes by default, the structure of man's struggle to weld his potency with his purpose in his struggle with alienation, uncertainty and non-recognition. He has shown us that there is a dialectical opposition between the social realities of production and reproduction, an insight Marx unfortunately missed. He has shown us why Life yields to Death as the primordial male experience. In doing these things, he offers us a historical ground and a philosophical foundation for a new transcendent philosophy of Birth and Life which must be the theoretical component of the feminist *praxis* which history now commands us to develop.

NOTES

[1]Excerpted with permission from mimeograph, "Group for Research on Women Paper No. 12," Ontario Institute for Studies in Education, 1977.

[2]G. W. F. Hegel, *The Phenomenology of Mind*, translated by J. B. Baillie (New York: Harper & Row, 1967 (1807)). Hereinafter referred to in footnotes as *Phen.*

The following abbreviations are used in this paper for Hegel's other works:

Love; G. W. F. Hegel, "On Love," *Early Theological Writings*, translated by T. M. Knox (Chicago: University of Chicago Press, 1948).

System; G. W. F. Hegel, "The System of Ethical Life," translated by T. M. Knox and H. S. Harris, unpublished, 1975.

P. of R.; G. W. F. Hegel, *Hegel's Philosophy of Right*, translated by T. M. Knox (New York: Oxford University Press, 1967 (1821)).

I would like to thank Professor Harris for permission to make use of his translation, and also his invaluable unpublished essay, "Introductory Essay to Hegel's 'The System of Ethical Life'" (1975). Like all students of Hegel's early writings, I also owe an immeasurable debt to Harris for his work in this heretofore rather misty area: H. S. Harris, *Hegel's Development: toward the sunlight* (Oxford: Clarendon Press, 1972).

[3]Whether Marxist theory is an adequate ground for such *praxis* is too large a question to be tacked on to a discussion of Hegel. However, it should be noted in passing that Marx does not transcend Hegel's generic one-sidedness, and may not, indeed, have so clear a notion of the dialectical structure of reproduction as Hegel has. Marx's theory is a prodigious exercise in the logic of necessity, but necessity has two poles, production and reproduction, and Marx conflates them.

[4]Plato's discussion is in *The Republic*, Book VIII, S546. For a discussion of the role of rites of "marriage" (*telete*) in the all-male mystery cults, see George Thomson, *Aeschylus and Athens* (New York: Haskell House Publishers, 1967), p. 127 and *passim.*

[5]Hegel finally dealt more broadly with the *Philosophy of Nature*, in which a more developed misogyny is historicized in a romantic vision of pre-history. A more elaborate feminist critique of his work on reproduction which centers on this work is my *The Politics of Reproduction.*

[6]The quotation is from the 1805-1806 lectures, which are not translated. It is quoted by George Armstrong Kelly, "Notes on Hegel's Lordship and Bondage" in Alistair MacIntyre, ed., *Hegel* (New York: Anchor Books, 1972), p. 198.

[7]T. M. Knox's explication of these terms cannot be improved upon. I have borrowed freely from it, but in a compressed way. See Knox's "Introduction" to *P. of R.*, especially pp. vii-x.

[8]*Idee*, to be distinguished from *Vorstellung*, which is idea in the sense of what one is thinking about--there is no such distinction in English.

[9]Simone de Beauvoir, *The Second Sex*, translated by H. M. Parshley (New York, Alfred Knopf, 1961(1949)), esp. p. 59 et. seq. where de Beauvoir argues that the Master and Slave argument applies much better to the relation of man and woman. De Beauvoir notes correctly that Hegel's discussion of sexuality argues from significance to necessity instead of the other way round (Ibid., p. 4). De Beauvoir's own error is to argue from *sexuality* to significance, neglecting the formal unity of reproductive process in which sexuality is but one aspect of the whole. See also p. 16 infra.

[10]Ultimately, there is a curious dialectical structure to Hegel's Universal notion of paternity, which is too obscure and extensive to be worked out here. Briefly, there is a suggestion of some kind of ideological inversion going on between the Concepts of Divine and mere biological paternity. In this process, Religion becomes Concrete, a unity of spiritual and actual, whereas human marriage

becomes essentially spiritual. It is very difficult to "prove" textually that this is what happens, and such a demonstration requires a theological sophistication and knowledge of Hegel's religious writings which I cannot claim to possess.

[11]*Phen.*, B. IV. A. De Beauvoir's argument (p. 12, f.m. *supra* that the Master and Slave parable would be more apt in a male/female context than in man and man, is, I think, a misunderstanding, for women are already "mastered," and without a struggle. They have no "separability" from the other to negate, for their tie to others (kin) is complete and their Universality in this limited sphere Conceptually complete (de Beauvoir, Ibid., p. 49 et. seq.).

[12]Of course, modes of contraception have existed for a long time, and many feminists have argued that these have been deliberately suppressed by men. In Hegelian terminology, these have been particular modes of contraception, but contemporary technology can realize "universal" contraception, a fact which profoundly transforms the social relations of reproduction.

[13]*Phen.*, VI. A. a.b.c.

[14]See Harris, op. cit., pp. 34-35, for a clearer account of Hegel's very opaque discussion of the structure of need as opposed to desire. Mere need, immediate gratification, is a subsumption of intuition under the Concept, logically and developmentally prior to the release of the intelligently directed labor which includes foresight as to future needs in productive terms. Reproductively, men and women are "equal" at the animal, intuitive state, but they are not "absolutely equal" (*System*, 425). It is never really clear just why.

[15]*System*, 421.

[16]The interjections in parentheses are mine. The textual interpolations in brackets are the translator's.

[17]*System*, 424, 425.

[18]Ibid., 425.

[19]Men, of course, are not wholly Universal in their Particularity, which includes biological needs, is concerned and ultimately socialized in Civil Society of existing with but transcended by political society, which is the realization of Man's Universality.

[20]*Love*, p. 307

[21]*Love*, p. 305.

[22]This is not the case in *P. of R.* (p. 112), where a distinction is made between ethical (married) lovers and mere philanderers, whose "physical passion sinks to the level of a physical moment, destined to vanish in its very satisfaction. On the other hand, the spiritual bond of union secures its rights as the substance of marriage, and thus rises, inherently indissoluble, to a plane above the transience of passion and the transience of particular caprice."

[23]*Love*, p. 305.

[24]*Love*, p. 307.

[25]*Love*, p. 307.

[26]*System*, 437, 438.   See also Harris, op. cit., p. 9. Possessions are realized, of course, by virtue of the alienated labor which is their essential content.

[27]"The pure infinity of legal right, its inseparability, reflected in the thing, i.e., in the particular itself, is the thing's *equality* with other things, and the abstraction of this equality of one thing with another, concrete unity and legal right, is *value*; . . . but the actually found and empirical measure is the *price.*" *System*, p. 437.

[28]*Love*, p. 307.

[29]Ibid.

[30]*Phen.*, p. 496.

[31]*Phen.*, p. 496.

[32]*Phen.*, p. 497.

[33]Ibid.

[34]*Phen.*, p. 496.

[35]*Phen.*, p. 497.

[36]Karl Marx, *Capital*, I. 3. VII.1.

[37]That this reality is a covert substratum to male-stream thought even at its most recondite levels, as well as its more overt manifestations in myth and literature, constitutes an uncovering challenge to feminist scholarship.

[38]The very long history of an association between the male ejaculation and death appears to have been of interest mainly to psychoanalysis.   Philip Slater, for example, is astonished that such a pervading literary and cultic theme

should be rooted in such a "trivial" reality. Slater does not recognize himself as the heir to centuries of alienation. See Philip Slater, *The Glory of Hera: Greek mythology and the Greek family* (Boston: Beacon Press, 1971). Apart from this brief opacity, this book is a very valuable study for students of the ideology of male supremacy.

[39]Thomas Hobbes, *Leviathan* (Harmondsworth: Penguin Books, 1968 (1651)), I. XIII.

[40]*System*, 449-460.

[41]Harris, op. cit., p. 50. In the interests of lucidity, I follow Harris' interpretive essay here, though in a simplified and perhaps over-simplified way. Harris notes some of the difficulties and ambiguities of Hegel's analysis, including the opacity which attends the emphasis put on single combat when Hegel appears to have already moved from the level of the family to that of society.

[42]Ibid., p. 62.

[43]Strictly, havoc is the second form: the first is individual combat, trial by combat in the *System*. In *The Phenomenology*, of course, it is our friends the Master and Slave.

[44]Ibid., p. 54.

[45]*Phen.*, pp. 471-472.

[46]*Phen.*, p. 476.

[47]*Phen.*, p. 477.

[48]Ibid.

[49]The young man does not appear to have been very happy, and died, with chilling appropriateness, a soldier's death from fever.

[50]*Phen.*, p. 784.

[51]W. Thomas Darby, "The 'New World' of Kojève's Hegel," paper read at the Edinburgh Congress of the International Political Science Association, August 1976.

[52]Ibid., p. 14.

[53]Ibid.

[54]Ibid.

[55]*P. of R.*, p. 134, #209.

[56]Darby, op. cit., p. 15.

PART THREE

Women, Health, and

Education

11

Learning to Win

One of the most important things I have learned about nurses since I switched careers in 1970 is that there is no such thing as an ex-nurse. Technically, of course, one quits, leaves, ceases to become a practitioner, even drops one's hard-earned license. Nurses do these things in significant numbers. Yet at a deeper personal and social level, the integrity, the we-ness of nurses, the sense of community is something which never seems to fade. When I meet a woman who says "I'm a nurse", I almost always answer "So am I". So I hope the reader will forgive me if I refer to "us," even if this is technically inaccurate. We-ness is more than organization, more than sentiment, more than shared interests, more than occupational solidarity: internally we are often healthily quarrelsome! But as a professional group operating under work conditions and a work structure imposed by others, we have had to battle for status and control of our work processes, and we have not always nor perhaps even frequently been victors in these battles. We have often found ourselves in environments in which our services are seen as a bit like mothering: absolutely necessary but somehow rather trivial. Working through this

---

Address to the Registered Nurses Association of Ontario in 1981.

contradiction of being both essential and low-status has
meant that strategies for change have never been clear-cut
and non-controversial.   Think, for example, of bitter
disagreements around the issue of unionization, of diverse
views about apprenticeship training and post-secondary
education, of attempts to redefine what we do in such
perceptions of team nursing, nursing process, total care,
whole patients and so forth.   Add to these the tensions
created by shift-work and the rapid development of divisions
in the theory and practice of what used to be called the core
task: all of these strains and others have made nursing a
high-stress occupation and the phrase "burn out" has become
one to which most nurses have an instant and visceral
response.

Yet despite all these and other divisive issues, nurses seem
to me to have retained a sense of "we-ness" which is
something deeper than the simple urge to close ranks against
a hostile world; something even more profound than the
shared humanitarian impulse which the ideologies of science
and technique have failed to extinguish. What I think binds
us, both current and ex-practitioners, is a shared but not
always articulated conviction that good health is the
necessary pre-condition of a good society, not only on ethical
but on very practical grounds. This view, instead of being
recognized as a legitimate and thoughtful piece of social
analysis, is often dismissed as mere sentiment. Yet nursing
solidarity, I think, does exist precisely because nurses
manage, often in the teeth of adversary forces, to unify
individual commitment with social good sense. That unity is
forceful and yet problematic, because it has to be put in
practice in a society where good health *is* perceived in much
the same way as motherhood is perceived. It is so obviously a
"good thing" that it can be taken for granted that no more
needs to be said; it is so obviously "necessary" that there is
no good arguing about what it actually means or how it is to
be attained. Health, like motherhood, is perceived as a gift of
nature rather than as historical creations wrought by human
action: society's job is simply to step in as Nature's
surrogate when things don't seem to be following the old
lady's prescriptions.   It is profoundly significant that the

vocations of being Nature's natural helpers in such fields as childbearing and rearing and caring for the sick are assigned to women. The *jobs* of assigning meanings to these things, of explaining how such essential services are so little rewarded and of fixing them when they go wrong: all of these are male responsibilities of high prestige and concrete rewards.

I have used this controversial word "vocation" quite deliberately, understanding it as signifying less a labour of love than working for nothing. For many years now nurses have properly distrusted the term, recognizing that to have a vocation has meant historically an exclusion from the ranks of those who work creatively and purposefully as well as for suitable economic reward. Vocational work is stuck in the realm of merely responding to necessity, and is much less prestigious than the innovative tasks of, say, making history. Yet the notion of nursing as a vocational commitment dies hard. A couple of years ago I was invited to speak to the Social Planning Council in a small Ontario town on the subject of health care. After delivering what I thought was a pretty good analysis of the dire results of the transformation from health care to the sickness industry, one of the women in the audience popped up as soon as questions were called for to ask if I did not *really* think that nursing was a vocation. Keeping my cool as best I could, I made one of these typically academic responses: that is to say, I moved the question into a different, in this case historical, context. I referred soberly and with much respect to the influence of Florence Nightingale on the development of professional nursing then went on to make a few critical remarks on the ideology of lamp-carrying manic-depressives. I referred to the unfortunate implications for nursing of the fact that the profession was not Miss Nightingale's major interest, and that the submerging of her concern for nursing into her wider concern for reorganizing the British army in an inflexible hierarchical structure had some unfortunate results for nurses. I went on to note that despite the problematic nature of this legacy, many nurses still wore the black bands of mourning for Miss Nightingale on their caps. I pointed out that she was really a much stronger and quite different woman than the ghostly legend suggested. I referred to her quite recently published letters, in which she boasted of having slept with women of every social class and nationality all over Europe. This rather heavy bit of debunking successfully closed off the conversation on vocation, but it also confused the local press. The following week they reported the event thus: Professor O'Brien said that Florence Nightingale claimed to have slept with women all over Europe and this is why nurses wear black bands on their hats!

We cannot, of course, hold Ms. Nightingale responsible for the limiting organizational forms in which health care has developed, nor indeed for the class bias which led her to want nurses to be ladies first and professionals only in the rather limited sense of doing nasty work with grace and tough-mindedness. We must always, I think, understand the historical context of the Sickness Industry as something a great deal more vital than an academic structure. The bureaucratic model for getting things done is endemic in complex industrial societies, both capitalist and socialist. It is an integral part of the development of the modern state and the proliferation of state political control into all the areas of existence. The modern state is a very innovative development, for it has transformed crude authoritarian rule by the strategy of procuring the consent of the governed to its policies and practices. While this is clearly an improvement on overt violent control, it obscures the fact that armed intervention is always available if consent is not forthcoming. We had a startling and bitter glimpse of the realities of political power here in Canada in 1972. In the October Crisis of 1972, French-Canadian nationalist groups murdered a Quebec politician and kidnapped an English diplomat. Pierre Eliot Trudeau, the Prime Minister at that time, advised Canadians to "read Sophocles" while he deployed Canada's tiny army on the streets of Montreal. The United States diplomatically moved troops to the south bank of the St. Lawrence river. We who labour in the sub-systems of the state must recognize that while we may not be subject to direct coercion, our institutions are very actively engaged in this business of the organization of consent. Thus, the proposition that what is now coming to be known as the "medical model of health care" is the only possible way--imperfect in detail though it can be acknowledged to be--is still the only rational, efficient and--blessed word--scientific method of attending to the health of the people. Old notions of shared caring and communal concern are only instances of the motherhood syndrome--charming in principle, hopeless in practice.

A letter recently appeared in the *Globe and Mail*, Canada's national print medium for the organization of the consent of the governed, from the secretary of the section on pediatrics of the Ontario Medical Association, rumbling on predictably about the dangers of home birth. This was done by very crude juxtaposition of dubious statistics, the triumph of computer symbols over language and common discourse. The good doctor refers to the practices of midwives as "primitive and bucolic", which is odd language, as much of the current home-birth movement is urban. Perhaps one should not be surprised that he doesn't know the meaning of the word bucolic: it is a long time since to be a well-educated person meant ease and precision with language, and the much vaunted statistical literacy seems to be indifferent to the death of actual literacy. The danger is that people think that they are expressing truth rather than guessing at the meaning of data. This notion of either/or, science or culture, is, in my view, both dangerous and slack minded, which is also the inadequacy of the consent model of the exercise of power--you have not only to buy the ideology but conform to the prescribed practice. Any other course is "primitive and bucolic". I suspect that by "primitive" the pediatrician meant under the control of women. What I want to suggest is that notions of caring and community control are *not* incompatible with either rationality nor scientific practice nor effective organization. They *are* incompatible with the notion that only one way of doing things controlled by one section of the community is the only way. What I think we have to do is to attempt to understand why the perceived incompatibility of organization and humanism comes to be understood as insurmountable and, more importantly, what might be done to challenge the actual power to define what knowledge and reality ought to be.

In practice, the bureaucracies which organize social life and individual choice owe their dominance to a wide range of controlling and manipulating factors: at the same time they may have to be able to convince us that we in fact make free choices or, at the very least, concede that, though nothing is perfect, we are all doing our very best. Another way to say this is to invoke the sociological cliché that institutions may claim legitimacy by virtue of their rationality, effectiveness in goal achievement, internal efficiency and commitment to the shared values of the society in which we live. Thus, a very broad range of human needs can be met organizationally--the need for social order, of course, but also the economy, social welfare, health, art, warfare, charity, education; all of these, and you can all add to that list, are seen as creating merely logistical dilemmas which have to be managed. Human needs are not seen as posing ethical and political problems which have to be acted on. You will notice that I have not included the venerable institution of the family in my list of social structures, for the conditions of social order are perceived to include not only the separation of private from public life, itself an organized and changing division which presents particular problems for women, but also the notion of health as private and illness as public. I shall want to return to that question, but let me note here that the claim that bureaucracy is rational obscures the sheer inefficiency of most bureaucracies, while the commitment to efficient health care delivery systems permits a gloss to be spread over older fashioned notions like justice and equality.

The claim to the scientific objectivity of organizational procedures makes it possible to shrug off--regretfully but firmly--the expression of personal or subjective criticisms by health care workers, which are redefined as the mere products of an enlightened self-interest. For example, claims that less stressful organization of working hours would benefit patient care cannot be taken seriously, for the definition of nursing care is already written in granite by some invisible force higher up the hierarchical ladder, disregarding the actual, experienced, day-to-day social relations of the agents or patients of health care systems.

The passion for order, that most intransigently conservative of political and organizational principles, permits all alternative options in terms of work organization to be dismissed as disruptive of the orderly achievement of institutional goals, thus obscuring the fact that institutions don't *have* goals: people do. But the presumed consensus that order for order's sake is a high priority for every thinking person is deemed to be absolute, and blind loyalty is thus a greater virtue than imagination or creativity.

We are all familiar, both theoretically and from our work experience, with the general trends of bureaucratic organization: centralization, well-defined pecking orders, obsession with technical problem-solving, the division of labour, the tendency for what is written to be considered more real than what actually happens. The phrase "scientific management" certainly sounds more benign than the more correct description of management technique as the exercise of raw power. The effect of scientific management on scientific health care is a very complex business. Tycoons in the business world operate above the bureaucracies which they control and which do the executive hatchet stuff and direct the people who actually produce. Similarly, the medical profession operates both inside and outside of bureaucratic structure: inside for power, outside for education, professional organization and rewards. With this inside/outside high-wire stuff, the medical profession exercises much power in health bureaucracies in terms of being able to prescribe not only treatments but *meanings*. Doctor power, even in its most primitive magical forms, has always rested on the consent of a given society to the power of medical men to give definition to what is health and what is illness and to claim these definitions as the only legitimate, certified ones. This power to name, to prescribe meaning, is the rockbed on which all political and social power rests. It also permits a hefty claim on social goods and resources, which helps to maintain that power over the generations. Beyond doctor power, health administrators have far outstripped the social and economic gains of other health workers. Doctors control knowledge and administrators control the actual work process, and both

work in close co-operation with the economic forces which
have found that the sickness industry is a very lucrative
market.

This control of work process is enormously important both
in conserving existing power relations and in the business of
organizing consent. The major strategy for this sort of
control is the ever more refined division of labour, developed
originally by--and powerfully symbolized by--the assembly
line, but now penetrating every kind of productive work.
This is why we spend so much time revising job descriptions,
which become longer and more lugubrious as the actual task
shrinks--it's always possible to throw in a few principles and
a bit of philosophy in a job description to achieve the goal of
never giving workers credit for all that they actually do and
to make sure that they understand what limited power over
the work process they actually have. Each part of each task
is carefully wiggled out of the whole, dusted off, analyzed,
isolated, described in a document, timed, costed, specialized
and assigned to a particular worker. It is reported in the
press that attempts are now being made to separate and cost
the symptoms of particular diseases and the time allotments
needed for attention to predictable vagaries of specific bodily
functions: we are close to computerized bowel control and a
scan of the proper way to throw a fit. There is, of course, a
heavy strain of irony in all this for nurses. Back in the
1940s, my generation was complaining because we were
supposed to do everything, but the remodeling of the work
process and the extreme division of labour which are features
of current administrative utopias tend towards the ideal
situation in which one worker does one thing all the time.
This was hardly the solution we sought.

The real effects of all this on the actual job are better
known to you than to me: the time spent in learning the
ever-changing rules and policies, in deciphering and
interpreting the directives, in providing data for more of the
same, learning one's place in constantly shifting work
procedures, checking that others are not invading shrinking
areas of responsibility, trying to win back lost prerogatives.
But most important is the fact that the whole thing never
really works: the tremendous gaps which the splendid,

totalitarian control process has managed to leave in the lived realities of health care must all be filled in. These gaps are precisely where the destructive fires of burn-out are kindled in those who have to deal with them whether they are on the schedule or not.

The management task of organizing consent is also complex. This is what is often called ideological control: the proposition that in general we have the best possible system and that any modifications have to do with particular problems which can be worked out within defined parameters of action. This process is primitively political, and the dominant model is the State itself. I have time only to touch on a couple of features of this complex system. I have already referred to the need to conserve the capacity to legitimize what is to be known as true, good and desirable in the hands of the controllers of the system. Consent relies on a perception by the public that, imperfect though a system may be, it is the only game in town. This does not imply that people in general are blind and stupid: it is because the medical model uses its power to create the appearance that it *is* the only game in town. Immense political energy is devoted to seeing that alternatives are nipped in the bud, rendered ridiculous, and never adequately funded. We may also note the tactic of co-option, which permits selected workers access to the lower levels of decision-making process: for example, we are not privy to a decision to cut staff, but our expertise is necessary to the working out of how staff cuts can be managed in the workplace. This is known as responsibility.

The medical profession also practices a tactic of fear: fear on the part of sick people who are convinced that health knowledge is so abstruse and inaccessible that they'll drop dead in short order if they don't get the right guy at once. Nurses assuage such fear for all of their working lives but their ability to do so effectively is constantly eroded by the ideology of medical omnipotence. There is also the real fear among health workers that the failure to conform with policies which limit personal work options--shift work, specialization--may mean loss of earning power. Then there is the reward system in which the hierarchy is constantly redefined and the gradations get tinier and tinier; endless and quite often meaningless categories are added to the pecking order to give individuals a sense of promotion, perhaps a little more money, but usually a large increase in responsibility-without-power. Another important tactic in the general strategy of consensual politics is the control of education, which is given some latitude for innovation as long as it does not challenge the basic structure nor the primacy of organization, technique, scientism, certified knowledge and hierarchical control. In my own workplace we are encouraged to study, improve and even reform educational practice, even to criticize it. The notion that we perhaps need to break up the whole system may even be voiced, though not too often. In any case, the Ministry of Education is supremely confident that the public approves of education in general, which it properly does, and educational bureaucracies can easily scorn radical suggestions as absurd and destructive proposals to tamper with the sacred right to education, and dissident intellectuals as having a long history of ineffectualness.

The picture I have painted is a dark one, and some of you may think it exaggerated. I don't believe it is exaggerated. Far more importantly, I think that there are signs that the prevailing consensus--the view that the medical model of health care is the best and only model--is beginning to show signs of fraying at the edges. It is my considered view that progressive forces in health care are beginning to emerge. They have always been there of course, and a lot of people at this conference have worn themselves out being part of them. There are signs that these activities are consolidating, and I want to share with you my view that the nursing profession is in the vanguard of this historic process. In fact, I see nurses at this time as the only major organized group which has the courage, the coherence, the experience, the true knowledge to deny the consensus, to say this is not the only possible system and it is not anywhere near the best that we can do. My we-ness springs proudly to life when I read--in small paragraphs to be sure but no longer necessarily in the women's section--that nursing leaders are telling it like it is, most recently in a measured but clearly passionate rejection of the imposition of user fees on patients. I glow when I see nursing groups in the marches--International Women's Day, peace marches, anti-nuclear marches: there we are, standing up and being counted. It is my view that increasing numbers of nurses will become involved with these movements and will bring critical intelligence and political will to the struggle for a new definition of health. I think it is nurses who will challenge the medico-bureaucratic mess in which the sickness industry currently languishes.

This is not a guess, but a reading of evidence--social, not statistical evidence. There are many reasons why this development is taking place, and many more why it is a difficult and slow and often willfully obscured process. Let me speak briefly of what I see as very significant developments of recent years.

Nurses have become increasingly politicized in a number of very concrete ways. This is something more than the single-issue politics in which all particular interest groups indulge. There are important professional interests around, for example, the Canada Health Act; but nurses are not resisting the Canada Health Act because it shafts nurses, but because it enshrines a limited and even dangerous definition of health. Particular issues are, of course, important, but politicization is also a response to the general definition which has been imposed upon nurses in the last few decades. Sustained attempts to "professionalize" nursing in terms of educational strategies, the redefinition of the "core task", and the struggles for decent pay have all in practice had mixed results. It would be too crude an exaggeration to say that we now have better-educated nurses doing more restricted jobs, but it is fair, I think, to argue that there has been a clear erosion of nurses' areas of responsibility, status and control of work process. The proliferation of medical technicians has shrunk the nursing role, and I would argue that what has been added on is division: separate and higher specialties (for example, in OR and intensive care) and a greater administrative role whose real function can be understood as the persuading of nurses to accept the new definition of who they are. Further, the division of labour has been at work within nursing. The system has had only indifferent success in replacing the exploited labour of the students in the old apprenticeship system, and questions of the scope and responsibilities of the various levels of nursing auxiliaries are difficult and divisive. It is quite clear even to external observers that auxiliaries are presented as cheaper and just as effective as professional nurses. But I would argue that the systematic fracturing of the coherence of the nursing task has had the salutary effect of forcing nurses to scrutinize the conditions of their work and their strategies for professionalization. This process has led to an increasing sense of solidarity in a political rather than sentimental or professional sense, the need to make a cold-eyed estimate not only of work process but of social standing and public reputation. To put it another way, in a search for an autonomous rather than an imposed definition of who they are, nurses have had to confront their institutional powerlessness and are less inclined to buy myths about "informal" power and influence--that we have our own cute little ways of getting the right pill in the right mouth, that we really push patients around quite a lot.

Closely woven with these developments has been the relatively swift embracing of union activism. When I left the profession in 1971 it was still quite difficult to find nurses who did not believe that union membership represented a loss of status, and who really believed that education was the road to climbing up the class ladder while unions meant falling down it. Large sections of what is falsely called the Canadian middle class have learned lessons about this the hard way--including, I may say, academics. To be sure, post-secondary education has produced excellent research and significant development in nursing care, but it has done so, in my view, at the cost of further splitting of the profession, creating an elite corps of nurses who lurk rather uneasily between management and practitioner categories. Still, despite these tensions, the mixed results of the educational strategy are basically positive. Education can produce new and successful recruits to bureaucratic conformity, but at the same time it provides the weapons for the critical analysis which many nurses have turned on the system. In the language of the organization of consent, education creates both consenters and dissenters, and this is a healthy trend in terms of innovative practice and leadership. The combination of increasing work dissatisfaction, the development of managerial skills, education and union activity are all factors which tend to make people turn to political interpretations and strategies.

At the same time, the emergence of feminism as a political force has had an obvious impact on this most feminine of professions. The fact that doctor power is patriarchally structured and that the managers who have crept into the administration-by-documentation process are mostly men is now seen by many of us as both problematic and political, political in the most vulgar sense of the crude usurpation of power. It is interesting here to compare the two traditional women's professions of nursing and teaching. My colleague Dorothy Smith's work shows that there has been a quite thorough and rapid takeover of the teaching profession by men since the economic gains for which women teachers struggled for so long became available. These men have appropriated executive posts--which have proliferated--consultant status and principalships, control of mixed teacher organizations, and all in very short order. Women teachers are losing ground. The problem in nursing looks less severe, for the increase in the numbers of male nurses, while significant, is much less than in teaching. It would be naive to take comfort from this, though; unlike teachers, the men who manage large numbers of nurses do not bother even to acquire nursing qualifications: they are administrators, systems analysts, personnel managers, time and motion study types and assorted esoteric manipulators. Men who practice tend also to favor technological specializations which are prestigious. They have also, with the Viet Nam war as inspiration, invented the new category of "medic", in which ten months training in a community college equips mostly male graduates for a health job which pays more than a nurse can earn after three years or more in university.

The recognition of and resistance to this kind of masculine workplace imperialism which has been generally recognized in the women's movement is reflected in health care by an increasingly critical analysis of medical and administrative pretensions and practices and by an increasing assertion of self-worth bolstered by sisterhood among nurses, as well as women in general. The innovative political strategy known as networking, which is one of feminism's major achievements, has led to co-operation between nurses and other groups, but has also been creatively developed by nurses in terms of particular issues: the Canada Health Act struggle, the midwife struggle (although we have to be careful not to let this one divide women), affirmative action groups and many others. Networking is the organization of dissent, the process by which women begin to see common collective interests which break down institutional and occupational barriers. Most radically, the artificial barrier between public and private life, which I believe to be the social lynchpin of male supremacy, begins to crumble. This magic barrier has already been breached by the number of married women entering the work force, a process which also exposes the class myths in which many dubious professionals have been seduced into making a merely ideological distinction between middle- and working-class status. The real definition of a profession is work controlled by and in the interests of men. The notion that wives "don't have to work" has been an important element of "professional" class consciousness. Like middle management, the middle class is a powerful tool in the manufacturing of consent, in this case to the inevitability and desirability of class division and patriarchal power. Back in the sanguine 1950s, it was popular to say in North America that we are all middle class now. In fact, that myth becomes increasingly difficult to uphold in the teeth of economic ineptitude and the transformations in work process wrought by the reliance on technique and the systematic degrading of human contact as skill.

The networking process which gathers women together brings laypeople into health concerns just as it takes nurses into wider social movements. In this process, we learn the political and organizational skills which enhance those already learned in professional organizations and unions. I think that increasing numbers of nurses recognize that professional exclusiveness is in fact a divide and rule tactic which must be resisted. The progressive nature of this still early and partial but already inexorable development is reflected in the new and exciting notion that service to patients is not simply care but a political service related to the civil right of good health care. The dichotomy is not in-fact between hands-on care and management skill: these are both essential and need to be unified and redefined in a non-hierarchical way. But the condition of such a unification is the radicalization of health care, the creating of alternative ways of keeping both individuals and the body politic in healthy equilibrium.

Which brings us to the third area of the radicalization of nurses: the development of the alternative health care movement. Nurses have been and are involved in many of these controversies: the movement for reproductive integrity, labelled by patriarchs and the crummier sorts of politicians as the abortion movement. Attempts to change this imposed limited image have not been too successful, and the language of "choice" is less resonant than the conservative carol about right to life. But we should at least call it the abortion plus movement, for it is of critical importance to us as women and as nurses and involves far more than abortion. There is also movement for the restoration and/or extension of midwifery, for community health care, industrial and environmental health and nutritional and fitness movements. These are the issues which the sickness industry cannot address--and it is not merely cynical to note that there is no immediate profit in them. Alternative health movements tend to unmask the raw power which lurks behind political consensus: nothing disturbs the power brokers of the medical model so much as alternative health care proposals (except perhaps suggestions that they let more people into medical school or content themselves with more modest remuneration). It is worth remembering that the National Health Act introduced in Britain after the Second World War proposed a health structure which gave equal weight to prevention and treatment of illness. It is now popular to say that the British Health Service has failed, but of course the truth is that one-half of the act--prevention--was never implemented. It is for this reason that the notion that state intervention alone can change perceptions of health care is problematic. This has nothing to do with the propriety or politics of state intervention. Of course we must use the State where we can, but we must also name those vague "powers that be" and confront them. In other words, we must work both within and against the State.

While the issues that I raise here are common knowledge among us, the notion of overt public political solutions is newer to us, as women and as workers. Conventional, within-the-system spaces for innovation and change are inadequate for tackling the problem of the unification of individual and collective health. We cannot simply abandon older strategies any more than we can walk out of the institutional arrangements of the sickness industry. What we did first was learn that we had a lot to learn. We have expended far too much energy, personally, professionally and politically, in winning far too little; in fact, even in losing some of the authority and public respect we once had, for as the public disillusionment with health care provisions has spread, some of it has stuck to our ancient profession. But I think it must be said that as both women and as workers we have in the past been taught to lose. What we are learning out of the stress and bitterness of this experience is how to win.

We know very well that this is a collective enterprise, not only for nurses but in fact for our species. In health terms the human species is rapidly becoming an endangered species, and we work in a social system which attempts to cover up these real dangers. It does this by insisting that health is a matter for individuals and that curing is more useful than prevention. Think for a moment about the cancer problem. The individualistic ideology of medical-model health care says that cancer is a disease which afflicts individuals, that the cause is not yet fully known, and that only specific, medically controlled therapies are even partly effective. It follows logically that the object of cancer research is to find an individual cure. The fact is, of course, that cancer is a historically and economically specific disease induced by the environments of advanced industrialism, that individual cures are an unscientific lottery, and that prevention rather than cure is the only rational strategy. However, given the causes of cancer, the prevention of the disease can only be achieved through political strategies, the disciplining of the powerful forces which pollute the environment for profit. There are few more obvious examples of the irrationality and inhumanity of the medical model than the plight of the victims of the cancer epidemic.

What is to be done? Powerlessness tends to breed in the first instance a sense of hopelessness and inaction: we are so concerned with the immensity of the challenge that we do not even notice for a while that we are changing things. We pessimistically believe that change is usually for the worse, for we look at the bizarre and exploitative changes wrought by the powerful and find them terrifying and debilitating. Further, we have to go on in the daily struggle, often beyond the rocky edge of strength and understanding, to try to reconcile the conservation of our personal dignity with the conditions of our work, to do our best for people's health in circumstances which we do not control. We are always being exhorted to "change our attitudes". What our we-ness and our growing political awareness has taught us, I think, is that those attitudes are in fact a rational response to the lived circumstances of our lives. Change is never wrought by the changing of individual attitudes, but by collective political action to change the lived conditions which breed attitudes. It is by this solidarity, this shared activity, the analysis and transformation of institutions, of power bases, of the definition by others of what is to become acceptable knowledge and transformative practice: it is this sort of approach which can teach us to win. With our experienced sense of the inadequacy of health care, of the shallowness of the accepted definition of health, of our own enormous collective potential, of our opportunity to break the bonds of occupational isolation; with all of these, united with a historical movement of resistance to the outworn ideology of man versus nature, we are ready to win, learning to win.

12

Hegemony Theory and
the Reproduction of Patriarchy

Hegemony theory and the notion of cultural reproduction have engaged the attention of feminists for a number of reasons. The first of these is the perceived shortcomings of contemporary Marxism. The most significant of these shortcomings is the transformation of structural dialectics to an ideological structuralism, a mode of thought which has tended to obliterate historical action in theoretical abstractions, a process trenchantly analyzed in E. P. Thompson's critique of Althusser.[1] Structuralism has also tended to obliterate women and grant to language an epistemological primacy which fails to notice the masculinist bias of all symbolic systems. Second, the fixation on class structure in the positivist mode, which we find in the "correspondence theory" of Samuel Bowles and Herbert

Excerpted with permission from "Civil Society, Education and the Reproduction of Patriarchy," *Critical Pedagogy and Cultural Power* David Livingstone, ed. (South Hadley, Mass.: Bergin & Garvey Publ., 1987), pp. 41-54; and from "The Commatization of Women: Patriarchal Fetishism in the Sociology of Education," *Interchange*, 15 no. 2 (1984), pp. 43-60. An early version was presented to the Canadian Research Institute for the Advancement of Women at Ottawa in 1982. Excerpted with permission from the proceedings, "Hegemony and Superstructure: A Feminist Critique of Neo-Marxism," *Taking Sex Into Account: The Policy Consequences of Sexist Research*, Jill Vickers, ed. (Ottawa: Carleton University Press, 1984) pp. 85-100.

Gintis,[2] for example, leaves little room for serious analysis of the significance of other social realities for educational practice. This provokes the strategy which I have called elsewhere "commatization," in which social activities related to race comma gays comma gender comma are simply added to class, with no attempt to analyze the actual relations and differentiation of progressive cross-class movement.[3] A third area of concern is the analysis of state power.[4] All of these considerations have significant impacts on education at many levels.

The debt of Marxist sociology of education to the theoretical work of Antonio Gramsci arises from Gramsci's important attempt to develop a more adequate theory of the modern state and the processes of consensual politics.[5] The conception of "civil society" in Gramsci's work also has clear resonances with the feminist concern with the structure and dialectic of public and private life. However, Gramsci postulates school and family as the major institution of civil society, but his analysis pays a great deal more attention to education than it does to family. The contemporary hegemony school is "sympathetic" to women, but the genuine desire to transcend the limitations of correspondence theory and abstract structuralism is seriously at risk where activist male educators are to replace sedentary male philosophers in the uncovering of the truth about truth-making. Male intellectuals, organic or elitist, may create counter-hegemonic strategies to undermine ruling-class monopolies on ideological reproduction and the definition of what can be known, but they will do so within a historically developed patriarchal hegemony which they may not consciously resist. There are few studies[6] of the particular constraints endured by women in all phases of educational process, such as, for example, Adrienne Rich's notion of women-centered "dehierarchilization" in education, which argues for the very practical priorities which must be given to the reorganization of day care as a precondition of educational innovation.[7] Michele Barrett advocates the unity of all socialist groups, while recognizing the difficulties involved in dealing with the supraclass nature of sexism.[8] Barrett understands very clearly that if such a unity is to generate anything more than "sympathy" for feminist aims, it has to be done within the dynamics of a theoretical position that does more than attempt to demonstrate the dependence of capitalism on a specific form of familialism and the correspondence of this form to the mode of production, however enriched and diversified that perception may be. The hegemony approach is enriched and diversified in that it attempts to escape merely reflexive relations for a dynamic dialectic of social action and social consciousness. It is impoverished in its failure not only to analyze but, more particularly, to theorize the social construction of gender relations.

Yet such analysis of education is vital: patriarchy is structured, ideological, and, it will be argued here, historical. It is also oppressive. The process of reification embedded in commodity production obscures the moral questions which arise in the context of economic oppression,[9] and even more so in gender oppression. Hegemonists share with feminists the view that these issues have ethical dimensions, and both consider value systems as something more complex than capitalist propaganda. Hegemonic analysis is concerned with uncovering processes of identification, formation, and persistence of values and knowledge, with the impact of class divisions on these issues, and with the impact of the issues themselves on class consciousness. This sort of analysis confirms that values are a strong factor in systems maintenance but does not, as is the case with Parsonian structuralism, separate value systems from their material roots or, like vulgar Marxism, bury them in the coarse soil of economic determinism. Furthermore, there is evidence that there are working-class values created by working-class practice, but studies in this area have tended to be about "the lads" whom bourgeois social scientists think of as deviant.[10] Hegemonic analysis attempts to unpack these socioideological processes of cultural reproduction without falling into the crevices of theology, economism, or barren structuralism. With such an approach, it is at least methodologically possible that hegemonic analysis might also cast some light on questions of the social construction of gender identity and the moral implications of male dominance. Such a project would require the broadening of relational analysis to gender relations and to the impact of male supremacists' ideology on curriculum and on the sociosexual activities of men and women of all classes.

Such an analysis is important for practical and political reasons. Feminists such as Jennifer Shaw, Jan Harding, and Sheila Tobias have begun to question the practical validity of coeducation and assumptions about feminine failings in math and science.[11] Politically, the time has come to provide some scientific substance to the notion that the personal is political and to analyze the revolutionary potential of the dialectic of state and family, of public and private life. Feminist scholarship has started to lay the intellectual foundations of feminist education, feminist politics, and feminist values. The difficult issue is how far critique of male-stream thought can go in such development. Neo-Marxism, which marginalizes women but understands the private realm as ideologically significant, may hold heuristic and analytical possibilities which its current androcentrism conceals. For this reason, it is worth looking at Gramsci's theory of civil society and the significance of his neglect of gender relations in the family.

Gramsci's effort embodied his keen sense of the inadequacy of theories of the state to comprehend totalitarianism, far less to resist it by relating theory to cultural reality and to political practice.[12] Like all competent dialectical logicians, he had to postulate the problem in terms of a dialectic of universal and particular. He therefore set out to analyze the relation of a historically generalized economic substructure and the complex particularity of superstructures. He argued that superstructures, in terms of culture and ideology, have their own dialectical dynamics, and that class antagonisms are mediated in cultural activities, which produce social and ideological formations. Ideology is not a product of naked coercion but of social practice in the realm of everyday life and thought where consciousness acts on the experiential social context in which the subject is immersed, and where men (sic) can only deal with the realities which history presents to them. The rise of the "corporate" fascist state had thrown into stark relief the centrality of the state in superstructural and infrastructural formations; the state had developed historically into much more than the executive committee of the ruling class. On the other hand, Croce's polemic against materialism and his positing of historicity as the essence of universal man was perceived by Gramsci to be the culmination of the defects of subjective idealism, an abstract individualism which lay like dead matter in the heart of the reality of community. For Gramsci, what was important was the creation of a universal class, which meant the abolition of class as such. Gramsci understood class consciousness itself to be dialectically structured, the site of a struggle between "common sense," or acceptable knowledge, and "good sense," which has the potential to overthrow common sense and its ideological baggage in the revolutionary struggle to realize true consciousness. Hegemony is the motor of common sense, defining reality and organizing consent, but in that very process it creates the possibility of counter-hegemony.[13]

Hegemony relies on cultural relations--and education is one of the most vital sets of these--to elaborate the axioms and practices of common sense, yet in doing this it creates the contradictory good sense, which challenges accepted definitions. There is nothing at all abstract about Gramsci's epistemology; working-class consciousness is based on economic reality, but this relation is not reflexive or reductionist. It is a *mediated* relation, mediated by the collection of practices which create culture or, in Gramsci's terminology, civil society. The significance of the hegemonic and mediative functions of the state in cultural reproduction become clearer when the state takes a totalitarian form. Gramsci's understanding of the state is that of class rule working on two superstructural "levels,"[14] political society and civil society. These together constitute "hegemony": the political level protects the hegemony of the ruling class "by the armor of coercion";[15] the other level, which Gramsci calls civil society, represents the needs of individuals and stands between the political level of state and economic structures. For Gramsci, this is by no means a formal model, nor does he utilize it with particular consistency, but what he does understand clearly is that the relation between substructure and superstructure must be *socially mediated* in the living relations of proletarians and bourgeoisie.

The economic substructure does not only produce goods, it "produces" social relations; but the ideological drama and "organic unity" of these relations is played out in the realm of civil society where autonomous cultural forms are developed.[16] The state attempts to form and reproduce a cultural consensus but when necessary will summon its coercive powers: it cannot and does not need to produce detailed blueprints as long as it can prescribe and procure general consent to acceptable outlines of "common sense." This principle has two implications for Gramsci. The first is that the working class must struggle to define and direct its own cultural formations and can in fact initiate cultural changes in *civil society*--"preformations," in Gramsci's terminology, of the eventual destruction of the state and transformation of the mode of production. Second, Gramsci suggests that the coercive aspect of the state must wither away if a universal classless society is to achieve its historic mission of the negation of class, for the state is not an abstraction but the living totality of class division.[17] A more ethical state will survive. Gramsci's debt to Hegel and Croce is very plain in this formulation. He argues trenchantly that, in practice, strong states rule more by hegemony--that is, consensual politics--than by tyranny.   Politics and education become inseparable in Gramsci's work: political action is education. In this broad sense, education is the key not only to the maintenance of hegemony but also to the breaking down of hegemony by challenging and eventually overthrowing consensus. Where, then, is this activity to be located? Theoretically and in practice in that social space and in those social relations which Gramsci calls civil society:

> What we can do for the moment, is to fix two major superstructural levels: the one that can be called "civil society" that is the ensemble of organisms commonly called *private*, and that of "political society" or "the State."   These two levels correspond on the one hand to the function of

"hegemony" which the dominant group exercises throughout society and on the other hand to that of "direct domination" or command exercised through the State and juridical government.[18]

This concept of civil society, so important to Enlightenment thought, is not treated systematically by Gramsci. For him, civil society is the realm of hegemony rather than coercion, but the political and civil realms are not separate. It is never quite clear, for example, whether political parties are civil or political or both. It is needful but not necessary for the ruling class to perpetuate itself by controlling the state apparatus, but in advanced states, civil society is complex and is in fact able to resist incursions by economic elements: Gramsci develops a whole series of militaristic metaphors in an attempt to explicate the relation of civil and political society.[19] Gramsci's society is more elastic but also more exclusive than the private realm as perceived by feminists, but he does lay a theoretical foundation for a cultural analysis which is materialist but not economically determinist. It does not, however, address gender hegemony at all.

The opposition of particular man and universal man is an axiom of Gramsci's dialectical logic, an opposition to be mediated by revolutionary class activity, which will abolish the coercive state in favor of a universalized (that is, classless and stateless) civil society. Gramsci argues strenuously against all notions of "man-in-general"; indeed, he scorns all human nature theories. The quest to identify the essence of man, so important in the history of political thought, is vehemently rejected: man, for Gramsci, is not a concept, nor is he "natural." He is a social product.[20] However, Gramsci's perception of "man" at no time denies his masculinity. Nonantagonistic forms of community will emerge from class struggle and the transformation of the mode of production, and this unification of individual and society will be brought about by political strategies which involve a preliminary struggle to transform "civil society." He does not, however, draw out the obvious implication that this struggle may mean transformations of forms of familial relations, including challenges to "the father as legislator."[21]

There is some relation between Gramsci's notion of civil
and political society and feminist concern with public and
private life, and his schema embodies at least some notion
that the personal is political.[22]   However, apart from the
obvious problem of the genderic particularization of universal
man, Gramsci's notion of civil society is circumscribed by his
conventional perception of family relations and his failure to
analyze these.[23]   Neo-Marxism shares this defect: it is one
thing to claim that the nuclear form of the family is the
specific form developed in capitalist society.   There is
historical evidence for this claim. It is quite another thing to
limit an analysis of the private realm to historical change in
the economic structure of households and the sexual division
of labor.   This kind of analysis opens the possibility of
reforming the economic life of women but still permits the
dismissal of social relations of biological reproduction as
ahistorical, or worse still, as an interest which tends to steer
inquiry into the muddy and unproductive waters of biological
determinism.[24]   The family, in this view, is functional,
reproducing labor power on an individual and species basis.
It also reflects property relations, though less so in modern
terms of corporate power and limited liability than in earlier
forms of patrilinearity. As understood by most Marxists, the
relation of the family to mode of production is at best
reflexive and at worst reductionist.[25] Its role in ideological
reproduction--in the socialization of young children, for
example--is rarely examined, and its role in the reproduction
of the social and ideological relations of male supremacy are
thought to be exhausted in the concept of the sexual division
of labor: there is thus a dogged evasion of the fact that
women of all classes are oppressed by men of all classes.

Hegemony theory zeroes in on education as a mode of
ideological reproduction and a set of social relations which
might actively be transformed in a way which could bring
real   change   to   civil   society   and   thus   create   the
"preformations" which are the necessary prologue to true
revolution and the abolition of class. Education provides a
step, as it were, into the interstices of actual and potential
forms of civil society. This interpretation of education, I
would suggest, blights the promise of hegemonic analysis

precisely because it shrivels the concept of civil society. Hegel knew better: the crucial dimensions of civil society were family relations and property relations, and Hegel argued the need for the family to enforce systematically the privatization of women.[26] Marx, in his critique of the *Philosophy of Right*, did not argue that the dialectical opposition of family and state was not real: he argued rather that the state is not "universal," as Gramsci, too, argues. Hegel's state is actually the production of one class operating within the relations of a historically specific mode of production; it abstracts from man rather than enriches him and institutionalizes the division of public and private life. For Marx and Gramsci, the ultimate universal is not the reconstruction of the state but the destruction of class division and the creation of community, but both neglect the social relations of species reproduction which are reproduced historically in the institution of the family.

What is to happen to women in these apocalyptic scenarios is an unanswered, indeed an unasked, question. "Civil society" is a useful term encompassing those social relations and cultural formations in which the impact of productive forces is perceived as hegemonic rather than causal. Civil society, we recall, is the realm of need rather than necessity: men need to be educated, both to meet economic imperatives and to develop consensual politics. It would seem to be more than merely needful that before they could hope to become educated revolutionaries, it is materially necessary that they be born, but a continued insistence that birth is merely a biological event persists in male-stream thought despite the fact that birth constitutes a basic *cultural* event in women's lives, as does the need to nurture--and instruct--very young children. In Marxism in general, the biological necessity to eat and to produce is given ontological primacy over sexual needs and the procreation and birthing of children. This core of evaluative idealism in Marxism's materialism is the product of patriarchal hegemony, and it needs to be theorized as such. The material ground of patriarchy is not the mode of production but the "ahuman" women's work of biological reproduction. All attempts to suggest that universal classless man will share *his* historic triumphs with women are as ideologically absurd as the canons of chivalry. They are absurd because women are not imperfect men with an inferior capacity for abstract thought and concrete action, nor is the oppression of women a sort of cultural by-product which illustrates the versatility of class hegemony. It is a mode of domination which emerges from the dialectics of reproductive process as patriarchal hegemony, culturally constructed, ideologically sophisticated, and intent on securing consent to the theory and practice of male supremacy.

Hegemony theory points firmly to the problem of false consciousness as a brake on class struggle and properly inquires into the processes whereby *partial*, ruling-class knowledge gains consent as *general* cultural truth. Gramsci, finding no room in a dichotomous model of sub/superstructures from which to give an account of the creation of consensual politics, insists that the private realm plays a significant part in ideological reproduction. "Mode of production" is therefore expanded to embrace the state, which regulates ungrounded *needs* as well as grounded *necessity* and ensures reproduction of labor power and the reproduction of consent to ruling-class political power and class-determined ideology. In collapsing "the reproduction of labor power" into the general category of production, a particular and necessary form of labor, women's reproductive labor, is negated. In collapsing women's productive labor into the general category of labor, the exploitation of women by men at home and at work is obscured. In collapsing the particular ideology of patriarchy into the general category of ruling-class (state) ideology, the systematic denigration of women and the legitimization of violence in procuring consent to patriarchal hegemony is ignored.

Marxist feminists have no difficulty at all in understanding that social change is a collective endeavor: we must surely be a little more critical of a collectivity in which birth has no historical significance. The assumption that women's labor is cheap labor must be changed. The popular notion that life is cheap is not, I suggest, a careless indifference on the part of a ruling class but a systematic indifference of a ruling sex to the value produced by women's reproductive labor. Only labor, Marx held, produced value, yet in denying the capacity of women's reproductive labor power to produce value and in failing to analyze and identify that value in social terms we are left defenseless in the face of idealist claims that the value of a fetus is the same as the cultural value of a human being. There can be no human value without human labor, no human value which is separate from the material necessity in which it is grounded.

All of these issues are posed in a still preliminary way. There is an ironic sense in which the understanding of how hegemony works might well be clarified in an ethnography of Marxist intellectuals. In Gramsci's terms, it may well be that Marxist intellectuals are not traditional because any claim they may have to be "organic" is destroyed in the vulgar teleology of the unicausality of productive modes on the one hand and the refusal to come to terms with the social construction of the ideology of male supremacy on the other. This difficulty cannot be cured by the extension of ethnographies to female subgroups or by limiting Marxist-feminist inquiry to questions concerning women in the work force and domestic labor. What is needed is a historical model which can given an account of male supremacy as an autonomous historical development. The crude superstructural model owes no debt to dialectical logic and can get along quite well with positivist methodology. Even Gramsci did not posit super/substructural relations as dialectically opposed, and the problem is not solved by the linguistic strategy of preferring to call substructures infrastructures. The dialectical relation, appearing by definition as class struggle, is found in both levels of structure, but the relation between the two levels is an unsolved problem. Hegemony theory goes some way toward resolution of this problem in Gramsci's theory of civil society as a mediating realm. What is being mediated however, is a relation which is not dialectical, namely, the realm of economic necessity on the one hand and the need of a ruling class to control the means of violent coercion on the other. Quite apart from the obvious but unaddressed question of why hunger is epistemologically more important than sexuality, this relation is not even dichotomous, far less dialectical. Thus, the conception of civil society is partial, promising in form but very limited in content. The content of civil society cannot be circumscribed by the notions of political party experience as true education, nor by faith in organic intellectuals bringing to the masses the knowledge which will make them withdraw consent to ruling-class hegemony. Such limitation means simply that the promise of hegemony theory is transformed to yet another tantalizing but ineffective mode of utopian thought.

The question is not simply one of scope, but of theoretical adequacy. In attempting to understand the historical development of the social relations of reproduction, it is necessary to demonstrate the material basis of its development, and to do that is to analyze biological reproduction, the material process on which reproductive relations arise.[27]

This analytical task in the first instance involves theorizing the dialectical structure of the process of human reproduction, which includes casting off the shackles with which men have tied the history and culture of birth to the prison of biological determinism. Models of historical development must, as Marx showed, be rooted in the realm of necessity, an existential condition of material survival involving the interaction of man and nature. The necessity to produce has as its basic postulate individual necessity: the relations of production become social historically. The relations of reproduction, however, are primordially social. One may reproduce oneself day by day all by oneself, given a favorable natural environment. No human being may reproduce another acting alone. Production reproduces individuals on a daily basis; reproduction unifies individual and species. This principle can only be understood materially in terms of the reproductive process itself, which is the ground of genderically differentiated reproductive consciousness.

Maternity is praxis, the unification of action (labor) and consciousness of action. The action itself, childbirth, is a mediation between the birth of the individual and the continuity of the race. Female reproductive consciousness is an integrative consciousness, linking the generations in a continuity over time and linking people as equal values. Its mediating force is physical labor, which is the ground of reproductive knowledge; knowledge of birth as process and of the child as value. Male reproductive consciousness, on the other hand, is an alienated consciousness, and paternity is essentially idealist: it is based on concept rather than experience and is dependent on a particular mode of reasoning, that of cause and effect. It is thus historical, for modes of reasoning are historical developments, and paternity must be understood in terms of the historical discovery of the causal relation of intercourse and pregnancy. It is a problematic discovery: the discovery of integration in general species reproduction is at the same time the discovery of the alienation of particular man from species continuity; paternity is the discovery of the uncertainty grounded in alienation of the male seed. Patriarchal praxis arises in the context of men's efforts to mediate the alienation of a particular seed and takes the general forms of collusion with other men, the appropriation of children and thus of women's reproductive labor, and the building of a hegemonic system to justify these procedures and to engineer consent of male interpretations of gender "knowledge." Historically, these efforts have been successful, but the material condition of their success has been the involuntary component of women's reproductive labor. The fight for the control of reproductive power has been, on the one hand, a fight to resist the alienation of men from reproductive process and, on the other hand, a struggle to maintain the involuntary nature of reproductive labor, to preserve men's reproductive freedom while canceling their reproductive alienation. It is precisely because the involuntary component of reproductive labor is now challenged by technology that the dialectics of reproduction emerge in new social forms which challenge patriarchal praxis as a denial of actual female reproductive experience and a willful transformation of female reproductive consciousness to male reproductive ideology. It is odd indeed that we have still to argue that reproduction is a form of knowledge with profound epistemological significance for women and men, but this fact is itself a massive triumph for patriarchal hegemonic practice.

Thus, I am suggesting that Marxist analysis must go beyond Marx and beyond Gramsci if it is to provide an effective tool for both understanding and changing historical reality. The variations of structuralism which have been so far proposed are hopelessly one-sided, for the relation of substructure and superstructure on which they rest is not a dialectical relation. As far as the sociology of education is concerned, there is more involved than the willingness to desist from commatizing women and to *the substitution of female for male subjects in cultural studies.* It must be recognized that some of the work regarded as seminal (sic) is indeed just that and, therefore, is one-sided. E. P. Thompson, for example, is properly admired for his considerable achievements, but it should be noted that the huge number of pages devoted to *The Making of the English Working Classes* are about men making men. Raymond Williams's work is intensely androcentric: the Long Revolution, he tells us "is a genuine revolution, transforming men and institutions."[28] He really means this literally. In speaking of political change, he cannot even bring himself to mention female suffragism but prefers a "neutral" expression: "the extension of parliamentary suffrage."[29] In his chapter on "Education and British Society," Williams allows one sentence to the subject of education for girls. This is hardly surprising, given his framework: "Schematically one can say that a child must be taught, first, the accepted behaviour and values of his society; second, the general knowledge and attitudes appropriate to an educated man; and third, a particular skill by which he will earn his living and contribute to the welfare of society."[30] Williams is critical of these aims in terms of their class content but does not even discuss their gender bias. He is generally more anxious to redefine educated man than to be concerned with undereducated woman.

There can be no useful analysis of hegemony, power, ideology, and the state unless it is recognized that cultural forms are not only reproduced in praxis but dialectically and materially grounded. Such a theory cannot arise where the "substructure" of history is perceived singularly: it is materially and theoretically incorrect to understand history as a dialectical process arising mysteriously from a unicausal necessity. The "material" realm--biological nature comprehended in human thought and practice--is itself dialectically structured. Production is the condition of survival imposed in the first instance on individuals; reproduction is the condition of species survival, the birth and sustenance of each succeeding generation. The concrete historical expression of the dialectic of history and nature has emerged as a struggle by men for domination of the natural world. In terms of production, scarcity, which involves the alienation of some people or classes from certain goods or a certain level of subsistence, is expressed historically in class struggle. In terms of reproduction, the alienation of men from species continuity has been expressed concretely in gender struggle and the domination of women in the private realm, an ideological realm in which patriarchal hegemony develops its perception of the separation of nature, history, and the mediation of this separation in violence. Production and reproduction are dialectically composed processes: further, the relation between the two is an opposition and mediation of individual and species needs, a point which is neglected in endless debates on the relation of the individual and society.

The implications for such a model in terms of hegemony theory go far beyond the formulation of research questions or appropriate ethnographic samples. The question of consent is broadened from the public realm to the private realm: not only why and how a consensual working-class consciousness develops, but why women consent to the ideology and practice of patriarchy. As the latter consensus shows more signs of erosion than the former, it appears as a promising field for both research and political praxis. As far as education is concerned, the preoccupation with schooling, the rehearsal for the separation of private and public, must take seriously the locus of gender identification and reproductive knowledge in the family. Further, the question of violent coercion cannot be held in abeyance simply because the ruling classes do not find it necessary at a given moment to unleash their sabres publicly: violence in the private realm is a ongoing mode of social control which *may* be related to capitalism but *is*, overtly and unquestionably, related to male control of reproduction.

Questions of the social construction of reality must take into account, as Marx noted, the questions which history presents to us. What Marx did not note was that this is done selectively by men in general as well as by bourgeois men in particular. The ruling class and the ruling sex have, at this moment, a joint historical mission. We cannot understand the current effort to get women back into conventional marriages and unpaid labor and to restore the patriarchal curriculum simply as reactions to capitalist crisis. We can understand far more clearly how this actually works if we also examine, for example, the social production of popular culture. One doesn't imagine that the state is sending out memos to songwriters to go back to sloppy lyrics about true romance, but they are being written. The state is unlikely to encourage citizens to subvert the political system, yet this is certainly happening in America in terms of education, in regard to divine creation, abortion, and homosexuality, all of which encourage violent resistance to the liberal state on the part of conservative ideologues. In Britain, of course, class manipulation is generally much clearer, and the major effort at retraditionalizing women seen in events such as the Royal Wedding and the subsequent christenings are chiefly remarkable for their capacity to mask the crudity of the ideological objective with the pomp of the ceremony.

At a more mundane level, women suddenly find that it is difficult to buy pants suits; the garment industry wants us back in skirts and gives us clothing for children which once more needs ironing. Movies have Dustin Hoffman showing us that being a single parent is tough on men and being a woman tougher, but it can be done if we let men show us how. The men, as ever, are being toughened up in boot camps and colonial and extraterrestrial wars. Novels remind us that men are prepared to give us "equality" in esoteric fields like espionage, but they will be the ones to make us over so that we can be little drummer girls,[31] or teach us that, like Sophie,[32] the only real choice we have is to acquiesce to the ethical primacy of male existence. These are hegemonic exercises in popular culture which proceed from state and individual initiatives rooted in the defense of the theory and practice of patriarchal hegemony.

NOTES

[1]For a critique of abstract structuralisms in the work of Popper and Althusser, see E. P. Thompson, *The Poverty of Theory and Other Essays* (New York: Monthly Review Press, 1978). For a feminist critique of exchange abstraction, see Nancy C. M. Hartsock, *Money, Sex and Power* (New York: Longman, 1983).

[2]Samuel Bowles and Herbert Gintis. *Schooling in Capitalist America* (New York: Basic Books, 1976).

[3]Mary O'Brien, "The Commatization of Women: Patriarchal Fetishism in the Sociology of Education," *Interchange* 15 no. 2 (1984), pp. 43-60.

[4]I have in mind particularly the work of Michael Young, Michael Apple and Roger Dale; Paul Willis and the Centre of Contemporary Cultural Studies in Birmingham; and the foundational work of E. P. Thompson and Raymond Williams. For a shrewd assessment of the Birmingham school, I am indebted to a recent analysis by Satu Repo, "The Problem of Working Class Consciousness in Marxist Cultural Theory," unpublished M.A. thesis, Ontario Institute for Studies in Education, 1982.

[5]*Selections from the Prison Notebooks of Antonio Gramsci*, edited and translated by Quintin Hoare and Geoffrey Nowell Smith (London: International Publishers, 1971) (hereafter *P.N.*); Antonio Gramsci, *Letters From Prison*, selected, translated, and introduced by Lynne Lawner (London: Jonathan Cape, 1975); Antonio Gramsci, *The Modern Prince and Other Writings*, translated by Louis Marks (New York: New World Paperbacks, 1957).

[6]Angela McRobbie, "Settling Accounts with Subcultures," *Screen Education* 34 (Spring 1980) pp. 37-50.

[7]Adrienne Rich. *On Lies, Secrets and Silence* (New York: W. W. Norton, 1972) p. 32.

[8]Michele Barrett, *Women's Oppression Today: Problems in Marxist-Feminist Analysis* (London: Verso Editions, 1980) pp. 13, 36-41.

[9]Michael W. Apple. *Ideology and Curriculum* (Boston: Routledge and Kegan Paul, 1970), argues (p. 124) that educational questions are always in some sense moral questions.

[10]Paul Willis, *Learning to Labour: How Working Class Kids Get Working Class Jobs* (Farnborough: Saxon House, 1977).

[11]Jennifer Shaw, "Education and the Individual: Schooling for Girls, or Mixed Schooling--A Mixed Blessing?" and Jan Harding, "Sex Differences in Performance in Science Examination," in *Schooling for Women's Work*, Rosemary Deem, ed. (Boston: Routledge and Kegan Paul, 1980); Sheila Tobias, *Overcoming Math Anxiety* (New York: W.W. Norton, 1978).

[12]*P.N.*, pp. 330-334. Gramsci discusses the unity of intellectual activity and common sense, the unity which can create "good sense": "Consciousness of being part of a particular hegemonic force that is to say, political consciousness, is the first stage towards a further progressive self-consciousness in which theory and practice will finally be one" (*P.N.*, p. 333).

[13]*P.N.*, pp. 323-324, 419-425.

[14]Hoare and Nowell Smith note (in *P.N.*, p. 5) that the Italian word "*cet*," which they translate as "strata," does not mean exactly that: for political reasons, Gramsci avoids the word "class." "Levels" also suggests a hierarchical relation, where Gramsci clearly intends a dialectical, mediated relation.

[15]*P.N.*, p. 263.

[16]For discussion of Gramsci's perception of civil society and political state, see Norberto Bobbio, "Gramsci and the Conception of Civil Society" and Jacques Texier, "Gramsci, Theoretician of Superstructures," in Chantal Mouffe, ed., *Gramsci and Marxist Theory* (Boston: Routledge and Kegan Paul, 1979).

[17]"It is possible to imagine the coercive element of the State withering away by degrees, as evermore conspicuous elements of regulated society (or ethical State or civil society) make their appearance" (*P.N.*, p. 263).

[18]*Selections from the Prison Notebooks of Antonio Gramsci*, p. 12

[19]See the discussion of "crises of authority" (*P.N.*, pp. 210-212), of parties and classes vis-à-vis the state. (*P.N.*, p. 227), and the discussion of the "trench-warfare" which the State wages against civil society (*P.N.*, pp. 234-235).

[20]Gramsci, *Il materialismo storico e la filosofia di Benedetto Croce*, p. 191.   Quoted by Leonard Paggi, "Gramsci's General Theory of Marxism," in Mouffe, *Gramsci and Marxist Theory*, pp. 122-123.

[21]"Every man, inasmuch as he is active, contributes to modifying the social environment" (*P.N.*, p. 265); that is, "all men . . . are legislators . . . to a greater or lesser extent . . . . A father is a legislator for his children, but the paternal authority will be more or less conscious" (*P.N.*, p. 266).

[22]Civil society is "the ensemble of organisms called 'private' which establish hegemony" (*P.N.*, p. 12). If it is not clear whether "organic" in Gramsci's usage is a metaphor for social interaction: it certainly embodies customs and mores, but "operates without 'sanctions' or compulsory 'obligations'" (p. 242).   This is the sentimental view of the family as a voluntary organization and is inconsistent with the notion of father as legislator.   However, Gramsci advocates equality of educational opportunity for "young men and women" (*P.N.*, p. 29).

[23]It should be noted that in his long imprisonment, Gramsci's concern for the education and welfare of his family (he had two sons, no daughters) was passionate and humane; his moving *Letters From Prison* attest to this.

[24]Barrett, *Women's Oppression Today*, pp. 12-13.

[25]Ibid., p. 12.

[26]G. W. F. Hegel, *The Philosophy of Right*, translated by T. M. Knox (London: Oxford University Press, 1952). See especially paragraphs 157-202.   The tripartite division of civil society, family, and state probably influenced Engels for whom, of course, civil society became "private property." See Joan B. Landes, "Hegel's Conception of the Family," in Jean Bethke Elshtain, ed., *The Family in Political Thought* (Amherst: University of Massachusetts Press, 1982) pp. 125-142.

[27]For a fuller analysis, see Mary O'Brien *The Politics of Reproduction* (Boston: Routledge and Kegan Paul, 1981) Chapter 1.

[28]Raymond Williams, *The Long Revolution* (Harmondsworth: Penguin Books, 1963), p. 10.

[29]Ibid., p. 160.

[30]Ibid., p. 147.

[31]John LeCarre. *The Little Drummer Girl* (London: Hodder and Stoughton, 1982).

[32]William Styron, *Sophie's Choice* (New York: Bantam Books, 1980).

13

Feminism as Passionate Scholarship

A slippery notion is embodied in the word *passion*.
Passion is by definition resistant to the notion of objectivity
embedded in conventional notions of scholarship. Perhaps
what passion and scholarship have in common is context:
passion never occurs in a vacuum--passion is passion *for*
something--and neither does scholarship occur in a vacuum,
all protestants of objectivity notwithstanding. But let us
start with the diverse contexts of human passion and their
versatile vocabularies. "He flew into a passion," for example,
evokes the transcendence of vulgar bad temper in a sort of
higher order of righteous rage. I say *he* deliberately: women
are arrested at the level of flying into a "tizzy" in a crass
exhibition of their existential shrewishness, at least in the
fading vocabulary of patriarchal assessments of gendered
emotional responses. But there is more to passion than rage:
there are, for example, expressive maneuvers in which
common or garden lust is exalted to grand passion; there is
also a way in which quite crude self-interest can be
transformed to a higher form of caring a great deal--the
passions for military and economic success, for example,

Keynote address to the University of Victoria conference, "The
Passionate Scholar," 1987.

which are presented as heroic activities undertaken for the general good of the community.   There is too, and more somberly, the religious sense of the word: I remember in my Episcopalian youth being much enchanted--and perplexed--by my Easter duties, which called upon me to both meditate on and exult in the passion of Christ.   Passion in this sense, one supposes, means a commitment unto death in defense of the ideal idea.   This level of passionate commitment is not one we normally think of in connection with scholars, except perhaps in more extravagant defenses of the institution of tenure or, to be just, the defense of a fuzzy but sincere commitment to academic freedom.   There is also, of course, the notion of passion in an orgasmic context, including the fairly common notion of male ejaculation as a small but passionate death.   In the scholarly context, one assumes that the passion for paternal certitude *is* a passion to know and to learn: the passion for knowledge is often ambivalent, for in the realms of passion knowledge itself is ambiguous.   For example, in a related way, the conflation of sexual passion and carnal "knowledge" is very ancient: "and he knew her" is a specifically sexual claim and embodies the implication that he had the power to make damn sure nobody else knew her, which is of course the most elementary patriarchal strategy to ensure paternity.   But it is also an exercise in power: the power to claim and name a woman's child can be passionate desire.   The need to confirm paternity, whatever the reasons for such an ambition--and they are complex--this lust for certainty in genealogical terms is only practically achievable if the man in question can control sexual access to the woman in question.   It is fair to note that men have made quite passionate historical attempts to develop the social strategies to consolidate the control of women's reproductive capabilities and have produced creative ideologies of legitimization of this control.

However, the purpose of this essay is not to discuss sexual passion and carnal knowledge, but scholarly passion and intellectual knowledge--though I hasten to add, as a life-long socialist, that I try hard not to disassociate knowledge from action.   The passionate activist is perhaps a better-known figure in popular terms than the passionate scholar, though I don't think either of those characters are necessarily perceived as model citizens. In speaking of the unity of theory and practice, the case of Karl Marx himself is instructive: as a young working class lefty, I recall, I was taught that the essence of Marxism could best be caught by his activities and addresses to the International Workingmen's Association without the intellectual stress of coping with *Capital* or the Hegelian-tainted early works. Yet the passions of these late political works were polemic and factional rather than a reflection of that passion for history which must certainly include him in the annals of passionate scholars. Also quite self-consciously passionate were people like Niccolò Machiavelli and Jean-Jacques Rousseau--I take my examples from my own discipline of political theory. Machiavelli, born in a time when one could still be passionate for Reason, which had not yet become the antithesis of passion, was certainly an activist, and he was devastated by his compulsory retirement from politics and diplomacy when he got caught on the losing side. But Machiavelli's passion was both scholarly and political. "I love my city better than my soul," he said, and his passionate imagination transported him bodily, and suitably clad in ancient finery, to the Rome which he believed to have been the epitome of the unity of political passion and practical justice. Rousseau's passions were a bit messed up in the tensions of trying to tame passion with reason, which was the premier intellectual ambition of his time, and his attempts to mediate between these currents are predictably confused. He didn't have it all together in his sex life either; indeed, none of these men found the notion of the faithful husband to be a rational one. Rousseau's notion of the education of women, if we are to judge by Sophie's curriculum vis-à-vis Emile's, was to direct her to the notion that total submission to her husband was the free choice of an educated woman. This pedagogical strategy foreshadows the gender contradictions inherent in the liberal notion that individual freedom is a condition for the pursuit of knowledge in the first place and the question of whether women are naturally free and indeed educable at all. This question is one which is never resolved in the history of male-stream thought, but until recently, the notion that some women could be learners of men's knowledge but not discoverers of knowledge was widespread, and mere receptivity is hardly a passionate posture--in any circumstance.   And domestic know-how is generally not thought of as either scholarly or passionate.

Thus, the capacity of women to direct their passions to the pursuit of knowledge has been deemed impossible or at least unseemly, and theirs is an outrageous history of destruction of women's intellectual products whether these were individual or collective. Indeed, from the *thiasos* of Sappho to the religious craft guilds of the Beguines and even today female intellectual energies have often been buried in bonfires, isolation, and denigration, to say nothing of the doctrine of perish before publishing.

It is probably fair to say that to this day the dialectic of passion and reason persists in an unmediated form for all scholars, though it is also fair to say that modern science believes that it has, by the development of modes of reason based on discernible regularities operating in passionless predictability, transcended this fruitless dialectic.   But I suspect that even supermen have a god, an unexcited and not passionate one, of course. I think his popular name is Roger, as in "Roger: there appears to have been a malfunction, Roger."   Meanwhile the whole explodes in millions of little picture frames and those passions thought to have been eliminated in the rites and rituals of boot camp now tremble on the edge of the humanity they have rejected. All this stuff can be represented as a moral quest for the enrichment of the conditions of human life. Who would deny that Newton and Kepler and Einstein were passionate scholars and felt their passion to know as a moral passion? Clearly, if the passionate scholar derives that passion from the principle that knowledge is good because it improves the lot of humankind, we are speaking of a moral fervor. Yet the age of Reason has traveled to an age in which the notion of knowledge for its own sake constitutes a challenge to creative minds.   I would argue that the notion of knowledge for its own sake is either a flimsy ideological illusion or a mode of decontextualization which is ultimately a form of neurosis. The passionate scholar must surely be of the world.

However, the difficulties in creating an ethically contextualized scholarship are twofold: first, understanding what knowledge actually is, and second, defining what is to be understood as the good. One could quibble about these issues forever, and indeed, much of the contempt for intellectuals, which is a fairly universal social tendency, emerges from their perceived failure to solve this Sphinxian riddle. I do not propose to address that impasse directly: what I really want to suggest is that it cannot be resolved so long as the notion of *the* passionate scholar is diminished in the inherent individualism of that concept of scholarship. I want to argue that the quest for knowledge can only transcend the ambiguities of reason, passion, objectivity, and subjectivity if the quest is a collective one. I have myself learned this in terms of feminist scholarship, and I would suggest that feminism, a loose community of differentiated individuals, has understood this in a unique way.

Now, I am not insensitive to the notion of "collective" as having chilling overtones. We do see passion, rage, and lust assembled in scary collectivities: the mob, the horde, the rabble, mindlessly destroying the imperfect but best-we-can-do social achievements of well-meaning and practical people who are callously indifferent to the rule of law and totally unfamiliar with Robert's Rules. To be sure, feminism as putative mob action has called forth the righteous rhetoric of the status quo, but it is frustrating for the Phyllis Schlaffleys of this world that the anger which undoubtedly infuses the feminist movement rarely takes traditional violent forms. Feminists tend to believe that strategies of violence are specifically masculine, except perhaps in the defense of children. Furthermore, women simply do not have access to the means of violence and are not socialized to the notion of violence as a problem solver. Women have, of course, taken their place in the past on barricades along with men, but these have usually been activities grounded in class structures which oppress men and women alike. Although the feminist movement is not lacking in rage, it has developed methods of dealing with it which are fairly constructive, all of which are based upon principles of collectivity. The most obviously successful of these methods is consciousness raising, not now practiced in its early form but still the passionate heart of the movement.

Consciousness raising is of interest to us in that it is a form of seeking knowledge which transcends ego preoccupation and lone ranging with a sense of a crucial politics of overcoming the isolation of women wrought in patriarchy's greatest cultural weapon: the separation of private and public life. Consciousness raising is an innovative pedagogy and an effective collective praxis and is neither objective nor passionless. Much of it now takes place in formal rather than informal situations: in institutions of learning, in community and special purpose organizations, in unions and on the job, in churches, in supermarkets, in neighborhoods, in artistic communities. But perhaps it takes place most insidiously in that most ancient and universal institution for the seemly control of passion, the family. This latter development is, of course, the one which conservative forces perceive as the most effective and the most dangerous effect of feminism. It is a revolution which has redefined revolution: no mobs, no barricades, but much political and imaginative passion and a significant increment of knowledge in relation to the development of possible and workable new forms of human cohabitation.

Also of note, in terms of feminist scholarship, is the outpouring of feminist publications, scholarly and popular, which we have seen in recent years. This trend is not simply an effect of more women going to universities: even Harlequin authors have modified their heterosexist fairy tales, and lesbian women can now read about their own integrity and adventurousness in works of pride and rage. To be sure, not all of this stuff transcends the more lugubrious textuality of conventional academic writing: the strategy is to write conventionally until you get tenure, then wing it. Still, at all levels, what seems to unify this outpouring of print is a collective passion for justice and integrity on the part of a loose collectivity which has transformed perceptions of human bonding and launched a passionate attack on human bondage. The content of this vast effort in scholarship has been enormous, not only in terms of the knowledge of events which have been suppressed, nor in the restoration of women's activities to the historical record, but in the development of theoretical and methodological innovations and, more radically, in the challenge to epistemological and ontological conventions which have developed to restrict both the parameters and the passions which have encased "legitimate" knowledge. I do not believe that the claim of the canons (or the disciplines) to bestow legitimacy on knowledge is any better grounded than the merely legal claim of the legitimacy of men's children. To be sure, some of the primary assertions of passionate feminist scholarship are as yet fairly primitive. Yes, women have a history which they have made themselves; yes, women are capable of recovering this history; yes, the creative imagination has moved women to write their reality and their pride and their oppression; yes, the passion for learning has stirred female minds, but the products of these meditations have too often disappeared in the self-serving and frightened defenses of patriarchal ideologues, who have their own passion to universalize our species as "man." Man, not as an abstract universal but in all too human forms, has progressively and over many cultures worked to the suppression of women's intellect and the sustenance of his own hegemony: universal man has passionately protected for himself the power of uncovering and interpreting reality in the light of gendered interests and ideologies rather than in the ethical mode to which he has paid bewhiskored lip service. And he has not, of course, done this without constructing a social context which reflects his claim to universality as well as canons of learning which defend it. The dualism of public and private life, the sanctity of the patriarchal family, the existential superiority of men, the historically developed organization of the power of the patriarchal state, the legitimation of violence as the ultimate problem solver in both private and public crises: all of these contribute not only to the sustenance of patriarchy but also to the limitation and stifling of scholarly imagination. All of these also represent the passionate foci of the patriarchal status quo and stand as challenges to the oppressed, whether by race, class, or gender. What seals the collective passions of feminist scholarship is a universal resistance to the denial that we are members of a species known with stunning arrogance as "mankind."

What we need in theoretical and political terms at this time in history is a general theory of oppression, so that the collectivities of resistants can combine and transcend the carefully cultivated compartments in which race, class, gender, imperialist, homophobic, national, and religious struggles are sustained, to contain the passions of the oppressed and to encourage the wastage of revolutionary energy in battles with each other. Here is a challenge to those who seek an imaginative and useful outlet for passionate scholarship. The question is not really that of selected members of these groups earning an entrance to intellectual elites: the real questions swirl around the integrated quest to discover and redefine what wisdom is, what is to pass for knowledge, whom it is to serve, how it can be good. And this must be, in my view, a collective endeavor; in our individualistic perceptions the litany of great names is too often allowed to set the limits of what can be known. I have no personal ambition to be a lonely passionate scholar, sweeping cartesian fluffballs from the musty corners of platonic caves while Minerva's owl molts away her wisdom and gradually loses the power to distinguish dusk from dawn. Heavy on women's intellectual struggle, too, and collectivizing it in a curious way, lie the ashes of those millions of lonely burnt women whose love of learning and passion for wisdom brought them steadily to the stake for 300 years or so, and not that long ago. Many of these women died precisely because of their solitariness in a time when communities of scholars were masculine and the only collectives available for women were the convent and the coven, and the convents were ultimately under patriarchal control. *Il pape*, the pope, the holy father was the ultimate status symbol of individual power and knowledge, and the witches' rejection of masculine authority over their minds and bodies was just as important, maybe even more so, in the rejection of canonical knowledge as it was in the political challenge to secular and holy power. Yet I have never heard the witches' ordeal by fire referred to as a passion, except perhaps in the case of Joanne D'Arc, and she had to wait for centuries for that understanding.

For me, then, the notion of the scholar is an ambiguous one, too solitary in its conception, too elitist in its practice, too sexist in pedigree. When I went to graduate school, at the ripe old age of forty-two, I was much struck by the way academics described their work. They tended to speak--and still do--about "my work," which means scholarly or research endeavors, and "my teaching load." An interesting distinction: it was as if teaching was the burden to be borne in exchange for the delights of intellectualism--rather broadly defined. This did not seem to be understood at all as a dialectical relationship, far less a creative one. Teaching feminist studies has taught me that it can be, though not of course without stress. The bureaucratic context, with its passion for hierarchy--expressed perhaps in its most obnoxious form in the subjectified inanities of the grading system but also in admission procedures, student "funding" (i.e., how to be passionate on the edge of the bread line)--the lust for specialization, to say nothing of the hegemonic control of the bourgeois state: all of this context does not enhance the joys of the teaching/learning dialectic. Furthermore, while the personal dangers and career impediments which were experienced by women on campus in the early stages of the feminist revolution have been curbed by collective action, they have not disappeared. In the east the duties of informally policing patriarchal privilege seem to have devolved on engineering students. Of course, this high-tech age needs a lot of engineers, and the manly mythology of engineering--the lone genius, spanner in hand, taming the jungle with asphalt and building bridges for modern Horatios to defend--combines with the traditional view that women are biologically unable to measure accurately. One suspects that engineers, truculently asserting their negative dialectic of brawn with brawn, feel deserted by their pure scientific fellows who have fled to the warmer reaches of untrammeled mind. In any case, the combination of rather puerile pornography and macho ideology which marks the publications of eastern engineering students has led to public melées in Toronto, Kingston, and Kitchener which have been dangerous for female persons, to say nothing of university and city property. But this level of public misogyny appears to be a sort of rearguard action by a group for whom passion is frustrated anger: the voice of Roger in his furious adolescence, perhaps.

Women's struggle for intellectual integrity is still a dangerous and exhausting one and is by no means over, but fighting for the simple right of access to canons does not seem to have snuffed the candle of scholarship. Indeed, I would argue that the subtle and crude resistances thrown in the way of feminist scholarship have contributed--painfully but ultimately in a strengthening way--to a stronger emphasis on precisely that collective endeavor which I am arguing is the most fruitful way to organize the production of new knowledge. But what does "new knowledge" mean? Many passionate scholars in the patriarchal tradition have spent their substance on the expansion of old knowledge--on *discovery*, of new applications, paradigmatic variations, theoretical refinements and so forth. Of course this is important stuff, but while it may expand or revise the content of the canons, of "acceptable wisdom," it still represents a corseted passion, an acceptance of a canonical content which can be revised without transcendence.

Transcendence is the movement of passionate scholarship--not to know but to know more, and how and why. This kind of scholarship ends the exclusion of women who have been taught that only the trivial, never the transcendent, is accessible to them. Feminist scholarship is a collective endeavor; patriarchy is a transcendent doctrine which holds that transcendence is masculine. The notion that the proper place for a woman is on her back is rather more than a vulgar and very unimaginative jibe. Patriarchal scholarship and individual ideologic design of paradigms structure the very language of theory, split ontology asunder, and sever the false universals of epistemology. This process has created man the thinker who sits, pensively stoned, in the shadow of man the phony universal. He may think straight, but surely we have learned that straightness makes an inadequate universal. He may think deeply, but deep thinkers do not necessarily escape the shallows of immersion in the status quo and, more seriously, sometimes do not know how to swim.

No, the passionate scholar must be in the first instance a passionate teacher, integrated in a community of doubters of convention, of canonical rectitude, of methodological corsets. She or he must be prepared to round up sacred cows and put them to the question--not, I hasten to add, in the Inquisitional sense of that word, the sense which forces conformity by torture--but in the sense of a collective pilgrimage which will leave no theorem, no common sense, no platitude, no convention unquestioned and in the sense that being in the world, actively, critically, creatively, and collectively is the condition of changing the world.

For is that not the ultimate objective of the passionate scholar? Not the mere increment of knowledge, but the moral lust for a different world based upon different knowledge and different values. Not the passion of the solitary pilgrim seeking pure knowledge, or the face of God, or even just elite colleague approval. Passionate teaching is not knowing for mere status, not a phony detachment from the ideologies embedded in one's pedagogy, not a distancing from the social, cultural, and ethical truisms embodied in conventional wisdom or from the power structure which controls the subject matter of pedagogy and inquiry and reserves the right to abuse the results. Teaching, unlike scholarship, can never be solitary; it is by definition social interaction, it involves collective effort, it draws no formal line between teacher and learner, for both are both. Passionate teaching struggles for the validation of new voices and different paradigms, and feminist pedagogy in particular struggles to resist the dualist ontologies which abstract analytical scholarship has thrust on us: nature/culture, subject/object, public/private, self/other, personal/political, the true and the false--the whole apparatus which splits apart everything that it can lay its hands or mind upon in the interest of the sum of the parts rather than in the collective search for wholeness. Existence before essence, Sartre cried, and then he left these terms in the abstract realm of philosophical discourse. Wholeness before particularity, feminist scholars say, and confer collectively in the recognition that this must be a political, practical, and pedagogical task directed to reforming and reproducing the world. The politicization of the task of reproducing the world has moved women from the obstetrical couch to the passion for knowing how to reproduce in collective historical and ethical terms as well as in isolated obstetrical adventures.

Feminism, then, is one place where, at this moment in time, passionate scholars may be at home. Feminism is also a collectivity, sustained with weariness, to be sure, but also with determination by those who are often far apart, a collectivity in which women and an increasing number of men seek--not necessarily with canonical approval--that which is common and do-able rather than that which is peculiar and merely knowable, that which is accessible rather than that which sees dignity in refined abstraction. It is a movement which asserts that "generalization" is not a strategy only of understanding, but a political strategy for the sustenance of commonality in spite of diversity in the collective organization of action and of knowledge. And central to this objective is the notion of teaching and learning as both an intimate and a social dialectical process which must be passionately maintained in a collective endeavor not only to know the world, not to seek intellectual proofs, but to develop strategies of collective human liberation which can form the basis of acting together in extending the boundaries of commonalty in humane purpose, the purpose of reproducing the world rather than destroying it. This purpose is the concrete universal, the challenge to scholarly, practical, and political imagination which is the vital task of our species. The task of making history has as its condition the reproduction of the world.

For me, feminism, with its commitment to collectivity (sometimes fractious); its commitment to the development of new forms of knowledge, a canonical fight whose lines are not yet clearly drawn; its commitment to the transcendence of violence as the world's star problem solver; its commitment to unifying theory and practice while rejecting blind orthodoxies: all of this is the ground for the unifying of teaching and scholarship as essential moments in the creative reproduction of the world. The life of Simone de Beauvoir, a passionate scholar indeed, is exemplary here. Solitary in her gendered sensitivity, she started life as a brilliant student of a brilliant teacher, learned early the need of the unity of theory and practice, suffered in the uncovering of the reality that the personal is political, and finally stepped from the dubious joys of existential elitism into the embrace of feminism as a collective, a movement. In her eighties, she marched as well as taught, learned as well as struggled politically, and tasted briefly but with enthusiasm and grace the stresses and rewards of sisterhood. Ah well, even collectivities need their heroes, and we are lucky that we had her and do not have, as is the case with so many female passionate scholars, to rescue her from between the churlish lines of the patriarchal record. De Beauvoir has taught us so much, cared passionately for scholarship, and finally understood that freedom and patriarchy are existentially incompatible.

So I suppose I have some kind of message to offer: if you would be passionate, then reject the lone ranger ideology and realize that unless we are equally passionate and equally disciplined in sharing our knowledge, and unless we understand that knowledge must be humanized in not just a collegial but a much broader collective endeavor and passed on in a skilled and creative commitment to sharing our knowledge, it will not ultimately enter nonexclusively the realm where alone it has ethical significance: the collective process which we call making history, or in my terminology, reproducing the world in a transcendence of ignorance and partiality. One could get passionate about that.

14

Political Ideology and
Patriarchal Education

When we speak of feminism and education we are immediately confronted by a contradiction. On the one hand, education is seen as a necessary and important part of action directed toward social transformation. On the other hand, educational systems and school curricula are structured hierarchically and are profoundly conservative: educational institutions are bastions of male supremacy and ruling class power. There are a number of ways of expressing this tension, which will be developed in this essay.

The preliminary point to be made is that education is political in both the broad and the narrow senses of that word. Broadly, educational systems are directed to what Parsonians call "system-maintenance"[1] and Marxists call "ruling-class hegemony" and "ideological reproduction."[2] The notion of education as an objective uncovering of the truth and a subjective passing-on of knowledge obscures the fact that truth and knowledge are socially defined and legitimated and that the power to define meanings and identify what is to be "acceptable truth" is very real power,

Excerpted with permission from *Resources for Feminist Research/Documentation sur la recherche féministe*, Vol. 12, No. 3, November 1983, pp. 3-16.

exercised day by day in the bureaucracies and classrooms of educational systems everywhere. It is also exercised in social situations which are less formally structured; and one of these, which is of acute concern to women, is the family. The notion of "socialization" embraces political and ethical questions, which is why raising children is both an educational and an ideological enterprise, an active reproduction of prejudice which is linguistically neutralized in the notion of "values education." Early childhood education is perceived as absolutely crucial to the good of the community and the welfare of the child, and therefore as work for experts to take charge of, but at the same time as an enterprise so simple-minded that it can quite safely be left to women. As it is "natural," women do not need to be educated (nor paid) for this task because they are equipped for it by nature. As it is sociopolitical, experts are highly trained and paid. The private realm is the "narrow" realm of education which is in fact crucial to the propagation of male supremacy.

The traditional view that childcare is a form of natural education which needs no special training has in fact faded to some extent with the development of a more highly bureaucratized society. In less-developed countries, this tendency takes place quite overtly as an exercise in putatively benign imperialism, and an endless number of foreign aid projects have taken the form of "black boxes,"[3] educational packages through which the children of the Third World are supposed to pass and be miraculously transformed into happier, richer adults, both more equal and more free. Ernesto Scheifelbein and Joseph P. Farrell note that educational intervention in the Third World tends to reinforce the existing class structure, but as far as the existing gender structure is concerned, they have little to say. They claim that their data make it impossible to count the female unemployed, for "one must assume that a significant, though unknown, proportion of the young women who are neither at school nor at work *have chosen not to seek employment.*"[4] This edifyingly pregnant sentence rather neatly encapsulates the deficiencies of patriarchal studies in education. First, there is the assumption that the goal of education is the production of wage labor for private or state capitalism, as a condition of affluence; these particular researchers are rather soulfully doleful about the failure of the black boxes to make much dent on either poverty or social inequality. Second, it is simply assumed that young girls in a patriarchal society *choose* not to seek employment when they are in fact *educated* to marry young, breed freely, and work for pitiful wages in their "spare" time. Third, there is the implication that schooling and wage labor of some kind are legitimate occupations, are *real* work as opposed to the desirable and stressless gaiety of maintaining a household, however impoverished.

These are the assumptions of patriarchy and economism, of the primacy of quantitative research, of the sliding over of the oppression of women by men. There is a refusal to concede that educational concern for system-maintenance is also the concern to forward the cause of gender and class hegemony in the definition and control of knowledge.[5] The need for a specifically feminist approach to education, however, grows out of far more than the gender bias of educational theory, practice, and research. It grows out of the fact that feminism is a historical and political movement of a progressive and momentous kind. This movement is radical in a very wide sense: not only does it demand changes in the life conditions of women, but it takes issue with the most strongly entrenched assumptions of male-dominant society. The position that we have just discussed briefly--the understanding of childrearing as education of an extremely important but simplistic kind--is something more than an affirmation of the cultural insignificance of women's work. If, in fact, the "proper" socialization of very young children is the precondition of the success of formal education in making acceptable wisdom acceptable,[6] it is quite clear that a transformation of the social structure of the family is an explosive political notion. Thus, feminism has been a major sociohistorical determinant of the extremist politics of neoconservatism: New Right organizers understand better than professional politicians the implications of feminist curricular innovation for family stability and ideological hegemony. The Right is equally dedicated to control of schooling. In fact, the major political ideologies of our time have carefully developed educational policies and ideologies. The purpose of this essay is to examine the ideologies of conservatism, liberalism and Marxism and their educational ideologies.

Conservatism and Education

The immediate notion of conservatism that education should maintain the *status quo* is really very misleading. Plato, the founder of this tradition in the West, had revolutionary or at least Utopian visions of the capacity of education to create good people--not everyone, of course, for the important notion of elitism as a goal of education, the idea of education as a device to identify "the best," is hardly *passé*. In our own times, much of the agitation for reform of school systems comes from the political Right, especially in countries such as Canada where school boards are elected by popular vote and are thus subject to electioneering tactics. Canadian conservatism of this kind is, however, derivative, and such American-based organizations as Renaissance International have been of financial and strategic assistance in setting up a move to control school boards in English Canada.[7] The quite different involvement of the Church in French Canada is of course long-standing, and its presence has survived *laicization*, a fact which makes policy documents on, for example, sex education, very ambivalent indeed.[8] The attempt to liberalize Catholic education produces a struggle different from that of conservatizing liberal education, but both are political struggles. The general complaint of conservatism is that educational reform has gone too far: in Ontario the educational reforms initiated by the *Hall-Dennis Report* are seen as demonstrably pernicious (though it may be noted that *Hall-Dennis* was not especially beloved of the Left, either). The New Right is, in a number of ways, "old" liberalism. It is a profoundly reactionary movement dedicated to totally free economic enterprise and individual freedoms, while training in the "feminine" family rather than in the "masculine" school is supposed to provide an ethical counterweight to the nastier

aspects of unrestrained competition. The social consequences
of free enterprise in the nineteenth century are clear enough,
but people like William Bennett, Ronald Reagan and
Margaret Thatcher believe that the price of worker
immiseration is worth paying in defense of "freedom" or, less
rhetorically, the free enterprise system.

The New Right's educational policy is expressed in polemic
but propagated by a very high-powered technological
communications system. Education and politics are wedded
in mail-order houses and mass media, and the ludicrousness
of the propositions--the return of creationism, for example, or
the ethical efficacy of corporal punishment, or the evils of sex
in print or practice--are integrated into a sort of survival-of-
the-fittest politics which blend capitalism, religious
fundamentalism, and radical individualism in a way which
quite clearly does not lack a certain popular appeal.[9] The
central tenet of New Right polemic, which is important for
feminists, is, of course, the devotion to a radically enucleated
patriarchal family form and the ideal of self-denying woman
lost in service to others.[10] The weapons for effecting this are
to be control of both socialization and schooling by means of
weakening state control and teacher autonomy and
strengthening local and parental authority. As a political
force, it gathers up a variety of people: those who genuinely
believe the state is too powerful, petty bourgeois interests
who are painfully aware of the tendency of big capitalists to
eat little capitalists, women who have invested their being in
the private realm and are nervous of stepping out of that
realm,[11] and those who prefer pseudo-spiritualism to the
hurly-burly of being-in-the-world. There is also an ugly
appeal to those who are not especially advantaged to find
scapegoats in other races and cultures, in the gay
community, and among the modern witches of the women's
movement.

The significance of this new conservatism for education,
and particularly for teachers, cannot be over-emphasized,
and it is important to avoid bringing rationalistic fallacies to
a judgment of New Right ideology as merely vulgar, thus
avoiding analysis of the very real anti feminist essence of
this movement. In patriarchal societies, educational systems

are historically grounded in patriarchal theory and practices in family and school, which are bastions of patriarchal control. The New Right, therefore, digs in potentially fertile soil. The perceived erosion of traditional values, especially in the 1960s, is one source of a certain social nervousness among large segments of Western societies which the New Right exploits. To be sure, the actual practice of the Bennetts and Reagans and Thatchers of the political world is considerably less radical than the rhetoric of Renaissance International,[12] but politicians are bounded by certain electoral constraints; these constraints may be weakening in the confusions of economic insecurity. Current activities in British Columbia will be instructive as to the success of New Right propaganda.

These considerations are important for feminist educators. Women teachers are as highly politicized as male teachers but often find their political options limited by their double workloads at home and school[13] and the urbane but real misogyny of the majority of men teachers and administrators. Many women are also oppressed by the hysterical homophobia of the New Right. There is not yet sufficient research evidence as to the historical contribution of lesbian women to education, though such work is now in progress. The current climate in education is hardly one to encourage lesbian teachers to "come out." Nonetheless, a feminist review of education must pay tribute to the contribution which lesbian teachers have quietly made to the education of children for centuries in the teeth of explicit threats from patriarchal pedagogy. The tendency for men to have increasing control of teaching at all levels--they have always controlled higher education--causes teacher resistance to the New Right and to patriarchal educational forms[14] to be both sporadic and problematic. The attempt to push women back into the home may be ideologically offensive to individual men but in the long run brings economic advantages to male teachers in general. This problem has to be brought into the politics of teacher unions: it is one to which the women teachers' associations are already sensitive.

Women teachers cannot alone resist the educational strategies of the New Right, even though it is clear that old-fashioned liberalism in economics, combined with traditional conservatism in family matters, constitutes an active patriarchal politics. The strategy of control of school boards has not appealed to feminism, which tends to be skeptical of organized politics in general. It is, however, a strategy which should perhaps be taken seriously: large cities such as Toronto and Vancouver have records of parent and teacher activism, and a number of progressive women have been elected, but there has been no organized feminist venture into school board politics. Perhaps the appropriate time for such a strategy is now.

Liberal Education

The very phrase "liberal education" is, like "liberal arts," tremendously evocative. The traditional faith in education as a means of creating a "new man" is integral to the theory and practice of liberalism, and its philosophical underpinnings were furnished in the modern era by Rousseau[15] and updated by Dewey. The patriarchal chauvinism of the early formulation was noted at once by Mary Wollstonecraft.[16] She did not challenge the notions of education as a liberating force nor the liberating potential of perfectible Reason;[17] she protested the gross sexism of the strategies in which women were not to participate as equals. Liberalism has also developed the notion of a *right* to education, a right which, in its early stages of development, grew up around the right to read scripture in the vernacular languages but rapidly developed into the property-based needs for men to be educated which were developed by John Locke.[18]

The main feature of contemporary liberal educational theory may be said to be indeterminism--the shifting, malleable center which liberals defend as pragmatism and the enemies of liberalism regard as simple political opportunism. This soft center has contributed to the recent decline of Canadian liberalism. The defense of free enterprise and radical individualism has, as we have seen, been taken over by the New Right, while liberal states have been preoccupied with economic intervention and welfare measures as a necessary condition of the survival of capitalism. Historically, liberalism has vested the notion of existential freedom in general in the promulgation of particular rights and has developed strong statist tendencies in the articulation, limitation, and defense of individual rights. The liberal state understands itself as protecting free economic enterprise by defending it from its own worst excesses but does this in the conviction that this slightly modified version of capitalist economics constitutes the road to as much individual freedom as is consistent with public order. Perhaps the most common way of expressing this development lies in the historical shift in the ideology of equality: equality of condition--wealth, life-style, class--is now considered to be not only a practical impossibility but to fly in the face of the human reality that everyone is unique. Liberalism has progressively substituted the notion of equality of opportunity for the putatively unattainable equality of worldly condition.[19] Education is the structure in which all children are said to start as equals. After that they are on their own, and the state has done its duty.

The soft core of indeterminacy in liberalism has many implications, not only for analysis but for lived lives. It is difficult to "name," far less define, liberalism: in Canada, for example, the mode of fuzzy liberalism practiced for forty years in Ontario is called progressive conservatism, while the social policies, as opposed to the radical language policies of the Parti Québécois, are essentially liberal. If there is one factor which perhaps distinguishes liberalism from other particular political forms of organization, it is the statist position to which I have referred. Liberalism regards the state as an organizational device to maintain stability and advance a wide variety of often contradictory policies, such as the support of private enterprise, for example, combined with a sometimes brash willingness to have the state intervene in production, or the devotion to the family while educational and social policy steadily erodes that venerable institution. Above all, the state apparatus serves to keep liberal hands on the levers of state power, to govern by poll results, and eschew the "strong" leadership which conservatives crave. This principle, which one might call "flexible indeterminacy," has until recently been politically successful. It has also been strong in terms of absorbing and neutralizing opposition: for women, it leads to some positions of moderate power in both state and constituency organizations. However, as feminism is committed to equality of condition rather than to equality of opportunity with its radically unequal reward system, many feminists, including myself, believe that liberalism is not ultimately consistent with feminism.

Despite the lip-service given to women's rights and the quite concrete gains--such as suffrage--which liberalism has grudgingly given to women, it remains fundamentally patriarchal in theory and practice. Further, it has not, in over 300 years or so, managed to say what it actually means by "rights" or "justice," as debates around the work of John Rawls[20] show. Liberal economics support differential wage scales for women and men in both public service and private enterprise, while fiddling about with vague policies of equal opportunity. Liberal support for women is not the fruit of conviction but of political expediency. In having given women the vote, it does what is necessary to keep as many of these votes as possible in the liberal column. Further, liberal statism has spawned an administrative mode--bureaucracy-- in which crass indifference to the much-vaunted rights of individuals is passed off as "objectivity" and "efficiency." Objectivity, too, is the myth on which liberal theory and research thrive; it forms the intellectual, or, for liberals, the "scientific" basis of liberal perceptions of knowledge. As liberal statism has grown and flourished to the point of bloat, the attenuated epistemology of liberalism and the notion of state organization and control of knowledge and ideology have been central to liberal strategy for the maintenance of political power. Furthermore, the major strategic achievement of liberalism--the vitiation of democracy by the political party system--ensures the limitation of women's political power. Parties remain firmly in the hands of men in all liberal democracies, and so do the state bureaucracies, which can make "concessions" to women while male hands maintain their sweaty grip on public and private power.

The liberal ideology of education, in sum, first posited education as an active instrument for the development of human potential and the affirmation of individual freedom and political right, notions much battered but still politically viable. In practice, liberal education has been and continues to be highly sensitive to the workforce and to the ideological needs of the capitalist mode of production.[21] In intellectual terms, liberal aspirations to epistemological sophistication and the development of scientific, empiricist, and structuralist research models probably owe more to capitalist political economy than to development of liberal philosophy. The politics of indeterminism are both stimulating and limiting, particularly in educational policy: liberal states in general have propagated the notion of individual rights to free, universal education while ensuring that curricula are attuned to liberal policies and "acceptable" forms of knowledge. Moreover, polls show that education is valued by the public,[22] and current efforts to cut back educational funding in capitalist democracies are volatile political footballs.

The central defect of the recommendations of liberal social science is that they do not treat patriarchy as an *essential* component of exploitation but as an accidental aberration. Feminist historians have been able to demonstrate that the teaching profession, for example, has *systematically* exploited women[23] and that church and state have combined historically to limit women's education to traditional domestic roles, differentiated by social class. Teachers are *like* mothers, though not quite so reliable; it has been argued that the brushing-off of this low status on male teachers may be a factor in teacher militancy.[24]

The myth of equality of opportunity and its educational underpinnings has been rather thoroughly exploded in the literature on educational elitism. Although John Porter clearly thought that gender was irrelevant to elite formation, he effortlessly achieved an analysis of extensions of suffrage without ever referring to women's struggle.[25] For liberals, equality is based on an atomistic view of individuality. Liberal individualism is clearly related to the notion of "private" enterprise, but in learning processes the significance of individual response cannot be summarily dismissed as mere bourgeois ideology. Individualistic ideology in liberal theory, however problematic in practice, has been a vital factor in the development of educational psychology and indeed of the "bourgeois" psychosciences in general. The question of how the individual actually learns, how s/he responds to emotional and instructional stimulae, and the significance of these findings for school administration, pedagogical practice, and student counseling have been widely studied.[26] The more mechanistic formulations of studies in the learning process have been conjoined with a concern for the psychological barriers to the learning process as well as for the shapers of that process. The work of Erik Erikson, with its assumption of generically differentiated views of time and space, has been subject to much feminist criticism,[27] and there is still much work being done around emotional factors as inhibitors/stimulators of the learning process. This sort of work, frequently illuminating, is liberal in its perception of the individual as the basic unit of social study, though the question of generalizing findings remains a vexing and unsatisfactory one. However, the work of many women in psychology moves attention from the individual to the group in a constructive way, challenging, for example, the trivialization of responsive interpersonal skills.[28] Mary Ellen Verheyden-Hilliard sees the psychologically trained woman counselor as a "potential superbomb" against school sexism,[29] which is a laudably optimistic strategy designed for use in counselor education at the individual level.

Liberal education is essentially a mode of conservation of the capitalist form of economic practice: this is a truism. It is also based on assumptions about the division of labor and the joyful competence of that inequity to nourish the good life. Liberalism also tolerates and even promotes change in the conventional family: the ideology of equality and the need for a mobile workforce has challenged conservative views of the socially and geographically fixed family since the late Middle Ages.[30] In education, liberalism has in practice permitted literacy for women and allowed a limited kind of social mobility to selected members of the lower classes and exploited sex. In such strategies lies the claim of liberalism to be progressive, and indeed, precisely such strategies have created the counterforces of the New Right. But the relation of liberalism to a radically inequitable economic system on the one hand, and to a defense of patriarchy in terms of who actually wields state power on the other, are precisely the factors which make it a problematic political ideology for women. The epistemological underpinnings of liberal education, with the conflicts of rationalism, individualism, dependence on abstract data, and the fascination with technological solutions to social discordances, is ultimately destructive of the humanism which many sincere liberals have hoped to nurture. Nonetheless, we in Canada appear to be stuck with liberal education for some time to come and may indeed have to defend it politically against the depredations of the New Right. Zillah Eisenstein may well be right in calling for discussions between liberal, socialist, and radical feminists.[31] Further, the feminist movement shares the liberal notion that education is indeed a vital component of *revolutionary* practice, though some feminists--including myself--have difficulty reconciling the need to be educated with the social and personal dynamics of existing educational structures.

The tenacious alliance of liberalism and education is clearly an enormous challenge to feminism. In fact, feminism has been innovative in terms of educational process: the social organization of consciousness raising developed in the 1960s in many liberal states was perhaps the most original educational enterprise since the development of socialist Sunday schools and Workers Educational Associations in the early part of this century. It has a shorter effective life span than these latter, although it is difficult to say whether it is simply in temporary limbo or changing its forms. Many feminist academics understand their pedagogy as consciousness raising and are engaged in research and practice in informal and innovative education.[32] Liberalism, in a classic demonstration of the expediency of indeterminism, has contributed to this development by the relatively rapid but carefully delimited incorporation of women's studies at several levels of education. In Canada, provincial governments have funded the development of curricular materials and guides, and women workers have seen to it that what was done was well done. An early and outstanding example was *The Women's Kit*, created at the Ontario Institute for Studies in Education in the mid-1970s. There are also provincial resource guides of high quality, such as *Sex-Role Stereotyping and Women's Studies* from the Ontario Ministry of Education and *Women's Studies* in British Columbia.

Feminist education in capitalist states is at present uneasily allied with liberal education, but there is a clear trend to work out educational strategies for feminism; these strategies, currently at a very tentative stage, encompass both formal and informal education. Thus, attempts to combine concern for specific cohorts--immigrant women, women of color, union women, lesbian women--with educational strategies do exist in a rather fragmented way, as do the combination of social objectives, politics, and education, which can be seen in the labor movement, the alternative health movement, the peace movement, reproductive politics and in feminist art and literature. The vital area of the school education of girls, however, is a particularly intransigent one, given the state's hold on schooling. Current research[33] does not yet show much more than statistical rearrangement--more girls but not too many more in math and science and so forth. The question of whether patriarchal science is an appropriate area for a feminist education remains moot. Some women scientists are critical of the hidden agendas of science but believe that the acquisition of scientific and technological skills are essential to scientific reform,[34] while other feminists cleave to a neo-Luddite position.[35]

The central problem for women in education may well be the statist, centralized, public realm definition of educational process. Research abounds to confirm that the preschool socialization process lays a cement foundation to the edifice of sexual stereotyping and discrimination to be built in schools.[36] The question is not simply a quantitative one or even a structural one. If gender is developed in the family, it is very important to see that socialization *is* education, and that the major impact of feminism in terms of concrete social change has been on family rather than school. Liberalism's commitment to sustaining the family as the basic unit of society while at the same time lauding liberty and equality (fraternity appears to have retreated a little) has produced liberal reforms of a somewhat parsimonious nature, but real enough. The education of women, the vote, sexual freedom, and reproductive rights, however imperfect, have been forced on a liberalism unwilling to admit publicly that the only individual right it cares about is the property right. Yet these imperfect reforms begin to erode the barrier between public and private life, which is a structural condition of patriarchal power.[37] In terms of the family, then, the impact of women's liberation combined with the internal contradictions of liberalism make the private realm the unprecedented locus of social change.

As the private realm is vulnerable to feminist political practice, this development is very promising; the forms of early childhood consciousness are being subjected to a dialectic of feminist transformation and high-tech ideological indoctrination. Something novel may be happening to Oedipus, and happening among all classes. A vital link is thus being forged between the oppressions within the social relations of both production and reproduction.

Socialism and Education

A distinction must be made here between the education of women in socialist countries and Marxist educational theory and analysis in liberal states and in the Third World.

Education in the Soviet Union and Warsaw Pact nations in general is burdened by an even heavier commitment to state control than that endemic to liberalism. Gender equality is making very slow progress.[38] Women are more heavily engaged in waged labor, with the familiar discriminations, and the family remains patriarchal. Abortion is readily available, but oral contraceptives are not, and even limited reproductive freedom sits uneasily with heavy social sanctions against sexual liberation. The "affinity between revolution and puritanism," as Heitlinger[39] describes it, assures the steady maintenance of a double standard in ethical judgment and male and female sexual expression.

Political education and ideological reproduction are more overt, a fact probably related structurally to one-party government. In politics, women fare poorly in central structures, though they are politically engaged as feminists as well as in cadres at local levels. The most sustained attempt to utilize educational process for improving the condition of women is perhaps that made in Cuba, but the evidence is that Cuba's attempts to use schooling and legal reform for deep cultural transformation in a specific strategy for the abolition of class appears to be stumbling a little because of, Nicola Murray argues, a state commitment to economic development over the liberation of women.[40] In the Third World, questions of education quite often have to yield to dilemmas of survival, though selected countries, India for example, have long and honorable histories of attempts to liberate women through education. The results are mixed and cast serious doubts on the capacity of educational policy to be a major force in political change, Paulo Friere's patriarchal genius notwithstanding.

The notion of revolutionary practice as an educational process has been important for the Left, but interest in formal education less so. Two things have happened to shake this indifference. The first of these is a growing concern among Marxists about the functions and powers of the singularly unwithered modern state. The second is the perceived necessity to give an account of the phenomena of ideological and cultural reproduction. These imperatives have grown from a number of events. One of these, clearly, is the failure of the proletarian in capitalist countries to expropriate their expropriators. The second is a Western Marxist uneasiness about the centralizing and heavily authoritarian structures of existing Communist states. Neither of these concerns is necessarily made specific, but they are at the center of Western Marxism. The location of these problems is perceived to lie in the continuing false consciousness of the proletariat, induced by the capacity of cominterns and capitalists to control the state. Of course, one of the main instruments of this control is education.

Marx's rather laconic dismissal of the state as the executive
committee of the ruling class is clearly inadequate to describe
the actual state apparatus prevailing in Western countries,
and (his theory) has difficulty in coping with the
omnipresence of Communist states in the lives of citizens.
Western Marxism has more generally preferred a critical
evaluation of capitalist states and has attempted to
demonstrate how the state is organized and what processes
contribute to the maintenance of false consciousness:[41] only
very recently have Marxist feminists recognized the
construction of gender consciousness as a historical
problem.[42]

Modern Marxist theorizing on the state is sophisticated
and complex; it is of interest here mainly because it has
taken education as a significant factor in ideological
reproduction but has largely neglected the education of
women. The question of whether class struggle in general is
the road to liberation for women or whether, in fact,
Marxism is intransigently sexist in theory and practice is a
divisive and difficult one for women socialists. However, the
notion of ideological reproduction or the maintenance of false
consciousness among workers is a useful concept which has
become theoretically and methodologically popular with
socialist sociologists. Clearly, democratic states rely on the
consent of the governed, and the manufacturing of such
consent by a variety of social practices in school, the
workplace, politics, and rather marginally, in the family is
the concern of the "New" sociology of education, which is
grounded in the work of Antonio Gramsci.[43]   Gramsci
attacked the vulgarity of crude structural reductionism
embodied in the notion of substructure and superstructure,
arguing that the relation between these two was far too
complex to be shrugged into a shriveled mold of mode-of-
production determinism. He posited a mediating realm of
social practice which worked, as it were, between the
objective parameters of the market economy and the coercive
power of the state. This area, which Gramsci called civil
society, embraced a wide range of individual, group, class,
and state activities: the function of these social activities
was basically to affirm the legitimacy of the state and elicit

the consent of the people to be governed. Gramsci believed that strong states ruled by consent, weak ones by force, but his theory of civil society and the consensual state is important to the present discussion because Gramsci believed that the two major social institutions which were responsible for cultural and ideological reproduction and the concomitant and necessary consent were family and school. He had, however, much to say of school and very little of family, at least in translated works.[44]

The new sociology of education has produced empirical ethnographic work and some stimulating theorizing on the significance of controlling and legitimating knowledge. However, the ethnographies have been mainly of working class lads.[45] Marxist educational research also puts a great deal of emphasis on the role that teachers can play in the development of a critical pedagogy and a more honest curriculum;[46] there is also emphasis on adult education, in unions and in less formal and static structures, such as distance education and the use of communications media such as that pioneered by Britain's Open University.[47] In a rather contradictory way, liberal notions of academic freedom have ensured the survival, with occasional purges, of significant cohorts of Marxist intellectuals in universities. In schools, Marxists tend to share the sort of life-in-the-shadows existence which is familiar to lesbian women, gay men and anyone slightly to the left of the principal. The relation of Marxist intellectuals and teachers is therefore no easier than that between feminist intellectuals and teachers, perhaps even less so. The interest in noninstitutional forms of education is therefore high among feminists and Marxists, but consciousness raising is regarded as highly suspect by Marxists, given its "bourgeois" appeal to subjective experience and its putative neglect of class consciousness.[48] Despite relative success in forms of adult education, both Marxists and feminists recognize the crucial nature of ideological training for young children, but they do so from radically different perspectives: Marxist-feminists[49] have insisted that while education is indeed preparation for adult life under capitalism, it is not only generically differentiated but prepares women for traditional no-pay or low-pay jobs.

However, questions of the material grounds of women's oppression remains problematic: many Marxists define "radical" feminism as ultimately immaterial, based on a tiresome infatuation with the Freudian account of the psyche and trammeled by a methodology which only points to untheorized examples of patriarchy.[50]   Heidi Hartmann correctly argues[51] that Marxism cannot offer an analysis of patriarchy until it develops an adequate theoretical understanding of the dialectic of production and reproduction, and such an understanding must take cognizance of the division of public and private life as structural rather than merely convenient.   Likewise, the attempt to absorb childcare and housework into capitalist exploitation--the apparently expiring domestic labor debate-- has to give way to a recognition that the historical oppression of women is not necessarily the product of property relations.   As far as education is concerned, study of the eroding consensus on the legitimacy of male supremacy, together with the feminist action and discourse which express this rebellion, are promising fields for sociological inquiry.

Feminism and Education

The education of women is likely to remain a contentious, creative, confusing, and vital issue for feminism.   The effort to see this phenomenon as a whole, or at least in terms of its integrative dynamic, is not a simple task.   If one starts from the assumption that androcentric education must be reformed, the immediate why, how, and when questions are difficult enough.   If one adds the need for a theoretical and analytical approach to the task which is uncontaminated by collective patriarchal power and the self-interest of particular men, one finds oneself bereft of language, concepts, and method, all of which have been developed in partriarchal forms.   This is not, as it seems on the surface, an impasse, nor is it, as men love to say, a "challenge."   It is the existential reality of women's life.   It is also, I would suggest, the condition of the exciting projection of a new epistemology.   The need for a future centered education is generally dismissed as Utopian, but the concerns of women have always been future centered; what shall we eat tomorrow? When will the child be born? It is men who have constituted a past which is a justification for the present, just as it is men who have contributed a neutral and objective science which can guarantee the integrity of timeless order-in-chaos. These disturbing considerations deserve to be taken seriously and, indeed, the notion of politics as a process of developing the future is currently vital in terms of planetary survival.

This does not mean that we abandon history and social studies. It does mean that we do them somewhat differently. The question of human values has always been a contentious one for women. For example, the proposition that women's values are ethically superior has emerged in many times and places, perhaps most specifically in terms of the suffragist movement.[52] Madeleine Grumet[53] has noted the "sentimentalization" of teaching and the advantages of motherhood ethos for social control, but Grumet also notes that sentimentalized teaching is fraudulent; in rhetoric familiar and tender, in practice such an ethos screens the process by which children are isolated from the private realm to be trained as consensual citizens. In any case, the movement from local schooling to systems of education which structurally and administratively ape the organization of corporations has overcome any predilection educators may have had for sentiment, which is not useful on assembly lines.

Education as a mode of social control is dedicated to the justification of the present by the past, and thus all forms of patriarchal education, irrespective of their political labels and the differences which I have sketched above, are, in terms of gender, radically conservative. What they conserve is the theory, justification, and social stability of male supremacy, which survive all reform and all pseudo-radicalism and libertarianism. The goal of a feminist education is not equality in knowledge, power, and wealth, but the abolition of gender as an oppressive cultural reality. Education and labor must be sexless in this sense. This goal demands the end of a "science," phallicly understood as hard or soft, and demands working toward an integrative historical process which can transform dualist perceptions and practice to the constitution of mediative relations between the natural and cultural worlds. The abolition of gender, as Ruth Pierson and Alison Prentice[54] have pointed out, does not entail the abandonment of the project of "maximizing female identity";[55] it *does* entail both the negation and procreation of knowledge itself and is thus a task which is profoundly concerned with education.

Education as it stands, powerful but fragile in its dependence on patriarchal ideology and state financing, is a necessary condition of acquiring critical and analytical skills. Feminist education is the process by which our skills can be utilized to bite the hands which have so confidently but parsimoniously fed us. The notion of knowledge as power, as danger, is an old one, which is why larger rations of education must be consumed by men, the ruling class, and the reliably upwardly mobile, and why it is accurately perceived that training rather than education is the proper strategy for preparing people to teach. But it is no longer enough to say that women must "define" what women's education is to be like, or even that we must reeducate men. An integrative curriculum must abolish gender, a sociohistorical category which really only marginally has to do with sexuality. That would be an impossible prescription if it were not in fact already happening.[56] This means that the superficially perplexing "how" question is not quite so intransigent as it seems. Beneath--not far beneath--the turmoil of feminist politics and women's resistance to oppression is a discernible process compounded of critical analysis, demonstration, speculation, artistic creativity, disciplinary rebellion, political will, and intellectual ferment which surpasses the Renaissance fervor which turned John Donne's world upside down. That Renaissance was a rebirth in which parents, child, and attendants were all male. This one is different.

NOTES

[1]Veronica Beechey, "Women and Production: A Critical Analysis of Some Sociological Theories of Women's Work," in *Education and the State*, Vol. 2, *Politics, Patriarchy and Practice*, Roger Dale et al., eds. (Barcombe: Falmer Press, 1981) pp. 116-120.

[2]Madeleine MacDonald, "Schooling and the Reproduction of Class and Gender Relations," in Dale et al., eds., *Politics, Patriarchy and Practice*, pp. 159-177.

[3]Ernesto Scheifelbein and Joseph P. Farrell, *Eight Years of Their Lives: Through Schooling and the Labour Force in Chile*, (Ottawa: International Development Research Centre, 1982), p. 9.

[4]Ibid., p. 130. My italics.

[5]Angela McRobbie, "Settling Accounts with Subcultures," *Screen Education* 34 (Spring 1980) pp. 37-50.

[6]Ann Marie Wolpe, "The Official Ideology of Education for Girls," Dale et al., eds., *Politics, Patriarchy and Practice*, p. 142.

[7]Gary Kinsman, "Parent Power, Patriarchy and Compulsory Heterosexuality," unpublished paper, Toronto, Ontario Institute for Studies in Education, 1982.

[8]Lise Moisan, F. Tremblay, C. Viver. "L'éducation sexuelle: Guy et Yvette dans la fosse aux lions," *La vie en Rose* (June-August 1981), pp. 14-25; Rachel Belisle, "C'est au nom d'Amour," *Des Luttes et des Rires*, 3, no. 4 (April/May, 1980), pp. 10-11.

[9]Gary Kinsman, "Parent Power, Patriarchy and Compulsory Heterosexuality," unpublished paper, Toronto, Ontario Institute for Studies in Education, 1982; William Buchanan, "The New Book Banners." *Mudpie* 2, no. 3 (March 1981); Charlotte Bunch, "Not For Lesbians Only," *Quest*, 7, no. 2 (Fall 1975); Ken Campbell, *Tempest in a Teapot* (Cambridge, Ontario: Coronation Press, 1975); Mary Douglas, *Natural Symbols* (Harmondsworth: Penguin, 1973);

David Stewart, *Moral Values Education in Ontario: The Crisis of Consent* (Ontario: Renaissance Ontario, 1978).

[10]Angela Miles, "Ideological Hegemony in Political Discourse: Women's Specificity and Equality," in *Feminism in Canada: From Pressure to Politics*, Angela Miles and G. Finn, eds. (Montreal: Black Rose, 1982), p. 220.

[11]Barbara Ehrenreich, "The Women's Movement: Feminist and Anti-Feminist," *Radical America* (Spring 1981); Andrea Dworkin, *Right-Wing Women* (New York: Perigree, 1983), Chapter 2, "The Politics of Intelligence."

[12]Ken Campbell, *Tempest in a Teapot* (Cambridge, Ontario: Coronation Press, 1975), and *No Small Stir: A Spiritual Strategy for Salting and Saving a Secular Society* (Burlington, Ontario: G. R. Welch Co., 1980).

[13]K. Clarricoates, "All in a Day's Work," in *Learning to Lose: Sexism and Education*, D. Spender, E. Sarah, eds. (London: Women's Press, 1980), pp. 69-80.

[14]M. David, "The State, Education and the Family: An Exploratory Analysis," paper presented at the British Sociological Association Annual Conference, Sheffield, England, 1977.

[15]Lynda Lange, "Rousseau: Women and the General Will," in *The Sexism of Social and Political Theory*, Lorenne M. G. Clark and Lynda Lange, eds. (Toronto: University of Toronto Press, 1979), pp. 41-52.

[16]Mary Wollstonecraft, *A Vindication of the Rights of Women* (New York: Norton, 1967).

[17]Ibid., p. 94.

[18]Lorenne M. G. Clarke, "Women and Locke: Who Owns the Apples in the Garden of Eden?" in Clark and Lange, eds., *The Sexism of Social and Political Theory*, pp. 16-40.

[19]Mary Jo Bane, "Economic Justice: Controversies and Policies," in *The "Inequality" Controversy*, Donald M. Levine and Mary Jo Bane, eds. (New York: Basic Books, 1975), pp. 277-303.

[20]John Rawls, *A Theory of Justice* (Cambridge, Mass.: The Belknap Press of Harvard University Press, 1971).

[21]Madeleine MacDonald, "Socio-Cultural Reproduction and Women's Education," in *Schooling for Women's Work*, Rosemary Deem, ed. (London: Routledge & Kegan Paul, 1980), pp. 13-25.

[22]D. W. Livingstone, D. J. Hart, L. D. McLean, *Public Attitudes Toward Education in Ontario 1982: Fourth OISE Survey* (Toronto: Informal Series #51, OISE, 1983), pp. 10-11.

[23]Marta Danylewycz and Alison Prentice, "Teachers, Gender and Bureaucratizing School Systems in Nineteenth Century Montreal and Toronto" *History of Education Quarterly* (1984).

[24]Myron Brenton, *What's Happened to the Teacher?* (New York: Avon, 1970), p. 44.

[25]John Porter, *The Vertical Mosaic* (Toronto: University of Toronto Press, 1965), pp. 370-379.

[26]Esther Greenglass, *A World of Difference: Gender Roles in Perspective* (Toronto: John Wiley & Sons, 1982).

[27]Ibid., p. 247.

[28]Jeri Dawn Wine and Marti Diane Smye, *Social Competence* (New York: The Guildford Press, 1981), pp. 29-30.

[29]Mary Ellen Verheyden-Hilliard, "Counselling: Potential Superbomb" (Washington: HEW Publication No. (OE) 77-01017, 1978).

[30]Madeleine Grumet, "Other People's Children," *Bitter Milk: Women and Teaching*, (Amherst: University of Massachussets Press, 1988), pp. 164-182.

[31]Zillah Eisenstein, "Towards a Unified Women's Movement" in *Women and Revolution*, Lydia Sargent, ed. (Montreal: Black Rose, 1981), p. 341.

[32]Jane Gaskell, "Stereotyping and Discrimination in the Curriculum" in *Precepts, Policy and Process: Perspective on Contemporary Canadian Education*, H. A. Stevenson and J. Donald Wilson, eds. (London, Ontario: Alexander, Blake Associates), pp. 263-284.

[33]Rosemary Deem, et al., eds., *Schooling for Women's Work* (London: Routledge & Kegan Paul, 1980); Isabelle Deblé, *The School Education of Girls* (Paris: UNESCO, 1980); Eileen M. Byrne, "Equality of Education and Training for Girls (10-18 years)" (Brussels, Luxembourg: Commission of European Communities. Education Series No. 9, 1978).

[34]Brighton Women and Science Group, *Alice Through the Microscope: The Power of Science Over Women's Lives* (London: Virago, 1980); Sheila Tobias, *Overcoming Math Anxiety* (Boston: Houghton Mifflin, 1978).

[35]Elizabeth Dodson Gray, *Why the Green Nigger: Re-Mything Genesis* (Wellesley, Mass.: Roundtable Press, 1979).

[36]Florence Howe and Paul Lauter, "Sexual Stereotypes Start Early," *Saturday Review* (October, 1971); Patricia Minunchen, "Sex-Role Concepts and Sex-Typing in Childhood as a Function of Home and School Environments," in *Women and Education*, Elizabeth Steiner Maccia et al., eds. (Springfield, Ill.: 1975), pp. 124-142; Anne Marie Henschel, *Sex Structure* (Don Mills, Ontario: Longman Canada, 1973), Chapter 6.

[37]Mary O'Brien, *The Politics of Reproduction* (London: Routledge & Kegan Paul, 1981).

[38]Alena Heitlinger, *Women and State Socialism: Sex Inequality in the Soviet Union and Czechoslovakia* (Montreal: McGill/Queen's University Press, 1979); Hilda Scott, *Does Socialism Liberate Women?* (Boston: Beacon Press, 1975); Wilhelm Reich, *The Sexual Revolution*, Theodore P. Wolfe, trans. (New York: Octagon Books, 1971).

[39]Alena Heitlinger, *Women and State Socialism: Sex Inequality in the Soviet Union and Czechoslovakia* (Montreal: Mcgill/Queen's University Press, 1979), p. 22.

[40]Nicola Murray, "Socialism and Feminism: Women and the Cuban Revolution," *Feminist Review*, no. 3 (1979), pp. 99-108.

[41]George Lukacs, *History and Class Consciousness* (Cambridge, Mass.: M.I.T. Press, 1971); Louis Althusser, "Ideology and Ideological State Apparatuses," *Education, Structure and Society*, B. R. Cosen, ed. (Harmondsworth: Penguin, 1972).

[42]Sandra Harding, "What is the Real Material Base of Marxism and Feminism?" in *Women and Revolution: A Discussion of The Unhappy Marriage of Marxism and Feminism*, Lydia Sargent, ed. (Montreal: Black Rose, 1981), pp. 135-164.

[43]Antonio Gramsci, *Selections From the Prison Notebooks of Antonio Gramsci*, Quintin Hoare and Geoffrey Nowell Smith, eds. and trans. (London: Routlege & Kegan Paul, 1971); Madeleine MacDonald, "Schooling and the Reproduction of Class and Gender Relations," in Dale et al., eds. *Politics, Patriarchy and Practice*, pp. 159-177.

[44]Mary O'Brien, "The Commatization of Women: Patriarchal Fetishism in the Sociology of Education," *Interchange* 15 no. 2 (1984), pp. 43-60.

[45]Paul Willis, *Learning to Labour* (Westmead: Saxon House), 1977.

[46]Michael W. Apple, *Curriculum, Ideology*, (Boston: Routledge & Kegan Paul, 1979), p. 23.

[47]Moira Griffiths, "Women in Higher Education. A Case Study of the Open University," *Schooling for Women's Work* in Deem, ed., (London: Routledge & Kegan Paul, 1980), pp. 126-142.

[48]Heidi Hartmann, "The Unhappy Marriage of Marxism and Feminism: Towards a More Progressive Union," in *Women and Revolution: A Discussion of the Unhappy Marriage of Marxism and Feminism*, Lydia Sargent, ed. (Montreal: Black Rose, 1981), pp. 196-197.

[49]Jennifer Shaw, "Education and the Individual: Schooling for Girls or Mixed Schooling - A Mixed Blessing," *Schooling for Women's Work* in Deem, ed., (London: Routledge & Kegan Paul, 1980), pp. 257-268; Madeleine MacDonald, "Schooling and the Reproduction of Class and Gender Relations," pp. 159-175.

[50]Heidi Hartmann, "The Unhappy Marriage of Marxism and Feminism: Towards a More Progressive Union," in Sargent, ed., *Women and Revolution* pp. 196-197.

[51]Hartmann, "The Unhappy Marriage," pp. 30-31.

[52]Carol Lee Bacchi, *Liberation Deferred? The Ideas of the English Canadian Suffragists, 1877-1918* (Toronto: University of Toronto Press, 1983.

[53]Madeleine Grumet, "Pedagogy for Patriarchy," *Interchange* 12:2-3 (1981) pp. 165-184.

[54]Ruth Pierson and Alison Prentice, "Feminism and the Writing and Teaching of History," in Miles and Finn, eds., *Feminism in Canada*.

[55]*Ibid.*, p. 107.

[56]For a discussion and guide to programmes and resources, see: Somer Brodribb, *Women's Studies in Canada*, Special Publication of *Resources for Feminist Research*, (November 1987) 252 Bloor Street West, Toronto, Ontario, M5S 1V6.

Ethics and Ideology in Health Care: A Feminist Perspective

There are few tenets more beloved of conservative thought than that which holds that the form which hovers over the sick bed and the death bed should be female. Historically, of course, these forms mostly have been female, but the notion of hovering has always been a largely fictitious one: it is difficult to hover on the trot. In any case there are many signs in the field of Western health that hovering is no longer appropriate: in our health institutions patients now appear to me to be as peripatetic as nurses are, whipping between O.R., I.C.U., X-Ray, C.I.U., O.P.D., and various other alphabetized mystery tours which make being incapacitated a call for prodigious activity. But apart from vast changes in what is now referred to as health care delivery--the commoditization of health, one perceives--there have been transformations in the structure of the health professions, the assignment of responsibilities and the therapeutic and technical infrastructure of health care. There have also been social changes--in educational preparation, in the growth of unions and in the intervention of the state. Insofar as health

Excerpted from "Health Begins at Birth," *The Whig-Standard Magazine*, vol. 6, no. 19, Kingston, Ontario, February 16, 1985. Lecture presented in the Chancellor Dunning Memorial Lecture Series, Queen's University, Kingston, Ontario, 1985.

is not only an individual good, but a question of species survival, recent developments in reproductive technology seem to me to be particularly significant--and I shall return to that discussion presently, for my themes are ideology and ethics--and there can be little doubt that, as a race, we have deemed species survival to be a great good. We have also developed some extraordinarily destructive means of endangering that survival. It is this contradiction which seems to me to be central to any serious discussion of what we intend by the notion of the cultural construction of good health in both theory and practice.

The traditional role given to women in health care and the highly specialized role of women in species reproduction suggest that women should be in the forefront of the battle to produce and reproduce good health, on an individual and species level. Whether they are or not depends on where one thinks the forefront is. If it is the front line, the trenches, then women are certainly there. If it is in the august chambers where decisions are made or laboratories where scientists work their dramaturgy with casts of cells on the stage of petri dishes, then women are less likely to be there. The forefront is actually in the political realm, for the notion of good health as a private matter is not affirmed by breathless joggers and fad dieters in advanced capitalist countries. The State has taken on responsibility for health care, a move now regretted perhaps, but not easy to reverse. Health issues are political issues and therefore the politicization of women in health care is a significant phenomenon. We see this clearly in the contemporary struggles of midwives, the growth of unionization and the development of male careers in the health "industry." The Grange Commission has done more for the radicalization of nurses than months of rational organization and development of alternative health strategies. There is a growing sense that the reform of existing health services through the traditional strategies of public inquiry, funding fights, political pressure and the endless writing of briefs is not sufficient to crack the hold of vested interests on the very definition of what health is. This is not to dismiss such activities as futile nor misplaced. We can and must meet problems and concerns which are presented by our living in the world, by our experience and by our practical possibilities.   But many women, including myself, and a slowly increasing number of men, believe that patriarchal politics, which have reached their gratifying if dizzy pinnacle in the Nation State, are *essentially* oppressive, intrinsically sexist, racist, and class-biased, and all the amendments to existing laws and the Constitution itself can only ameliorate and never really transform this repressive relation.

Thus, we see ever more clearly in the everyday definitions of good health the "good" of the economic system, of the powerful, of the electoral needs of political parties, and a systematic marginalization of the young, the poor--countries as well as people--in the health market.   We also see differential criteria developed for the definition of women's health and men's health which is damaging to both genders. Men are to be strong enough to be permanently ready to die for their country.   These ideologies persist in the face of population explosions and the universal destructiveness of modern warfare.   Such considerations, however, do not mean that we can sit back and wait for the contradictions of our social existence to burst asunder and then start over.   What it means in terms of health and political issues is that not only do we have to struggle, but we have to struggle on two fronts: we have to identify, by hard analytical and theoretical work, a consciousness of the actuality and relationship of events, of where we are and where we are going and of what our ends and purposes are.   At the same time, we must meet individual issues as they arise, whether these be issues of techniques, of organization, of particular modes of ill-being--such as, for example, the halt in the search for a safe mode of contraception in favor of the computerization of species reproduction; the rape of the environment; the adulteration of our food and the starvation of huge populations--we must meet these issues as they arise in all their complexities.   We must also, of course, earn our living, care for our kids, get ourselves educated, cultivate our gardens, learn to know and care for each other as women, and so forth.   We all know, of course, that women "don't work" and that if we are fatigued it's all in our heads.   Pop another Valium!

This constant effort means that good health is not a distant objective but a day-to-day struggle. It is, as is clearer every day, a *species* struggle, but the traditional role of women in conserving good health as a family responsibility--a sacred duty rewarded only by the satisfactions of healthy and well-socialized children, if one is lucky--makes the struggle one in which women are existentially and historically immersed, but which we do not--yet--control. I do not want to make the unimaginative and misleading leap from the health of people to the popular notion of a sick society. I understand health as the care of our physical being at the personal level and the reproduction of the species on the historical level. Metaphors of disease have always been popular but are in fact a cop-out--an attribution of organism to events and circumstances which are the result of human actions. Samuel Beckett speaks in *Waiting for Godot* of how men blame their boots for imperfections of their feet, obliquely drawing our attention to the fact that we can control how we make boots but we do not in practice make them for healthy and unstandardized feet. We make them for profit, for fashion, for work and for wearing out fast so that we need new ones, promoting the economic health of shoe companies and keeping podiatrists busy.

Let us eschew the seductions of health metaphors in favor of a clearer view of health and a more realistic perception of physical and moral well-being: pornography, for example, is not sick. It is evil. We go burbling on about the evil of censorship, when the legal issue is not that of censorship but of incitement to violence. Sickness is not what the violator experiences, but the ruin of the good health of the violated. To speak of a "right" to health in a society which legitimizes violence and pollution is to pretend that the only enemy that we encounter in terms of our well-being is disease, and that medicine is the royal road to health. Further, we conceptualize disease as an individual affair. To be sure, people do get sick, are treated, are cured or die. But in an individualist society, such as ours, we can never have any "right" to be well but only to be treated with some semblance of equality when we are ill, and it is supposed to be our personal responsibility to keep fit. Thus, we see all these persons jogging along (not necessarily in the right boots) doing their twenty-minute workouts, painfully withdrawing from the addictions which made our society a tiny bit more tolerable, swallowing their cereals, pumping in the vitamins--all of these individual initiatives which are based upon the view that we somehow control our own health. If we consider the current epidemic of cancer, for example, we see the ideological tangle of our perceptions of good health in all its massive contradiction. Because cancer is a disease which attacks individuals, we must search for an individual cure. If, however, the premise is incorrect--as many believe it to be--if cancer is an environmental scourge on community rather than an unfortunate individual fate, then we have these young one-legged heroes--with whom, being one-legged myself, I have deep sympathy--we see them running across the country to raise funds, millions of dollars, for something called cancer research, which consists of a search for an unknown cause and an individual cure. To be sure, there may be unknown microbes and bandit genes concerned, but we do *know* that cancer is a by-product of environmental pollution, increasing radiation, lousy diet and bad habits. But we raise funds for the medically controlled cancer societies which insist on the ideology of personal health and individual cure. It would make little difference if our one-legged heroes ran for environmental protection agencies either, for the forces which profit from pollution are much stronger than those which try to resist it. Health and welfare become strategies for amelioration, the worst excesses of irrational economic systems.

I believe that the interest of women in health care is a crucial issue here: I am arguing that good health is a physical, social and moral issue, that it is a question not only of individual health but of species persistence, not, you will notice, species *survival*--a counsel of desperation--but of persistence over time--a counsel of unified species action. Mere survival is O.K. for all those ants which men like Edward O. Wilson think should be our moral mentors as well as our in-laws: "The female of the species," Wilson asserts, "is quintessentially a producer of eggs." The quintessence, you will recall, was an abstract essence which the ancients

invented to cover those material things not readily
describable as earth, air, fire or water; it was thought to be
the substance of which the heavenly bodies were formed.
This does not seem to be what Wilson had in mind, so
presumably he actually means essential, but uses the wrong
word to suggest that this is not an essential task which
women do but their *only* significant one. The fact that this
view--the notion of women as essentially breeders, preferably
of healthy children with clearly accredited fathers--is in fact
a historical and cultural elaboration which, if it is the
quintessence of anything, is that of the systematic relegation
of women to the private tasks of personal needs rather than
the public task of making history. As this is a partial view
of women's reality, it may be defined as ideology, which I
understand as an attribution of meaning to phenomena
which ignores their human and social content. The classic
case of ideology is that arising in Marx's description of
commodity fetishism. In the practice of re-defining the
products of human labor as values in the marketplace, Marx
noticed, human products become things, and the social
relations embedded in them are obscured in the market
relations of the exchange of things. This is an important
issue nowadays in terms of the health industry, in terms of
health itself perceived as a thing rather than as a communal
activity, a historical creation. The transformation of nurses
into managers, of doctors into entrepreneurs, of patients into
statistics and of community health into a salvage operation:
all of these developments are ameliorated by the care and
concern of struggling individuals, but the basic process of
turning good health into a commodity advances in spite of
these efforts. But the ultimate contradiction in
contemporary health care emerges at the species level, not at
the level of the solitary sufferer. Our two largest public
expenditures in the modern world are for health and welfare
on the one hand and for species destruction through weapons
development on the other. To talk of "public health" in the
age of destruction is to posit a moral question and then
refuse to take it seriously. The notion that the well-being of
individuals depends on their willingness to finance the means
of destroying both the natural and human world is

profoundly ideological, a radical separation of the real needs and aspirations of people from actual strategies to conserve and re-create the species.

The whole question of health is drearily circumscribed, in my view, by the Western fixation on liberal individualism. There is no point in having a "right" to health if we do not have the will and the means to produce and reproduce it, or even a clear idea of what it is. What we actually have, as has often been noticed, is not a health service but a sickness industry, a conception of health rooted in the passive notion of the patient. Patient, I would remind you, is the opposite of agent. Women, of course, are doubly exploited as both patients and agents of the sickness industry and are exploited as both producers and consumers of health care. To be sure, men are consumers and producers of health care too but their situation is quite different. In the first place, they have no history, no tradition of being "natural" tenders of care, and they are not therefore frowned upon when they make no bones about the fact that they are in the business for reward, not as a labor of love. When women seek rewards--usually of a more modest scale--they are considered to be attacking the sick and the taxpayers with equally unnatural venom. A couple of years ago, during a hospital strike in Ontario, an angry hospital worker--a woman-- screamed in the phlegmatic countenance of the premier of the province. The media solemnly opined that she had done the cause more harm than good all that vulgar screaming you know, in the face of that dear man who certainly prefers to be patient rather than agent. Implicit in this view is the endless slur on women--that they ought to be, have a moral obligation to be, patient and dignified, that they have tedious and unlovely vocal pitch, that they should leave action to men and, I suspect, at a deeper level, that it is their natural duty to cherish and nourish the sick and unseemly to expect decent wages for doing so. It is now common to note that nurses are "very well paid," but the salary of a nurse with three years in college is still about $7,000 per year less than such other public servants as policemen, who have six months training. We might note, too, that men, while they have no tradition of vocation, except perhaps as priests and soldiers, do have a tradition of power and decision making, of definition and control, of strength and rationality.

Why have women put up with their identification as natural carers, not even inspired by ethics but determined by biology? This is not an easy question to answer--that women have been incarcerated in the private realm for centuries not by choice but by force, by the twin strategies of economic deprivation and physical violence, is not deemed an acceptable answer within the categories of patriarchal interpretations of family life. But I shall come back to this point. First, I'd like to comment on some of the tensions arising from the situation of women as consumers/patients on the one hand and producers/agents on the other.

When we speak of women as agents of health care we must ask: agents for whom? Is this the "agency" of practice, of control, of policy making, of ethical deliberation? No. Clearly, women health workers are agents of the people of the community they serve, the consumers, and this is traditionally and sometimes actually a relation of trust, an ethical as well as a practical relation. At the same time, health workers are agents of the state system of health care. This is quite often a relation of suspicion and antagonism, of industrial conflict. This dialectic of suspicion and trust in the working lives of health agents causes much tension. The ideology of health care also posits the relation of doctors and nurses as one of trust, but the hard reality is that this is a relation of dominance/subordination in which gender plays a compelling role. This is true of the relations with the increasing bureaucratic presence in health services.

The relation of health care workers to the health industry means that, whatever the myths and sociological fantasies of professionalism, health care "professionals," apart from doctors, are in fact workers, and increasingly assembly-line, hourly rated workers. Nurses, for example, now recognize that they work for a large corporation--the state--a company in which we all are forced to buy shares but whose dividends are distributed in a way which might fairly be called uneven. The state of course is not a corporation in the strict sense of limited liability, and certainly has shown no aptitude at all for capital accumulation. It is not in business to make profits, but to dispense its products, to give away the shareholders' money, not a strategy in most of the corporations we know and love. Quite a bit of what is dispensed does in fact find its way into the coffers of other corporations. Nonetheless, the definition of species health in terms of individual disease gives health workers a vested interest in ill-health, which constitutes a moral dilemma of which many workers are acutely conscious. So are some politicians, hence the trickle of funds to public health, well-baby clinics, seniors day care, home care and so forth, though no funding for the politically contentious health issues related to species reproduction, such as midwifery and reproductive control, from teenage pregnancy to termination of pregnancy. But it is a central contradiction in the lives of health care workers that there is a gap between what they think they ought to be doing--promoting well-being--and what they are actually doing, which is depending on ill-being for their livelihoods.

A further contradiction, especially acute for women carers, arises from the fact that the health industry, like all modern industry, is blindly infatuated with technology. I do not mean only scientific and medical technology, but technology in general--in administration, in work process, in the division of labor, in "processing" the patients over against whom workers stand as agents of heath care technology. It is, of course, difficult to be critical of technological development in a society in which ET is everyone's favorite wee brother, and in which demurrals are written off as neo-luddite survivals from the nineteenth-century resisters of reason and progress. None of us, I imagine, would deny the advantages which technology has wrought in the diagnosis and treatment of disease in very wide areas. One would not like there to be no vaccines, no dialysis, no anesthetics, no pharmaceuticals at all, but I could manage without assembly-line nutrition, routine blood tests, the preponderance of Caesarean sections and about 80 percent of X-rays. I think I might want to do without nuclear medicine too, but I have been too frightened to find out what it is. Management technology, too, has transformed the lives of nurses in radical ways, in which the maintenance of documents has become more time-demanding than the care of patients, documents which give an illusion of scientific health care but which distract health care workers increasingly from patient care. The debate about hands-on care is lively. The greatest trial for a patient in a hospital these days is to be suffering from a discomfort which doesn't appear on your care plan--if it's not there, you must keep it till the shift changes and new rounds are done. The sickness industry is subject to the famous norms of efficiency which govern modern organizational and management theories. One of the consequences for nurses and other health workers is that they are forced to practice guerrilla tactics to force a caring comportment into work structures developed with an eye to cost control rather than health promotion. A basic component of this strategy is the increasing division of labor and the tendency to insist that written records are more real than what actually happens.

When I was a head nurse--in Scotland in the 1950s--I had no written job description. Tut tut. But a brief look at the job is illuminating: it included not only the core tasks--as they later came to be called, though the phrase had a short life span--of doing and supervising hands-on care, keeping the doctors contented and maintaining relatively uncomplicated written records. But it also involved educating students; supervising diets and serving meals; admitting and discharging; checking out home situations with colleagues in Public Health; directing domestic staff (augmented, of course, by student nurses); organizing patient recreation (this was a sanatorium with an average 18-month patient stay); collecting blood and urine samples and doing certain tests on the ward; regulating linen supply, visiting hours and religious services; caring for oxygen and ether equipment; controlling drugs; maintaining sepsis; and scheduling staff off-duty. Whether this sort of versatility was desirable and productive is a matter of debate, but it does provide a way of demonstrating how the division of labor works over time. These jobs--this job--now requires social workers, assorted technicians, dietary aids, ward clerks, various therapists and, of course, the institutional separation of nursing education and nursing practice. Many of the functions--diet, sepsis, laundry, lab work--are contracted out, giving private enterprise its share of the state funding. But the job was never boring and in fact carried considerable authority and responsibility. Paper work was at a minimum and evaluation was by results. However, the financial rewards were minuscule, and nurses took the view that they could only increase these by strategies of professionalization, involving education and a firmer and more clearly circumscribed job description.

I think it doubtful that the prestige of health care workers has been in fact raised by these strategies, which were in any case overtaken by state intervention and the proliferation of management techniques and the strengthening of the institutional power of doctors and administrators. Further, while the question of increase in efficiency via the division of labor is moot, there can be no doubt that as a strategy it serves to create tensions between categories of workers and ultimately helps to keep workers in line; it facilitates control and creates a division of interest as well as a division of labor, an often hostile clamoring to guard one's tiny space against competitors. This, of course, is not new. Feminist scholarship has shown how divisive these battles have always been. Jean Donnison in her excellent book *Midwives and Medical Men* has documented not only the struggle between midwives and doctors, but the struggle of nurses, led at that time by the formidable Florence, against midwives. A hostility between nurses and social workers was virulent in the late nineteenth century, and shades of that hostility live on. I was taught that public health nurses were cop-outs who preferred weekends off to caring for patients. The division of labor in the health industry has undoubtedly raised divisions among women, divisions which are only now being challenged by the development of the women's movement and the marginal but significant development of health alternatives.

As patients/consumers of care, women are perhaps even more disadvantaged. In this process, one sees very clearly the significance of both gender and class divisions, but I would argue that gender is the prime analytical category for understanding the exploitation of women as health agents and patients. Health care is, of course, differentiated by

class for women and men: extra billing is the pragmatic
recognition of this, which is why elected politicians with
ideologies of equal opportunity dislike it so much.   But gender
is a far more significant factor in the analysis of women's
roles as agents and patients of the health industry.   Women
simply do not come to the marketplace of commodity health
on equal terms with men of their own class: consider the
longevity of shelters for destitute males compared with the
very recent efforts to find shelter for "bag ladies," and even
middle-class women do not necessarily have access to the
hard cash which buys health care.   More basically, we do not
come to that marketplace with a historically verified version
of our well-being which says that we are fundamentally
strong, in control of our bodies, or even reliable witnesses of
our own signs and symptoms.   To be sure, if there are men
who actually correspond to this ideological formulation, and I
didn't come across them in my twenty-five years in nursing,
it doesn't do them much good unless they can confront the
super-experts of the illness industry on equal socio-economic--
that is, class terms.   Women never come to the merchants of
the industry on those kinds of terms; the historically verified
picture of women's well-being and ill-being is one which
women themselves have not created.   We do not control, and
have not controlled for centuries, the bottom line of the
species economy, the quintessential creativity embodied in
the labor which reproduces the race.   We do not yet control
who we are, culturally nor intellectually, or who we might
become.   Female well-being is continuously subjected to an
interpretation filtered through a long-dominant ideology of
male supremacy, through the liberal myths of equality and
freedom of our own political ideology, through the ideological
equation of physical health and the brute strength, the
power to violate.   These can never be the bases of an ethic of
caring, but the material source of such an ethic in women's
lives which has transformed the meaning of birth itself,
placing it technically as well as ideologically in the control of
the patriarchate.

The historical record of male problem-solving, based upon
domination of the natural world, on violence, on a
preoccupation with death and a contempt for the "animal"

act of birth, does not seem to me to promise a moral deportment towards species continuity, a unity of morality and good health which would seem to me to be the condition of the continuity of our species. Yet reproductive technology has enormous potential for women. When we consider the historical ways in which men have attempted to mediate their separation from species continuity--a subject which I have addressed at length in *The Politics of Reproduction*--and the realities of male and female reproductive consciousness, we must arrive, I think, at the conclusion that while birth itself appears to be a biological event, it is much more complex than that.

When I was a young midwife, somewhat thoughtless, I used to like to claim that I was a member of the second oldest profession. I thought this a clever wee joke. If one wants an example of what existentialists mean by bad faith or Marxists by false consciousness, this is an excellent sample of both. It is clear that the caring for biological being must be aeons older than prostitution: prostitution requires the historical development of an exchange market and the commodification of sexuality, none of which suggest themselves as "natural" phenomena. What is as old as the race itself is the vulnerability of the organism to injury and disease, to death, to hunger, cold and pain. The fact that women have historically attended to these needs does not mean that they have done so "naturally," but as the human vulnerabilities of the newborn are among the most acute, and the front line of infant well-being is the breast, it is not at all difficult to understand that the construction of cultural responses to such needs might well have been undertaken by women. Almost as vulnerable is the childbearing woman herself, engaged in sweaty, dangerous, painful labor and quite often dying in the attempt. Men's relation to birth is quite different, and there are no historical records of men dying in the act of impregnation, although the ancients made this connection poetically: "Let me die," Ovid asked, "as I come to the foot of Venus," a phrase which raises interesting etymological questions about the verb "to come." What men lose in the act of ejaculation of course is not their life but their sperm, an act which separates them from the

continuity of the species in a material way. History attests
that this alienation from species continuity has caused them
some anxiety, and created a lot of activity around the claims
of paternity. The law recognizes this in its magisterial way:
Mater sempa certa est, pater est quem nuptiae demonstrant.
The mother is always certain, the father is he to whom the
marriage points. Fathers are, in one sense, legal fictions.
But the efforts of men to reduce the uncertainty of paternity
are not, I would suggest, psychic longings nor responsible
choices, but an ancient effort to deal with the alienated
reality of the species status of the male. The efforts of men
to affirm paternity are not recorded in history books, just as
the reproduction of the species--an absolute condition, a
necessary sub-structure of a human history--does not find its
way into theories of history. I believe that a recognition of
human reproductive experience and significance has to be
restored to our notion of human history. Women's
reproductive labor is, after all, a highly integrative process.
It affirms experientially the continuity of the species and
creates a different perception of time--as continuous--and of
the practicality of a mediated relation between the human
and natural world. Yet this integrative consciousness has
been derided as inferior, as naturalistic, ahistorical,
hopelessly in thrall to uncontrolled nature. The natural
continuity of women's experience of continuity over time, the-
integration-through-labor aspect of reproductive experience,
the concern for the helpless, the care of the body and the
peace of the mind--all of this has been considered sub-human
and prehistorical by the men who are biologically alienated
from the experience of species continuity.

What I am suggesting here is that our conception of good
health is a product of certain definable social strategies by
which human societies deal with contradictions between the
way we reproduce ourselves in species continuity and
individual births and the way we reproduce ourselves in the
production of economic and cultural needs. I am not trying
to set up a model of biological determinism, though I do think
that intellectual denigration and hysteria produced by *any*
notion of determinism is one of the more exaggerated
genuflections to the notion of freedom which liberalism posits

as existential. What is not biologically determined, as history shows us, is the cultural forms in which we deal with biological realities--the needs for food, shelter, sex and so forth which are clearly of biological origin. The notion that we must overcome nature, enter into a permanent struggle for transcendence of the natural world, is one which patriarchal culture values highly. As it has led to strategies of domination and violence, it might at least be subject to some kind of critical evaluation.

The only force in Western society which aims to challenge the validity of very fundamental questions of how we can know, understand and change our human experience is feminism. Patriarchy is not healthy. It legitimizes violent solutions to historical problems in ways which casually destroy whole species, the natural environment and the well-being of individuals; it is preoccupied with death and infatuated with power; it claims to transcend contingent nature while it invents sexism, racism and genocide. It is, further, profoundly ideological in the sense that it posits an absolute breach between history and nature which leads to a valuation of nature as both inferior and endlessly threatening to man's aspirations. I believe that the biological uncertainty which separates men from species continuity in the act of ejaculation has been a factor in the development of this dualist view of reality. It has also led to the definition of woman as part of nature, due to their reproductive functions, and as radically unfree creatures. The natural continuity of women's experience over the generations through the pain/pleasure dialectic of childbirth; the concern for the helpless, the care of the body; the peace of the mind; the survival of the species; the notion of a respectful partnership with the natural world: all of these are considered in male dominant society to be "soft" issues. "Hard" issues are war, politics, law, economic, racial and gender power. Softness, of course, is feminine. It has clearly been perceived as important to keep women, who epitomize soft values over hard ideologies, from ganging up on men, to prevent the morality of life and well-being from challenging the hegemony of domination and control. The major cultural device for achieving this control has been, in Western society,

the separation of public and private life, the cultural
expression or gender ideologies and the related ideology of
male supremacy.

This separation is one reason why we have difficulty in
defining good health.   Public and private reflect the
existential tensions of our existence as both individuals and
members of a community, but there is no evident reason why
that should be perceived dualistically. The split is reflected
internationally in the major ideologies of our time, liberal
individualism   and   communism,   which   both   insist--
ideologically--that we must be one or the other when in fact
we must learn to be both. The notion of health can never be
one of static equilibrium, of commodity production, of
reification, or of that alienation from the natural and
biological being which is a condition of but which does not
determine the possibility of health. Health, in my view, must
be holistic, not in the still limited but promising ways being
developed in holistic medicine, but in an attempt to integrate
individual well-being, species strength and care of the
environment in political action to redefine radically our
notions of the good.

Which is easy to say, but hard to do. I have spoken of the
historical transformation of health to commodity and the
subsequent proletarianization of workers in the sickness
industry. I have spoken of health as a species concern. I
have spoken of conceptions of good health as ideological
reflections of unmediated contradictions.   I am therefore
suggesting that any useful perception of good health must be
materially related to the historical means by which we
attend to the need to both produce and reproduce--to
reproduce individuals on a daily basis and as a species, to
unify productive and reproductive strategies in an
integrative way. I have also suggested that the oppression of
women is the suppression of the significance of reproductive
relations in any notion of history which men have produced.
I believe that at this moment feminism, which grapples with
this significance, is the political force which has a
progressive understanding of what is at stake here.
Feminism, we should note, has already redefined revolution·
long understood as violent action in the public realm, the

feminist revolution hinges on non-violent change in the private realm. This revolution is quite clearly under way, and is now an irreversible force in our society. Given the basis of women's experience, it is obvious that the sphere of reproduction will arise as a politically significant social formation in this new revolution. The moral character of these developments has taken as its primitive form the struggles around abortion, women's work, child care, sexuality, violence and peace, and environmental concern. These are the "soft" issues which the phallic imagery of patriarchy distinguishes from the hard issues of power, warfare, riches and death.

The notion of defining good health has been central to the abortion struggle, as has the question of morality. The inadequate abortion scenario produced with a progressive flourish by the then Minister of Justice, Pierre Eliot Trudeau, in 1967, embodied a definition of health for the use of abortion committees which was deliberately vague. Abortion committees in practice had to have a working definition, and it turned out to be a broad one--much more so than the actual workings of these committees, which turned out to be inadequate, narrow, parochial, and uneven. Opponents of abortion are outraged by a definition of health as the state of social, mental and physical well-being to which democratic citizens are perceived to have a right. The executive director of the Alliance for Life was reported (*Globe and Mail*, January 12, 1985, p. 18) as saying that this definition is Utopian, and that the definition of health should be looked at and given "stringent definition." In fact, the anti-abortion movement *has* produced a narrow but hardly stringent definition--health is life. Now, that *is* biological reductionism; it also calls for another definition, as the defining game always does--the definition of life as such.

The abortion issue has been a difficult one for feminism, and I would like to argue that this is because it has become trapped in ideological formulations which are alien to considerations of the good. The parameters of the abortion debate have become two abstractions: "life" on the one hand and the "right" to free choice on the other. As is often the case, abstract formulations, especially those which do not

know themselves as abstractions, prove to be deficient tools
of analysis of meaning, to say nothing of practice. This is
not surprising. As I suggested earlier, paternity itself is
abstract in the sense that it is basically uncertain, and is
confirmed by cultural constructs rather than subjective
experience. Maternity is confirmed in labor. As men make
laws, we can expect male laws related to birth to reflect
men's alienation from birth and their cultural need to control
the definition of reproductive reality. The major strategy for
this control historically has been men's appropriation of
women's children, which is also the appropriation of labor
embedded in the child; institutionalization of children in a
wide range of cultural strategies such as naming; marriage;
the separation of public and private life; and differentiated
moralities for male and female sexual expression and
reproductive responsibility. Most fundamentally, men have
produced odd definitions of what constitutes life itself. The
conservative definition of a "right to life" is a positing of
conjoined empty abstractions and is in fact theoretically
indistinguishable from the liberal marriage of right and
choice, which are also abstract terms. The fight is over the
way of transforming these abstractions to actions. Abortion
is a disturbing issue for feminists who aspire to create an
ethical politics and find their non-violent persuasions
seriously challenged by the act of aborting. The liberal
solution to this impasse, which is the retreat to a situation
ethics, is not a very satisfactory one. The conservative
position of sticking mindlessly to patriarchal ideology is even
less so.

We cannot bring about social change by changing the
meaning of words. But, I have been suggesting, we cannot
build ethical perceptions of the good in good health by
starting with ideological formulations. I could argue that the
definition of "life" which patriarchy has produced is
profoundly ideological, precisely because it emerges from
men's alienated experience of conception rather than
women's integrated experience of birth. Life is not
specifically human: Edward Wilson's quintessential eggs,
duly fertilized, bring forth life in myriad forms. If life itself is
an absolute value, then we must never swat a fly, fumigate a

fungus, never catch a fish nor boil an egg. What we actually do is privilege human life, attributing to it a difference: patriarchs have usually attributed this difference to the possession of rationality, a quality more satisfactory in theory than visible in practice, and always problematic in terms of women. This reliance on abstract "life" has led to the extraordinary quarrels over when in fact a foetus becomes human, and a deflection from the issue of women's control over their own bodies.

This obscure and abstract debate can only take place in a world in which men have abrogated the right to give a meaning to experience, including the experience from which they are biologically excluded, that of giving birth. The transformation from life in general to human life in particular comes, I would argue, in the *historical* labor of women. Marx defined labor as the creation of value, but he did not heed the value produced by women's reproductive labor. This work is a unification of bodily labor with human consciousness, a unity of knowledge and experience which defines the human as the species which knows what it is doing in the act of giving birth: it is creating value, the value of human life, a cultural and individual value which is assessed by the consciousness of the laboring reproducer. Life-as-such can have no value, for value itself is ethical and rests on a conscious interpretation of experience. The infant, produced by a combination of labor and consciousness, of culture and biology, of women and nature, is the human reality of life as opposed to that abstract "quintessence" of life-as-such, undifferentiated, brute and consciousless. The foetus in utero is all of these things, and the notion that it is already human is one which rests upon the limp fallacy of the creative power of the alienated sperm and ignores the whole issue of men's historical "right" to women's bodies. Neither pregnancy nor abortion are rights, but are existential choices related to the *historical* relations of reproduction which partiarchs pretend are not historical but natural. It is an odd world in which we casually destroy millions of people, the valuable products of women's reproductive labor, and find these killings ethically defensible in terms of patriarchal ideologies of power.

Yet those who defend this sort of power can also become violent in the defense of a collection of cells unvalorized by labor, uninterpreted by conscious experience, but nevertheless regarded as sacred by those who think of male sperm as the messengers of a holy ghost. The decision to have a child is not one to be made on the basis of a swelling uterus: pregnancy is not yet a choice for women. Pregnancies result from the oppressive ideology of *men's* sexual desires, the exaltation of lust, the condoning of rape, the economic and social disadvantagement of women, the ideological   undermining   of   women's   self-awareness. Pregnancies also result from the failures of patriarchal science to develop contraceptive techniques; from the neurotic dread of women's sexuality, which is rendered "scientific" in patriarchal psychiatry; from the separation of public and private, which exempts men from caring for the living in the exercise of power, militarism and imperialism. The fact that few men can live up to their ideological billing is irrelevant: what is relevant is that it is men who render life abstract, make nature their enemy, claim a clamorousness for their sexuality which makes their claim to rationality absurd. "Life" is both abstract and absurd where women's sexuality is defined as both a commodity for men's use and a threat to masculinity. The argument about the "sacredness" of life is simply ludicrous in a world of ever more effective strategies of destruction.   "Life" is not mere nature, but is defined by social and historical reality.   For women, that reality now includes--unequally,   often   dangerously   and   always politically--the capacity to make a decision whether or not to carry a fertilized ovum to term. It is not selfish choice but an agonizing and responsible decision-making process based on the realities of women and children's lives in a patriarchal world of inequity, hate, violence and misogyny, complicated by the well-meaning but basically servile women who have bought into patriarchal culture.

All of this deflects our attention from the much more vital issue of reproductive technology. Women are understandably ambivalent about this; childbirth is no fun, whatever the subsequent joys.   Technology, a male preserve, is the most successful device we have seen historically to award to men the control of species reproduction, which has been available to them so far only by socio-historical strategies for controlling women's sexuality and reproductive potency. This is not a reason for a sort of generative ludditism, but it does mean that we must address the implications of reproductive technology much more seriously and thoughtfully than we have done. Women will perhaps eventually gain by the escape from the hazards of labor, but the species may lose from its blindness to the ethical dimensions of childbearing, usually dismissed contemptuously in the phrase "motherhood issue." Motherhood may well be the ethical issue of the coming decades, with the implications of caring and conserving life, which men have taught women to understand as mere sentiment but which in fact have a capacity for mediation of dualism, for integration, for reproducing the world, a capacity which is absent from the sterile deductive categories of axiomatic ethics.

There is only one way, ultimately, to create good health, a goodness which can transcend ideological formulations and rest firmly in praxis, in the unity of thinking and doing. That is to recognize that health must begin at birth, which means that it is not only an individual concern but a species concern; not only a physio-biological process but a historical process; not only a national concern but a planetary concern. In other words, under existing notions of how we can know anything, it is impossible to know what good health is, far less produce and reproduce it. The sickness industry cannot do this, nor can science and technology reified as independent historical forces, neither can class struggle nor the geopolitical ravages of male imperialism. It cannot be legislated, formulated, simulated nor defined a priori. It cannot survive the agent/patient dualism, the producer/consumer dichotomy, the gross hierarchies of prestige and reward, the evasion of the relation of health and environment, of individual and species, of nature and history. In other words, health is community, politics and humanity. It is fundamentally *process*, and is thus part of the larger struggle to make history, and to make that history a history of the development of material realities and moral strength.   Feminism takes such tasks seriously, and unless we take feminism seriously as the preeminent progressive force of our times, we cannot begin to understand the radical nature of the species crisis with which we are confronted.